Truth Never Changes: The Genesis of the Path

By Michael L. Kilday

Illustrated by Deborah T. Kilday

To Patricia

Past is Prologue

Michael L Kilday

9/14/2012

© 2011 Green Dove Press

No part of this book may be reproduced, stored in a retrieval system, or transmitted by any means, electronic, mechanical, photocopying, recording or otherwise, without permission from Green Dove Press.

ISBN-13: 978-1466279100

I dedicate this book to Plato
for lighting the path for the
sincere seeker of knowledge.

Table of Contents

Disclaimer from the Author 7
Past is Prologue 11
The Scientific Angle on Earth Changes 23
A Journey Begins with a Single Step 39
Kubrick's Interpretation of Genesis 53
Darwinism Unveiled 59
An Encounter of the Most Unnerving Kind 77
Atlantean Genesis 83
The Coin is One 101
Opening a Vista on The True Faith 113
Feeling Your Way 117
Independence of Mind 125
The God-Concept 135
The Quest for Knowledge 145
An Armageddon of the Mind 155
Striving to be the Perfect Being 163
Reclaiming Your Idealistic Purpose 169
Sectarian Salvation Comes with a Price Tag 181
The Declaration of the Son of Man 191
The Road Ahead 199
Index 215
Bibliography 219
Endnotes 221

Truth Never Changes: The Genesis of the Path

Disclaimer from the Author

The purpose of this manuscript is to make sense out of something which is characterized as being speculative. When one dabbles in the realm of intuitive sensibility, no one else could validate the findings but the receiver. Thus interpretations can shift like the prevailing winds. The quest for knowledge is justifiable as a legitimate fact-finding mission into a twilight realm. This manuscript serves as the annotated travel log. One may accept or reject the findings as stated, but one should not doubt the sincerity of the provider. The quest for understanding probes the boundaries of what rational men and women might say is at the fringe of reasonability. Yet it is a place one visits every single day if one professes a belief in an unseen ethereal life force that underpins human existence.

The circumstances under which some of the information is compiled to write the manuscript border on the surreal. The determining factor of whether or not the content of it is believable should not be the manner in which some information is received. Some may use that as an excuse to suspend belief for whatever reason they choose. Excluding the testimony of Spirit simply because the transmitter is unseen shouldn't be just cause to invalidate the statements made. They stand or fall on their own merit. It is no more radical a concept than deeming the words of the Bible to be *divinely-inspired*. By nature, statements of spiritual import often fall into that category. One should be open-minded enough to realize there is a multitude of ways to acquire knowledge. With the close-minded, the source takes priority over the content. That is the main problem with their approach.

At the deep-trance session described in TRUTH NEVER CHANGES: EARTH CHANGES (Kilday, 2009), the first book of this series, I had been informed that six Atlantean masters [i] surrounded me, ready, willing, and able to answer *"all that you may wish to know"* as Spirit put it. To be honest, I must admit my skepticism; for I am first and foremost a rational man. I am not given to leaps of faith, or an initiate of secret doctrines. Like many others, I have doubts such things really exist. If they do I am suspicious that they have hidden agendas. Instead of a twilight realm of fancy and fiction, I live in the real world. I put my pants on one leg at a time like everyone else. I do not pretend to be anything else, but an inquiring mind. If anything sets me apart, it is in being a progressive thinker. That opens a vista to new and different ideas from unusual sources. That is precisely why I received this information, rather than someone whose preconceived notions wouldn't allow them to be open to the possibilities. That would have been a waste of effort on the part of those who delivered the message. Hence the question of *why me* is answered to my satisfaction.

If I am to give credit to where credit is due for the content of this manuscript, I would suggest it is a conglomeration of my ideas, and ideas from the Other Side prepared in a mulligatawny stew. The ideas expressed cannot be separated or assigned. Every thought is derived from the same source and is colored by the human channel in every manner of disclosure. Whatever this manuscript contains I must assume responsibility for as well as its perception. I will never make the claim that anyone or anything speaks for me. The manuscript speaks for itself. The stance it proposes is for the betterment of humanity or the information would never have been disclosed. I am compelled to reveal what I know; not to curry favor, but to set the record straight. After a two thousand year legacy of ideological brainwashing, fear-mongering and misguided attempts at constructing a spiritual box, someone has to show the way out of it.

I am without a calling or an agenda except to speak and act forthrightly. I am not chosen to do anything. I choose to do it. What I have chosen to do is to relay to the rest of humanity what I have received, cleansed of the taint of ideology. Therefore the suggestion that anyone should think they are chosen becomes a source of agitation. In actuality, it is only one's quality of awareness that makes the difference. All life is unique and precious without qualification, but none is more so than any other because each has its place. A problem arises in that feeling of being special -- separate and distinct for whatever reason one chooses to imagine. It tends to pervert the message and separate humanity into contentious factions vying for supremacy of what humanity rightfully shares – an identity and a goal. From it comes an understanding of why we are here, and a purpose for life.

The main reason for the lapse of time in producing the manuscript is that providing illumination without offering any hint of solutions is disingenuous at best. I do not have an ideology to preach or a cause for which to pass the basket. Neither do I wish to add one more solitary voice to the public outcry for a course change without careful consideration of where it leads. Until I could lend a constructive solution to the debate, I abide by Falstaff's insightful comment from KING HENRY IV PART 1 (Shakespeare, 16th Century). He said, *"the better part of valor is discretion, in the which better part I have saved my life"*.[ii]

A chance encounter with Elwood Babbitt, insofar as anything is chance, re-energized my initial investment in the secular humanism of Woodstock Nation[iii]. It has been refined into a personal quest to promote a renaissance of the human spirit because it is long overdue. By advocating a change in perspective, this manuscript will set the sincere seeker on the path to participate in a renaissance of the human spirit. It will educate the sincere seeker in how that could be accomplished. Enacting a personal solution begins with casting oneself in the role of a sincere seeker. It is the only way to attain the knowledge one seeks to realize the innovative solution required to liberate the mind. The goal of this communication is to enable a transformative process.

Freeing oneself from the mind games imposed by imprudent ideologies begins with answering important questions. How can one recognize the truth when they hear it? Once one has placed their feet upon the path, which direction should one go? How does one know they are going in the right direction? These questions are for the seeker to answer, but if he or she pays close attention to the content of the communication that follows an epiphany will dawn. It points the way to ideological self-sufficiency. Be assured only a free-thinker can tread this path. Now the reader has his or her prerequisite. The hope is one understands the need for prudence because the thoroughfare is cluttered with the vainglorious jockeying for position.

At this juncture, the question a reader may be asking is: why should he or she accept the interpretation of this author? Validation of the ideas presented here or consensus on their veracity is not being requested. It is only required that each individual searches his or her own heart for confirmation. Understanding it is always wise to be cautious of a researcher's motivation, engaging in critical analysis often necessitates dispensing criticism of some kind. It goes with the territory. You do yourself a disservice by blindly accepting or rejecting anything. It is the reader's responsibility to prove to him or herself that there is a reason to believe. Having the subject matter of these investigations questioned is not offensive to me. It merely invigorates the resolve to provide a more convincing argument. Arbitrarily being labeled as a crackpot or a heretic is offensive however. Any sincere seeker would feel the same way because the sincere seeker prides him or herself on being a rational thinker as well as a competent researcher.

If nothing else, the sincere seeker is a pioneer. Breaking new ground and treading on virgin soil is part of the job description. One should not close the door on any possibilities if the evidence presented is persuasive enough to walk through it. The sincere seeker is obligated to ask why, and pursue the investigation wherever it leads. As far as this manuscript is concerned, all I ask is for the reader to suspend judgment until the last page is read. And to allow the ideas presented to resonate with the wisdom that is imbedded in one's heart; then contemplate the evidence offered and take the appropriate action to free one's mind.

Truth Never Changes: The Genesis of the Path

Past is Prologue

Through nationally-renown channel Elwood Babbitt, a forecast of future events was initially received in 1979. That encounter was described in the first book in this series, TRUTH NEVER CHANGES: EARTH CHANGES (Kilday, 2009).[iv] The narrative was composed of a memoir of the deep-trance session featuring communications from the Other Side. It continued with a detailed analysis of the prevailing prophecies concerning Earth changes and the investigation undertaken to reveal their meaning. It concluded with a provocative statement on the prevailing human condition. Considering what was transpiring on the economic and ecological fronts in the first decade of the 21st century, it indicated to those in the know prophecy was being fulfilled. The stipulation was that each individual carved out his or her own destiny within the parameters of global change. Therefore it mattered less if one embraced prophecy or denied it, and mattered more how one adapted to events on the ground as they unfolded.

The requirements for surviving the events forecasted or succumbing to them lay in how one perceived what those requirements actually were. Like the words etched on the side-view mirror of your automobile -- objects were closer than they appeared to be. Furthermore the objects usually were not what they seemed to be at ground-level when seen from the stratosphere. It was only when one delved into the content and purpose of the matters close at hand that the underlying Truth was revealed for what it was. Dates did not tell the story. Events on the ground did. Ideology would not carry the day; people would when they spoke from the heart. Furthermore no white knight in shining armor was riding to the rescue whether it was John Nelson Darby of England, Al Gore of Tennessee, or even Jesus of Nazareth. Each had their say and could do no more than what they had. Human problems had to be resolved by humanity. Any legitimate prophet told his audience that in no uncertain terms. Beyond that he or she could do little more than prepare the way for change. Ultimately it meant becoming aware, adaptable, and pragmatic. In this case, it was positioning oneself for the best opportunity for survival.

TRUTH NEVER CHANGES: EARTH CHANGES (Kilday, 2009), described the scope and complexity of the imminent Earth changes in considerable detail. In the second offering in the series, the intent was not to revisit the evidence already gathered on prophecy or rehash the details. That had already been done sufficiently for the reach of the first book. The reader could take it or leave it for what it was. The expressed purpose of book two, subtitled THE GENESIS OF THE PATH, was to clarify *the why of it*. Earth changes were not the invention of a seer's vivid imagination or a prophet's urgent admonitions. In this case, there was a scientific and philosophical authenticity supporting the claims of prescience if one was patient enough to investigate them thoroughly. Chapter two laid them out for the reader.

The second book in the Truth Never Changes series, TRUTH NEVER CHANGES: THE GENESIS OF THE PATH, explored many of the same themes as the first book, but focused more upon illuminating the path one must take ultimately to connect with the One. It will explain where we came from and where we were going. The Creative Life of which every living thing was a part was a process with purpose. Because it had purpose there was an underlying truth that needed to be grasped before it could be fulfilled. To be an initiate was enough at the start of one's quest. That only inferred one realized one didn't have all the answers. One was merely looking for a venue where the appropriate inquiries could be aired. Enlightenment was a noteworthy goal, but it was a lot to ask. The uninitiated may equate it with being a journey into the nether regions of an undiscovered country. But an epiphany of the human condition was central to completely understanding the impact of so-called Earth changes upon humanity. One may consider it to be the deciding factor of a series of seminal events.

Furthermore TRUTH NEVER CHANGES: THE GENESIS OF THE PATH was an attempt to redefine spirituality as a personal objective devoid of ideology; the goal being an embodiment of Truth. No commitment to Church or State was required; only one's recognition there was something to know. It began with a search that should be undertaken by the average man or woman when the self-appointed guardians of ideology did not answer one's inquiries to one's satisfaction.

Either those guardians could not or would not provide the answers for reasons only known to them. It was conceivable they didn't possess the answers themselves. Therefore the assumption they were withholding information may be unfounded. They may not have any to give. Therefore one was compelled to seek the answers themselves from whatever source they could find.

In spite of Earth changes, finding the Truth was a noteworthy goal at any time, in and of itself. The challenges offered by Earth changes were just added incentive for one to be alerted to the possibilities they offered because the shadows were lengthening. It was imperative one must avoid being caught unaware. That way one would not succumb to the banal claims of those who claimed to have a customized solution for whatever ailed you. The profiteers claimed to have control of the situation, but the Great Purification [v] was beyond the scope of human control and would proceed despite any attempts to deny its reality, or capitalize on its effect. Such efforts attracted the vainglorious opportunists who wished only to affix a price to salvation and extract that pound of flesh from whoever they could while they could. Thus even this opportunity for deliverance was being treated like it was the produce of entrepreneurship. Distasteful as that was to the ideological purists, essentially it was what new-style religion, evangelical and New Age alike had become. Blood in the water always drew the sharks and they circled the prey in anticipation of the kill.

This manuscript will encourage the reader to aspire to be a sincere seeker of knowledge, and it suggested a path one must traverse to acquire it lie over rocky terrain. The course one was obligated to follow was predicated upon choice. In a series of dissertations from the Atlantean masters, it will be described how one could prepare oneself for *coming out of the cave*.[vi] That would be to acquire the key ingredient of enlightenment -- understand what it means, how it goes and one's role in it. That understanding was the result of one's investigations alone.

Throughout the course of human history, every seeker had walked the same path. Being assailed by the naysayers, a seeker may find it difficult to keep to the path. But because one blazed the trail, one traversed it alone, and reached one's conclusions based upon the knowledge gained. The urgency for taking that journey at the present time was that humanity was on the cusp of transformational change in the Earth as well as in ourselves. Hopi prophecy referred to it as the fifth age of Man. Energies to induce transformation had been deployed to assist humanity in developing a new consciousness to welcome the incoming age.

The signs of impending catastrophe were prevalent as we turned the page on our civilization. Among them were human deprivation, ecological disturbances, and a spiritual crisis of confidence. Our deprivations were evidenced by what was happening in human society at present – economically, morally, and psychologically. The ecological disturbances will be in the form of a host of natural disasters: earthquakes, volcanic eruptions, tidal waves, hurricanes, tsunamis, and cyclones. The problem will not be that these occur because they always had, but rather their frequency and severity. Our spiritual crisis of confidence stemmed from a lack of understanding what it all meant. It culminated in the fear there was nowhere to turn and nowhere to hide.

Our societal upheavals were deemed to be inevitable because the point of no return was reached in 1967. That was the year when Israel reacquired the city of Jerusalem after the six days war. It fulfilled biblical prophecy. The first step in the prophetic scenario was achieved in 1948 with the re-establishment of the state of Israel. The final step was the rebuilding of the temple of Solomon on its original site – the temple mount. At present a Muslim temple, the Dome of the Rock, occupied that site. It stood to reason the destruction of the Muslim shrine, and the subsequent erection of Solomon's temple would precipitate the Final Conflict. The roots of the conflict between estranged sons of Abraham ran deep. It had simmered like sleeping volcanoes that would awaken in due time, and explode in full fury. The catalyst of thousands of years of antagonism will fuel Armageddon. But the match will still need to be struck to light the fuse. And one knew full well it was more likely to happen than not. It was not a matter of if. It was only a matter of when. But the course was conditional because it had to be chosen.

As counterpoint 1967 was also known as the *summer of love*. In retrospect, that celebration of love did little to change the course of Western Civilization; mainly because it did not reverberate throughout Society as a whole. It operated at the fringe as an attempt of the hippie counterculture to affect a change in course, highlighting peace, brotherhood, and music as the way to make it happen. It appeared to have little effect except to make tens of thousands of hippies contented for a weekend. But it still showed there could be hope if people wanted to entertain hope. It was a direction to go which the public at large chose not to pursue. The opportunity to put humanity on the correct path toward global awakening was lost. Instead civilization took a detour that put humanity on a collision course with destiny.

That was long before we reached critical mass on our consumption of natural resources and corruption of the biosphere. That course had already been set by economic policies of manifest destiny. Moreover the effects of thousands of years of genocide, persecutions, and warfare could not simply be put aside. Attitudes that were too quick to condemn and too slow to forgive could not be changed by acclamation. Some attitudes were ingrained and behaviors were habitual. It took generations to unlearn bad habits, and it took considerable effort to instill good ones. The greed, debauchery, and gluttony of the civilized world were fueled by a mind-set that materialism was the way of the world, profit was earned, and usury was a legal right. For centuries now, greed is good had been the mantra of human civilization. Unfortunately few were inclined to listen to the small, still voice inside that reminded it was not.

When the Roman Empire was rotting from within from the same disease Western Civilization had contracted, the populace was distracted from taking any corrective measures by games in the Coliseum. While the powers-that-be silenced their critics by any means at their disposal, the games provided a diversion. In those days, the powers-that-be killed those who told them to share their abundance. The shoot-the-messenger mentality they employed was their undoing because it showed only a violent reaction could change the social dynamic in their Society. Today the powers-that-be used different techniques to gloss over societal problems, including mass media entertainment and political misdirection. The institution of Democracy made that necessary because no citizen could be ordered to do anything. Currently the powers-that-be used more covert means than the Romans to convert those who told them to share their abundance, including brainwashing, bribery and extortion techniques. The shoot-the-messenger mentality they employed would still be our undoing because it delayed a societal reaction until it was too late to apply corrective measures. Ultimately any empire that neglected the metaphysical needs of its citizenry invited decay and destruction.

There was every reason to believe that if Rome fell any civilization could. In recorded history, no civilization had held sway, economically and politically, over the known world for as long as the Roman Empire did in its time. The American Empire was its facsimile in the modern era. But civilizations rose and fell. That was the natural course of human events. The historical record was clear on that account. Humanity has had numerous opportunities to reform its ways and live in harmony, but they had been squandered each time. Another opportunity was approaching. All that was required was to part the veil over one's eyes, think clearly and act righteously. There were many steps along the way whereby the Light was revealed by systematically removing the veils that filtered it. All it took was to change one's approach.

Much of the advice given during the deep-trance session in 1979 was geared toward preparing oneself spiritually for the upcoming Earth changes. It was the process of transformation to which the Mayan elders referred in their explanation of the 2012 experience. That included positioning oneself for change on an evolutionary scale. Continuing on the theme of the Canopy of Light that was introduced in the first book, it was the vehicle for transformational change. This manuscript focused upon how change would be manifested in human beings who embraced the message as opposed to those who chose to deny it. This was touched upon in the first book of the series, but there was much more to add. A book called THE CHILDREN OF THE LAW OF ONE AND THE LOST TEACHINGS OF ATLANTIS [vii] (Peniel, 1997) provided some of the inspiration for this book. Recognizing the profound influence of the Children of the Law of One upon the change scenario was vital because of their Atlantean roots. The reader will note the influence of their philosophy in the chapter entitled "Atlantean Genesis" and those following it.

At the beginning of the 20th century, the founders of the Theosophical Society[viii] presented a provocative view on the history of the Earth and the Ages of Man. It focused upon an intuitive perspective on Egyptian mysticism and how it dovetailed into a consideration of the Ages of Man impacting humanity's development. With a new sidereal year beginning on 12/21/2012, the Age of Aquarius, the findings of Theosophy tended to agree with the Hopi and the Mayan predictions that profound change in human evolution was not only imminent, but predetermined. That change was predicated upon certain astronomical events and astrological aspects occurring once every 25,920 years. Nostradamus had noted them in his predictions with rare planetary alignments that only occurred at the threshold of a change in the sidereal year – from Pisces to Aquarius for example. Also some mystical organizations were floating theories about Nibiru, referred to as Planet X. According to legend this planet was a sister world of Earth. More or less the legend postulated the inhabitants of Nibiru were the space brothers of forgotten lore.

However the Theosophical prospective focused upon the Egyptian Mysteries. It centered upon the cycle of death and rebirth of Osiris. According to the Osiris/Isis mystery, a metaphorical scenario played out at the change of each sidereal year. Osiris, symbolic of the human divine self, was murdered by Set, symbolic of the human ego self, his half-brother. Set betrayed Osiris and usurped his throne. Set had the body of Osiris dismembered in 14 pieces, and hidden across Egypt. Isis, his queen, searched and located his body, reassembled the pieces, and with the aid of Thoth's alchemical formulas and the appropriate rituals brought him back to life. Once the missing phallus was found Isis was impregnated by Osiris and a new age was born in the person of Horus the Child. That was the plot-line of the story. The setting, characterizations, and thematic content were supplied by the trappings of the Age.

What was worth noting was the Egyptian belief that at the start of each sidereal year, the gods lived again. They returned to Earth in the form of adepts and avatars to reinvigorate human civilization; a civilization the Egyptians credited them with beginning untold ages before. In essence the deities were returning to Earth to set things right once again. The Egyptian Mysteries referred to it as the Great Return. In his recently published book, EGYPT, CHILD OF ATLANTIS: A RADICAL INTERPRETATION OF THE ORIGINS OF CIVILIZATION (Gordon, 2004), author John Gordon, a senior fellow of the Theosophical Society of England, wrote about the significance of the aforementioned Great Return being the essence of the Osiris/Isis mystery religion. In the following passage he suggested the possibility it would include alien visitation to be timed with the beginning of the sidereal year in 2012. It appeared to roll up the Nostradamus, the Hopi, the Mayan, and the Planet X prophecies into one neat package. Gordon explained the true import of

Michael L. Kilday

the sidereal year prophecies in the following section of his book, entitled "The Real Significance of the Great Return".

> *While many readers might well be prepared to recognize and admit the astronomical allegories just described [sidereal year prophecies], experience leads one to believe that much less credence will be given by the scientifically sophisticated minds of the intelligentsia of our time to the practical aspects associated with "soul evolution". Almost certainly in the train of what has just been suggested here, we shall now experience a plethora of authors confirming that it is these cyclical periods just mentioned that "spacemen" arrive from other, more advanced solar systems in order to further the evolution of our mentally or spiritually backward humanity. While such a materialistically literal translation can hardly be avoided as a product of our times and will thus just have to be accepted, we make the point here very firmly that this is what the ancient Egyptians (whoever they were) were intent on putting across in their metaphors and allegories. Not only did the ancients, as we have otherwise seen, believe in the actual existence of gods, daemons, and souls as entirely real entities, but they regarded them as the very core of their philosophy of life as well. Without them, as we said at the very outset, their belief that the periodic return of the gods as divine influences was not only a matter of fact, but that it was also entirely dependent upon a synchronicity of sidereal cycles. To imagine then that such a civilization, whenever it existed, could put together a vast, exactly working model of our local universe without a highly meaningful spiritual rationale, allied to a huge amount of detailed scientific knowledge, and instead that they merely indulged in fantasy about the spiritual life animating and guiding the mechanism of the universe, is plainly fatuous. What we see in their stupendous allegory is a gift of information and prophecy to future generations of humanity who would be able to perceive its hidden meanings. Of that there can be little doubt. For in none of the historical records of the last 6000 years or so is there any indication whatsoever of anything even nearly approaching such an intelligent civilization [Egyptian] in existence on the face of the earth. That alone leads one to surmise that theirs had to be a far more ancient culture and civilization than is presently recognized, and that it almost certainly disappeared by prior design, at its allotted time, in conjunction with the conclusion of a major sidereal cycle. ...*

Truth Never Changes: The Genesis of the Path

That leads us directly back to the idea of "seasonal cycles" affecting the growth and decay of human civilization and culture. It also answers the paradox of advanced scientific knowledge being found in the hands of young civilizations that could not possibly have derived it themselves from mere personal observation and empirical rationalizing over the period of a couple thousand years. It also otherwise leads on to the supposition that even though the mass of highly evolved mankind may depart this planetary sphere in due cycle, some must remain behind, somehow, in order to maintain the continuity of existence and the natural momentum of the evolutionary process. That in turn implies that the dynasties of Manetho [ancient Egyptian priest] are no work of fiction after all; that his dynasties of gods, demigods, and heroes actually did exist; and furthermore, that they will continue cyclically to reappear on Earth.[ix]

When considering the Great Return to be an actual event, the implications were intriguing. A cryptic statement offered during the deep trance session in 1979[x] now seemed to make sense in that context. In reference to the prospect of alien visitation, Dr Fischer had noted in passing, *"When these things of which I am speaking about come to pass, the aliens that now trod your earth will make themselves known".* Until recently the inference of this statement had been lost on me. But in the context of the Great Return, the suggestion was to imply one's *gods* were coming for a scheduled visit. One might argue the term *gods* could be substituted for *parents*. Moreover it would behoove one to get one's house in order before that happened to save oneself the potential embarrassment of not living up to their expectations. Every ancient civilization, Mayan, Aztec, Tibetan, Egyptian, Sumerian, and Persian anticipated a visit from their *gods* at regular intervals. In some sense, each of their respective prophecies foretold of such events. When each one of them adhered to a similar if not identical view of the Great Return, would that qualify as mass delusion? Or as in the case of the myth of the Great Flood was it a shared remembrance of actual events occurring in the distant past?

So it appeared the Egyptians were either the greatest innovators of mythology of all time, or they were privy to knowledge our civilization was not. If the latter was true, it indicated their advanced civilization was far older than anyone could possibly imagine. Considering the sophisticated and erudite quality of the Egyptian Mystery religion, it was inferred the roots of a much older civilization had been transplanted there. Only a very ancient civilization could possess the perspective required to comprehend and catalog the cyclical nature of Earth changes occurring on the basis of sidereal time. They also postulated men and their *gods* communed for their mutual benefit at regular intervals. It was something one could only learn through experience. Few civilizations were old enough to grasp the intricacies of the cosmic forces in play. But strangely enough the Hopi knew it. The Maya knew it. The Tibetans knew it and the Egyptians obviously knew it. It was apparent also contemporary men didn't know it. Younger civilizations could only surmise what had occurred in the distant past when they didn't have any records to refer to. And one could only assume it was because they had been cut off from their roots. Whether it was intentional or unintentional, science, technology, and institutionalized religion had effectively accomplished it.

Evidently 6,000 years before the Common Era when civilization began as recorded in the Bible, it was viewed by its interpreters to be a fresh start with no carry over. Plato's accounts of Atlantis were basically treated as if they were fiction. He was considered to be a storyteller rather than a historian. Primarily this was because no records could be found anywhere to indicate that Atlantis wasn't simply a fairy tale concocted by Plato. Modern scholarship went so far as to infer the stories in THE CRITAS and TIMEAUS (Plato, 4th Century BCE) that wove a tale of the Greeks repelling an invasion by the Atlanteans were simply political propaganda. Supposedly its purpose was to extol the fighting prowess of his homeland against a potent adversary. This interpretation was consistent with the political spin we put on everything in Western Civilization -- evidence of a preoccupation with manifest destiny.

As far as the existence of Atlantis was concerned, no evidence presented had been conclusive enough to prove or disprove its existence. Either the devastation of the continent was so complete nothing of the previous civilization remained or the whole thing was merely a fabrication. But if it was a pre-historic fantasy, why would so many words be written on the subject by so many different authors, and why would so many devote their lives to looking for a lost continent that never existed? Was it evidence of delusion or prescience? Regarding the probability of the kind of catastrophic events occurring then which could make an entire continent disappear, it was another matter entirely. Modern scholarship simply did not want to consider it was possible. And their stance was logical considering no one alive today ever witnessed mass extinction level events of any kind, only gradual change. But that didn't mean it couldn't happen; only that the events could not be substantiated. It would be presumptuous to believe any event not witnessed simply didn't happen. Normally anything unseen was relegated to a matter of conjecture.

Presently what could not be explained away was the environmental phenomena astrophysicists, geologists, and climatologists were observing and commenting on at the turn of the 21st century. That evidence suggested the cyclical changes ancient civilizations knew quite well were in fact, real and actual. Something was happening in the Earth modern science was struggling to explain. Events appeared to be timed with the change in the sidereal year. These events were the result of scientific measurements rather than a showcase of events and conditions following a pre-determined prophetic script. When it was realized that these events made science and prophecy converge on the facts, it showed the concern over Earth changes in some quarters was genuine. It indicated the events were definitely not the result of a self-fulfilling prophecy, but rather an actuality that could be demonstrated by cause and effect. For the free-thinking individual what it amounted to was a paradigm shift in attitudes and prospective.

Michael L. Kilday

The Scientific Angle on Earth Changes

After the first book in the Truth Never Changes series was published additional information came to light which should be noted here to complete the Earth changes prognosis. The patient who reported the aches and pains may dread hearing it, but the diagnostician would be remiss in his duty not to tell it like it was. The update to the prognosis included recent scientific findings, media investigations as well as the Hopi perspective of the 2012 phenomenon. They were presented here to make the reader aware there was a reason for all of this, and an underlying cause that made it necessary. There were several new items of interest indicating that radical environmental change was in the offing, and the powers-that-be knew it. They just weren't being forthcoming with what they knew. It was one thing to scorn the predictions of psychics and prophets. It was quite another to malign or disregard the evidence gathered by the scientific community. And when the scientific findings confirmed what the psychics and seers had been warning of for millennia, one had to wonder if there was a reason for the conspiracy of silence from official sources.

Firstly, NASA recently discovered that the Earth had changed its wobble. The wobble in the rotational orbit of the Earth kept it in balance as it orbited the Sun. From a report in December of 2009, it was learned that Edgar Cayce had predicted this change in the wobble back in the 1930's. His concurrence with the scientific evidence was cited in the following item off the NASA web site (webmaster, NASA document on the Chandler wobble, 2010).

> *This anomaly (the wobble of the Earth) will be of significant interest to fans of Edgar Cayce, the famed sleeping prophet. He predicted during the 1930's that a new cycle of the shifting of the poles would begin in 2000/2001 and thereafter an increase in the 'upheavals' in the Earth. Since this anomaly has appeared in a 'cycle' of Chandler's wobble which began in 2000, just after the completion of the min phase in 1999 [regarding solar flare activity], we are now seeing Cayce's prediction fulfilled with remarkable fidelity.*[xi]

To confirm this finding, in the first several months of 2010 there had been a rash of earthquakes and volcanic eruptions. Most of them were along the Pacific Rim, known as the Ring of Fire. During that time span earthquakes had occurred in California, Mexico, Chile, Oregon, China, Taiwan, Japan, Sumatra, Indonesia, The Philippines, Haiti, and New Zealand. The bulk of them had measured over 7.0 on the Richter scale. The massive 8.8 quake in Chile actually caused a change in the rotation of the Earth by making the day a few milliseconds shorter. In addition the Earth's crust moved 3 inches. Scientists anticipated it would eventually move back to its original position. As if on cue, late in 2010 Chile had another massive quake in the 7.0 to 8.0 range. Also previously inactive volcanoes in the Atlantic had abruptly awakened on the islands of Montserrat and Iceland.

On March 11, 2011, Japan experienced a 9.0 earthquake that devastated the northeastern section of that country. A series of tsunamis inundated the coastline. In the aftermath the containment walls of five nuclear reactors at the Fukashima Daichi power plant in the region had been breached and at last report radiation was pouring into the atmosphere and the Pacific Ocean. The Japanese government was telling its citizenry who lived within a 19 mile radius of the plant not to go outside. There was little else the plant management could do but flood the affected reactors with sea water in a desperate attempt to prevent a core meltdown. That crisis was being played out as this book was being compiled. The final tally on loss of life wasn't official yet, but it was likely to top 20,000. The numbers were climbing each day. The numbers were actually low because Japan was the most prepared nation on the face of the Earth for these kinds of seismic events. As with the 8.8 Chilean earthquake of the previous year the wobble of the Earth changed again. Reportedly it caused the length of the day to decrease by 3 milliseconds, and the Earth's crust moved 8 feet this time.

Many of Edgar Cayce's Earth changes prophecies predicted numerous seismic events occurring on the Ring of Fire, prior to the pole shift event. It signaled a period of geological instability in the Pacific Rim that Edgar Cayce began forecasting seven decades before. He also indicated volcanic eruptions and earthquakes of mammoth proportions would continue increasing in frequency and severity until the pole shift event. Now it appeared his predictions were deserving of another look by the naysayers. Whether or not one ascribed to the notion that the sleeping prophet as he was known was privy to information normal human beings were not, he was proven correct. When one is proven to be correct over 90 per cent of the time it would be wise to pay attention to what he did say. Devising rationales for why he could not be correct, didn't serve humanity's best interests.

Secondly, an article from December of 2005, entitled "NASA CLAIMS POLAR SHIFT DUE IN 2012", posted on the NASA web site (webmaster, NASA document on magnetic pole shift, 2005), noted a magnetic pole shift had occurred on the Sun in 2001. It further stated a second one was anticipated in 2012 at the height of the solar flare activity. For someone who was not an astrophysicist it was difficult to understand what it meant exactly, but a giant, turbulent spot on the sun that emitted a great quantity of solar flares would be pointed directly at Earth in 2012.

> *Solar System – Did you notice? In February 2001, the Sun did a magnetic polar shift. The next one is due again in 2012. NASA scientists who monitor the Sun say that our star's awesome magnetic field flipped 22 months ago, signaling the arrival of a solar maximum. But it wasn't so obvious to the average human. The Sun's magnetic north pole which was in the northern hemisphere just a few months ago, now points south. It's a topsy-turvy situation, but not an unexpected one. "This always happens around the time of solar maximum," says David Hathaway, a solar physicist at the Marshall Space Flight Center. "The magnetic poles exchange places at the peak of the sunspot cycle. In fact, it's a good indication that Solar Max is really here." The Sun's magnetic poles will remain as they are now with the north magnetic pole pointing through the Sun's southern hemisphere until the year 2012 when they will reverse again.*[xii]

Moreover for the last few years information had circulated periodically claiming magnetic north was shifting into Siberia. According to some sources the pole was moving eastward at the rate of 34 to 37 miles a year.[xiii] According to an article in National Geographic News from December of 2005, the north magnetic pole was moving at a clip of 25 miles per year. In the 20th Century the pole had moved 685 miles from Arctic Canada toward Siberia, according to Joe Stoner, a paleomagnetist at

Oregon State University. At its current rate, Stoner suggested, the pole could move into Siberia within the next half-century. He further indicated that this hadn't happened for at least 500 years. A Geomagnetic scientist at Natural Resources Canada, Lorne McKee confirmed that Stoner's assertions fit his own readings; adding "The movement of the pole definitely appears to be accelerating" (Vastag, 2005). Exactly what the ramifications were was a matter of speculation.

Edgar Cayce had stated in his readings a magnetic pole shift was destined to occur on Earth; so this news did not come as a surprise to anyone familiar with Cayce's predictions. According to some in the scientific community excessive pole wandering was a prelude to pole shift. That was the basic premise of THE EARTH'S SHIFTING CRUST by Charles Hapgood.[xiv] If one desired a greater understanding of the dynamics and prerequisites of geographical pole shift, that was a good book to read. Time and space didn't warrant a full disclosure of the details at this time. One may note that Hapgood's book featured a preface written by Albert Einstein supporting Hapgood's theory. That fact alone demanded it be taken seriously, even if one thought the concept was complete rubbish. A great many in the scientific community did, but that was before the theory of plate tectonics was introduced. The greatest scientific mind of the 20th century didn't think Hapgood was off his rocker. Why would any mind of lesser stature automatically assume he was?

Thirdly, also on the NASA site (webmaster, NASA document on Earth's magnetosphere, 2009) it was noted that readings taken of the Earth's magnetosphere indicated a potential problem. A giant hole was found in the protective helix that deflected harmful gamma, x-ray, and ultraviolet radiation away from the surface of the Earth. Presumably this would permit harmful radiation from solar flares to penetrate Earth's natural defenses and strike its surface. Since it was already known that the highest concentration of solar flare activity on record was predicted for 2012 by NASA, it was worth noting. Whether or not it meant harmful radiation would actually strike the Earth in 2012, no one knew for certain. The potential existed, and NASA would be remiss in their duty for not reporting it. No one could say with certainty what exactly would occur when the solar flare activity was at its peak. A wait and see attitude seemed appropriate. Aside from moving human populations underground or into caves, there was little to nothing anyone could do about it.

Truth Never Changes: The Genesis of the Path

The 2009 movie, KNOWING (Proyas, 2009), utilized that information in its plot scenario. In its climatic scenes, a massive solar flare literally incinerated all life forms on Earth. The chosen few in an alien-assisted, Rapture-like exodus were taken to another planet to begin life anew. To believe a Deus-Ex-Machina intervention could even occur was a matter of choice. While it may be the epitome of wild-ass guesswork at the fate of mankind, the Rapture angle had been tried before. Recently a self-proclaimed Biblical scholar by the name of Harold Camping had announced the date the Rapture would occur on May 21, 2011. The day came and went and nothing of note happened. Due to the fact many would like to believe this could be true, he had achieved notoriety, and an internet site to go along with it (webmaster, Harold Camping, 2010). Over the years, Mr. Camping had amassed quite a fortune. According to reports, his company, Family Radio, was worth 72 million dollars. Apparently to protect his investment, his first reaction of "flabbergasted" at his May prediction no-show was followed up by a statement. Camping now asserted, *"The whole world is under Judgment Day and it will continue right up until October 21, 2011, and by that time the whole world will be destroyed"*. Soon he will be 0-3, and set the all-time record for End-of-Days futility.

Currently Camping shared the record with William Miller, a self-proclaimed Biblical scholar from the 19th century[xv]. Camping's first stab at a date was in 1994. Needless to say that didn't happen. And like William Miller before him, upon his first failure Camping resorted to his Bible and recalculated his formula to come up with the second date. It was difficult to take Camping's mathematical formula seriously when posted on his web site was a contention that the Creation of the Universe had occurred 11,000 years ago. For a scientifically-minded person from the 21st century that was quite enough to cast suspicion upon any of his other findings, however intriguing they appeared. Currently astrophysicists calculated the age of the Universe to be approximately 14 billion years old. Furthermore for a professed follower of Jesus, it was difficult to believe Camping would not take his savior at his word when he said that no man not even himself knew the appointed hour of Judgment Day. Only the Father knew[xvi]. This would leave Camping and Miller and any others who wished to presume they knew better on shaky ground.

Camping's mathematical formula may have been elaborate but it was still founded upon assumptions. Primarily these were founded upon his usage of esoteric Biblical numerology. One must access his web site to understand what this meant. Suffice it to say, for those who didn't necessarily want to be part of a bad emotional investment again, all one could say was *"caveat emptor"*, and leave it at that. Intriguingly Camping's date for Creation coincided with the timing of the final destruction of the continent of Atlantis, give or take a thousand years. Therefore in the correct context the date may have some validity as a new start for humanity after a major cataclysm, rather than as a Creation date for the Universe. It would only require a realization that their literal approach presumed too much.

Regarding the proposition presented in the film, KNOWING (Proyas, 2009), admittedly a Hollywood movie was not proof of anything, but the information it was based upon was obtained from scientific sources. Therefore it was so noted as a possibility. One factor not considered in the movie was the polarity of the solar flares striking Earth. The film assumed the Earth would attract a solar flare and the result would be total annihilation of the surface of the Earth. This made for good theater, but it didn't reflect reality. In actuality, the polarity of sun at the time the solar flare was emitted was critical in determining its impact. The existing polarity of the Earth could attract the solar flare or it could be deflected into space. This could mean anywhere from total devastation of the Earth's surface to a mild disruption of the magnetic field. However even with a mild disruption the power grid could be a casualty and that would be enough of an impact to warrant concern.

In 1989 a solar flare of significant magnitude did strike the Earth and it caused the power grid for the entire province of Quebec to be knocked out for ten hours.[xvii] (Times, 1989) Such an event would cause civilization to collapse if the duration of the outage stretched into years or the power grid was lost permanently. To use a Cold War metaphor, the net effect would be like being bombed back to the Stone Age. In large part, Western Civilization existed because of the power grid. Our technology depended upon it. Without it our lifestyle would regress a few centuries at the very least. It was doubtful humanity was prepared for that. How could it be? In 2012, no one knew what the circumstances would be at the moment of solar flare impact. To say the potential effects were speculative was an understatement of the highest order. It was wise, however, to understand the probabilities and respond accordingly.

Fourthly, the scientific evidence being gathered concerning potential pole shifts, earthquakes, and climate changes had been nothing less than prodigious. Not only scientists, but biblical researchers and makers of public policy were examining the possibilities. The reality of these cyclical events was being proven by Science notwithstanding what seers and prophets contributed via prophecy, or the Federal Emergency Management Agency (FEMA) via public policy, and scientists via environmental impact. The premise for putting all of this information together suggested the Earth was moving from a long era of Uniformitarianism to one of Catastrophism.[xviii] Relative uniformity in climate and conditions represented gradual environmental change, while dramatic alterations in climate and conditions represented radical change. The changes experienced in the Earth would be relative to alterations in its systems and processes. Gathered from numerous internet sources[xix], the data showed that the Earth and its inhabitants were potentially in for a very bad day if the worst happened.

The prognosis was laid out in graphic detail in the following array of *facts* compiled by researchers. It mattered less who these researchers were as opposed to what was being researched and what the research indicated. Some were acknowledging that there was a connection between physics, biology, philosophy, and metaphysics. At some point it congealed into a coherent expression. A case in point was an organization named what the bleep[xx] had already claimed to find concurrence between the physical sciences and consciousness with their new theories of quantum mechanics. A new holistic faith was spreading – proposing that everything was truly connected like a network of mycelium in a rain forest. Were the seen and the unseen attributes of a single expression as the theoretical construct of as above, so below suggested?

Fact one; It had been reported the geological record showed that at least 175 times the geomagnetic fields of the Earth had diminished to zero, and a magnetic reversal of the poles had occurred. Another source contended it was 400 times in 330 million years. It was inevitable the geographical poles would be shifting to new coordinates again. But there was no guarantee a magnetic reversal and geographical shift would always coincide. The primary reason was a geographical pole shift required a displacement of the Earth's crust. That displacement could only happen if certain changes were exhibited in the Earth's core first. A super-heated core was the first requirement, and then energy was needed to cause the Earth's crust to slide. Needless to say a geographical pole shift was a more dramatic shift than a magnetic one, but didn't occur as often. Scientists contended the last geographical pole shift had occurred approximately 780 million years ago. Frankly one doubted crustal displacement was predictable, and it was not something for which one could prepare. Like the Siberian mastodons that were discovered flash frozen with undigested buttercups in their bellies, humanity would simply awaken one day to a change of scenery. By the way, buttercups didn't ever grow on frozen tundra, not then or now. They were ingested by the mastodons when their surrounding environment was temperate. It was extremely doubtful the mastodons would intentionally migrate into a climate zone where there was no food source. [xxi] (Veilikovsky, 1950) Other environmental factors for a geographical pole shift were in play that will be discussed in other facts.

Fact two; when the gauss rating[xxii] of the geomagnetic field was reduced, it allowed unfiltered solar energies to flow unimpeded into the Earth's crust. That created extremely low frequency waves. Coupled with large air pressure changes they could create an electrical stimulation. These stimulations could bring on seismic events in the form of earthquakes. In the first decade of the 21st century the Pacific Rim was very active as if on cue. As the gauss rating continued to decline the threat of severe and frequent earthquakes tended to rise. At this writing, the geomagnetic field was measuring between 0.4 and 0.7. That didn't offer much protection. Whether or not the low frequency waves cited earlier were sufficient to cause the crustal displacement required for a geographical pole shift, probably could not be known until the fateful day arrived.

Fact three; besides facilitating pole shifting, earthquake triggers, and deflecting solar radiation, the geomagnetic field also served as a shield to deflect stellar bodies from invading the Earth's atmosphere. For the Earth, it provided some protection from comet and asteroid impacts. In addition, as previously mentioned it also prevented the harmful effects of solar radiation from impacting the Earth's inhabitants. Being bombarded with an abundance of ultraviolet, x-rays and gamma rays was not conducive to living things, their tissues or cells. Nothing would live long under those circumstances; barely long enough to procreate. It was probable a declining gauss rating would see a complementary rise in the reported incidents of skin cancer.

Fact four; the jet streams in the atmosphere and the giant oceanic gulf streams all carried an electrical charge. The solar electromagnetic storms affected these currents. They diverted ocean currents, potentially affecting air and water temperatures. Also directly affected was the atmospheric pressure by creating low pressure troughs associated with severe weather changes such as hurricanes and typhoons. Charged-up atmospheric weather conditions were responsible for generating more storms than normal, and the altered ocean currents carried those storms to where they didn't used to go. Hence incidents of severe weather in the form of tornados and hurricanes would be on the rise. In 2011, a rash of killer tornadoes raved the Southeastern section of the continental United States.

Fact five; the stability of the Earth's crust was also being compromised by the previously mentioned slowing in the rotation of the Earth. Since 1965, the speed of the Earth's rotation had been slowing down by 9 milliseconds per day. Although it would appear to be insignificant and barely perceptible, a tremendous amount of energy was used to keep the Earth rotating. The lost energy potential had been transferred to the crust of the Earth causing an increased risk of earthquakes. Because the energy transmitted by earthquakes had been known to affect volcanoes, it was anticipated that volcanic eruptions were liable to occur as well. Theoretically that energy transference could supply the force needed for crust displacement. Probably other factors in addition to the low frequency solar waves penetrating the compromised geomagnetic field would include the China syndrome effect of a nuclear core meltdown sinking into the Earth's core. One would never have imagined the latter a possibility, but when Japan constructed a nuclear plant in the proximity of a major fault line they enhanced the possibility. The El Diablo nuclear plant in Southern California erected on the San Andreas Fault line presented the same potential problem.

Fact six; the fluctuations in the atmospheric and magnetic currents was causing the Earth to increase the wobble in its rotation. NASA had already reported this finding. In 1835, the geographical pole and magnetic north were located, in close proximity, near Ellesmere Island, Canada. Between 1850 and 1950 the meandering of the magnetic north pole had averaged about two miles per year. During that time the magnetic north pole had moved over 200 miles. The facts discovered in September of 2008 that huge sections of the ice shelves on the western edges of Ellesmere Island and Greenland were breaking away from these land masses was a further indication that the pole was moving toward the east.[xxiii] (webmaster, 2010) By rough estimates, the wobble had doubled during that same time period.

When the magnetic north pole reached its destination, the theory was a toppling of the earth would occur. When a top spun a wobble was noted. As the top slowed down the wobble increased until it caused an object to topple over. This would be manifested by the erratic movements of the sphere experiencing the shifting of weights within it; effects inherent in an object in the process of tumbling in space and falling over. That explanation was not a guess but applied physics that could be demonstrated on a tabletop with any spherical spinning object. Scientists maintained that magnetic north was heading toward a point in northern Siberia. When it reached its destination point, the poles would readjust, find their points of stabilization, and the equilibrium of the Earth's rotation would be reestablished. In the meantime, the Earth tumbled it way through space until the fateful moment. To be honest, no one could predict when that moment would occur.

Fact seven; the increased penetration of solar radiation, coupled with moving jet and gulf streams, had shifted the flow of warm and cold water. It had caused an increase in the overall temperature of the global climate. In addition, it had changed the weather pattern in various climates around the world and their ecosystems. In Antarctica, a curious phenomenon was occurring that scientists could not explain. A section of the western shelf of Antarctica called the Wordie ice shelf was warming up while the eastern section of Antarctica was cooling off.[xxiv] This was the actual affect of global warming. But also global cooling was occurring at the same time because hot and cold counterbalanced each other. It served to confirm that the phenomenon should have always been called climate change instead of global warming. The latter only told half of the story.

A change in definition was appropriate because in essence the ultimate impact was a shifting of balance between hot and cold. In 50 years, the fact that the global temperature had risen nearly 3 degrees Celsius meant the balance across the globe was in favor of hot. The measurement of global temperature was an average of temperature across the globe. A warmer climate overall, however, was a threat to the 65% of the Earth's population that lived along the coasts of the continents. The accelerated melting of the ice shelves of western Antarctica and Greenland was causing the ocean levels to rise. Inevitably when sea level rose to its maximum, either one grew gills in a hurry or drowned, there was no in-between. The only question to be answered was how high and how fast the seas would rise. Projections had been made but it depended upon the confluence of a number of factors[xxv]. The forecast seemed more tenuous when the facts were based more upon probabilities than events. That didn't mean it was impossible to decipher but rather it would not be decoded until a human being appeared who possessed the tools and the expertise to make the correct inferences.

Fifth, if that wasn't enough to be concerned about from a scientific standpoint, a telecast of the show, "CONSPIRACY THEORY" aired in April of 2010 on TruTV reported that a six-level underground city was being constructed under Denver's Stapleton airport.[xxvi] (Ventura, 2010) Host Jesse Ventura made the disclosure and attempted to prove the installation existed by venturing to the site to investigate. The closest he got to confirm its existence was that some workers on the facility testified off-camera that the underground city existed; not exactly iron-clad proof. They were dry-wall installers that claimed to be working on it at the present time. No pictures were shown of the installation; so there was no hard evidence it actually existed except for the word of laborers. While one could not accuse them of lying about the existence of the installation, one would be wise not to jump to the conclusion it did. But why would the laborers lie about it? If notoriety was the reason for the disclosure, one would think they would have made their assertions on camera. Therefore if one was so inclined one may assume it existed. The operative question was however what prompted the decision to build it?

The host also visited a similar installation that had already been erected in Mount Weather, Virginia (Ventura, 2010), and was protected by armed guard. He was not allowed to enter nor could confirm what the interior looked like. Armed guards were in place to prevent the public from entering the Mount Weather facility. Perhaps what Jesse Ventura had to say about that was most notable; that being, the installation under construction was for government officials, dignitaries, and noteworthy

Michael L. Kilday

personalities – another concession for the rich and famous. On camera, he noted *"power had its privileges"*. The general public was not invited in the case of a catastrophe. When the guard was asked what measures would be taken to keep the public out, he tapped his sidearm in response. It appeared the public would be *discouraged* from entering the facility if the worst happened. It may only indicate the government was taking the NASA reports seriously, and preparing for the worst. Perhaps they were hedging their bets, or maybe they knew more than they were willing to say publicly. The suggestion was people in high places had been reading the NASA reports.

There was one last piece of information to relay. Potentially it correlated what was happening in Nature to what was happening in human nature. All of this scientific evidence indicated change was moving Nature steadily toward planetary equilibrium by way of catastrophe. First however the planet had to pass through a baptism of fire. One could liken it to experiencing the pain of child birth. Humanity was passing through its own kind of tribulation; emotionally, psychologically, and philosophically. There had to be changes in the human condition that corresponded to match that movement toward natural planetary equilibrium with metaphysical equilibrium on the part of humanity. One affect had already been noted. That was the appearance of the hippie counterculture forty years before that forecasted an unprecedented era of peace and harmony. It was embodied in coming of the Age of Aquarius, as being a foreshadowing of what the Hopi Indians foresaw in their prophecy.

In the Hopi prophetic tradition, as recounted by Frank Waters in his book, THE BOOK OF THE HOPI (Waters, 1963), one of the culminating signs in the Hopi apocalyptic scenario was the appearance of a new world religion. The forecasted religion was said to be a potential catalyst for the renewal and rejuvenation of the human race. The prospectus was if it could gain some traction dire catastrophe on our planet of human invention could be averted. The Hopi elders were adamant about their prediction of a third world war that they referred to as a *"third great shaking of the Earth"*. That interpretation was presented by Lee Brown, a Cherokee activist and shaman. An internet video that was posted split his presentation into five parts. It encompassed a recounting of the entire Hopi prophecy given to the Indian tribes gathering in Alaska in 1986

(Brown, 1986). In the excerpt below it identified the Baha'i faith as that long-awaited catalyst[xxvii] for the salvation of humanity.

> ... And so they [the Hopi elders] say there's going to be the Third Shaking of the Earth. It's not going to be a good thing to see but we will survive it. We will survive it. And when we survive it, then there's going to be another attempt to make a circle of the human beings on the earth. And this time the Native people will not have to petition to join but will be invited to enter the circle because they say the attitude towards us will have changed by then, and people will let us into the circle and all the four colors of the four directions will share their wisdom, and there will be a peace on earth. This is coming close. A lot of times when I share this message of the prophecies, people say, "Can't we change it? Could we stop it?" The answer is yes. The prophecies are always "either/or". We could have come together way back there in 1565, and we could have had a great civilization, but we didn't. Always along the path of these prophecies, we could have come together. We still could. If we could stop the racial and religious disharmony, we would not have to go through this third shaking. The elders say the chance of that is pretty slim. It seems to me like it's pretty slim, too. But they say what we can do is we can "cushion" it. The word we use is "cushion". We can cushion it so it won't be quite as bad. How do we do this? We do this by sharing the teaching that will reunite us. The Hopis in their prophecies say there will be a religion that comes here. Maybe it will be true and bring unity, or maybe it will not be true and not bring unity. If it does not bring unity, a second religion will come, and the people of this religion are known in the Hopi language as the Bahani, the people of Baha. Ni means "people of". So I was looking for the people of Baha. I wondered who the people of Baha were. I was a Baha'i for quite a while before somebody told me that Baha'i means "people of Bahà". I thought, "Oh my God!" Here I was looking for it all these years and I never even noticed it! And I found it! I was stubborn and didn't want to become a "Baha'i but my grandfather who passed away, you know he must have found out about it in the next realm because he came back to me four times to tell me, "Hey, look at that again, look at that again. Look one more time." Bahà, (it) means "light or glory". Baha'i means "follower of the light", or the "people of Baha". We've been waiting for these people for a long time. They say they will bring a Teaching that will unite the earth. So we need to share this

Michael L. Kilday

> *Teaching. They say the fire will come from the North. So here we are, in a circle, in the North, talking about the Bahànis, the "people of Bahà", and the teachings of Baha'u'llah. When I heard about these [Hopi prophecies], none of them made any sense. Now most of it has come to pass. Last I heard on the news, they said the "house in the sky" will be put up in 1996. It was going to be put up sooner, but it's been postponed for four years. Maybe it will be postponed again. But in not too long it's going to go up. The earth as we know it is going to change.*

In 1979, a statement presented by Dr Frederick Fischer, a disembodied entity who was one of deep-trance medium Elwood Babbitt's *controls*, echoed a sentiment similar to Lee Brown. The session was detailed in the first book of the series, TRUTH NEVER CHANGES: EARTH CHANGES[xxviii] (Kilday, 2009). During that session Dr Fischer, had said:

> *A canopy of light enters the lives of all concerned which brings with it a harbinger of change. All will feel its effects quicken the pace of the life-beat as it is played upon the heartstrings of all those who now trod your earth. And what you will see in your 'New Age' is the complete understanding of spiritual life and force that is now obliterated by the misunderstandings propagated by the teachings of your churches, temples, and mosques. They manipulate the truth to meet their need and in the process cast darkness over all those who are eager to live the Truth. The kernel of Truth they present in their teachings has become so distorted by their manipulations it is unrecognizable to those of us who live in the Light.*

The *complete understanding* referred to may very well be the world's oldest religion; namely the teachings of the Children of the Law of One.[xxix] The Baha'i faith[xxx] had originated over a century ago in Persia and came from the same root. It was the latest offshoot of the legendary faith of Atlantis. If taken to heart, humanity could actually save itself from a cruel fate, and peace could reign on Earth. Conversely if the Law of One failed to connect with the populace, humanity would suffer the consequences of a final conflict to end all conflicts. Even if humanity survived it, it was likely to be a time of devastating upheaval in every sense of the word – geological, emotional, and psychological. Like Lee Brown noted, "*the prophecies are always either/or*" because humanity had choice. He confirmed the belief that peace and understanding could not be forced upon the world. The people of the world must want it for the right reasons for it to become a reality. A sense of harmony and brotherhood could not be mandated. It had to be a collective effort, freely-given and self-governing. To make this happen, it was the inner landscape of human thought and emotion that provided the most challenge.

Moreover if some were inspired to change they would need somewhere to take that inspiration. Thus began a quest to discover what the options were. If nothing else this manuscript will confirm there was something worth knowing that too few actually had the correct perspective on. Generally it didn't mean they couldn't know it; it meant they didn't know yet how to recognize it. Given the scientific evidence presented, change was no longer a matter of *if*. It was only a matter of *when*. Given the metaphysical evidence presented, humanity could save itself if it was so inclined. Whether or not it would choose to was another matter entirely. However it was incumbent upon each individual to take matters into their own hands. On a cautionary note however what Geoffrey Chaucer said in the 14th century held true today: "*time and tide wait for no man*".

Our planet will proceed through a period of cyclical realignment and it had already begun. A cyclical process was in motion. The scientific evidence provided showed this to be actual fact. The word *tribulation* had been used to describe this time period by Biblical sources, while psychic sources preferred the word *transformation*. Regardless misfortune and hardship would be a pretty apt description of either choice of characterization. Even if the least traumatic shock of the prophesied Earth Changes occurred and our power grid went down, the consequences would still be grave. If our modern conveniences were wiped away in an instant, it would lead to mass hysteria, insanity, and starvation; not necessarily in that order. However speculating on the fate of humanity was primarily conjecture because of the influence of cause and effect. Free will complicated the scenario, opening vistas or closing them depending upon choices made. How would millions of people who had no actual survival skills fare? What would happen to those who were self-medicated? What would happen to those who could not fend for themselves? Ask yourself: what was self-sufficiency worth given those circumstances?

Truth Never Changes: The Genesis of the Path

A Journey Begins with a Single Step

Since the deep-trance session in 1979, the idea of meditating on a regular basis lurked in the back of my mind. Shortly thereafter, Spirit's advice was taken and my experimentation with meditation began. Having little or no experience with meditation, Spirit's advice was taken literally. My methodology was to sit still for as long as possible with my intention focused upon my breathing and repeat the mantra given, *'Be still and know that I am Spirit'*. As soon as it was a regular practice, it was also apparent it wasn't working as anticipated. Chalking it up to my inexperience with meditation in general, some research appeared to be in order before it could be mastered.

Picking up a book on RAJA YOGA[xxxi] (Vivekanada, 1980), an attempt was made to familiarize myself with the concepts involved. What was learned about Raja yoga was that it was yoga of the mind, rather than the body. As such all of the exercises were mental ones. While the focus was on one's breathing, the lessons the book offered encompassed the mechanics involved; such as proper body posturing and relaxation techniques. The objective was to focus attention on one's breathing so that thinking and breathing would be synchronized. But it also included techniques to clear the mind of wanton thoughts. After joining a local yoga center so the proper techniques could be practiced, it started to fall into place.

To meditate wasn't as difficult as was originally imagined. The challenge it presented lie in determining if the correct results were being achieved or any results for that matter. At the yoga center it was assumed that enlightenment was everybody's ultimate goal. In their lingo, it was accomplished by opening the chakras and awakening the kundalini. As it was explained, the kundalini was a coiled snake that symbolized the bio-electrical energy one stored at the base of one's spine. They called it *prana*. A chill up the spine was a crude way to describe the effect but it was an adequate description. If you could imagine a bio-electrical charge of unknown voltage traveling at light-speed, you got the point. Certain meditative procedures were employed to release it, and care had to be taken to ensure the release was controlled. To do it abruptly and carelessly invited damage to the mind of the practitioner. Whenever the conversation shifted to explaining what the kundalini was and how it operated, the in-house yogi treated it with utmost seriousness. As far as the potential dangers were concerned, they were likened to putting a lethal weapon in the hands of a novice. The image that stuck in the mind was a 45 caliber revolver in the hands of a child. One could only imagine there were reasons why it was so dangerous, though it was never adequately explained what the potential damage could be. That was left to the imagination. It was merely stated one would be unable to control their mind; inferring insanity would be the result. Thus it was wise to get some instruction and exercise caution.

The ultimate goal in releasing the kundalini was to raise one's consciousness to a level where one could achieve enlightenment. By observation it appeared everybody had a slightly different definition for it. It depended upon the person. It's not so much that anyone saw it differently. Rather everyone had different reasons for wanting to achieve it. While some practitioners wanted power and prestige so they could profile on their accomplishment, others would just settle for a little peace of mind. Some it appeared were just following the latest fad in the hopes it would prove to be more than a fad. Others treated it like it was the greatest invention since the wheel, and endlessly extolled its virtues to any who would listen. Sometimes experienced practitioners would just smile that thousand-fold smile of the Buddha and say virtually nothing about what they were feeling. One could only assume they had reached their goal, and if you followed the same path you could also.

But truthfully one usually didn't even know what one wanted until one accidentally tripped over it. If that was the case, how could one know what they needed? From what one could gather, the majority of the practitioners didn't have any perceived goals except for peace and tranquility in their own lives. Any knowledge gained in the process was a bonus. It also came with a price because *donations* to the center were requested for the dispensing of this information. Churches, temples, or mosques also had a collection plate for their compensation; so it was not unusual the yoga center would follow suit. They fancied themselves to be on a par with these other religious institutions at least in the way of tithing. Whether or not that's appropriate under the circumstances, it's a mute point. Their place among them had been secured by representation.

Truth Never Changes: The Genesis of the Path

The community had always been asked to contribute something to the operating expenses of one's choice of faith. This was no exception. Technically being a house of worship, the yoga center qualified as a place where one could practice their faith at the very least. How effective it was strictly a matter of opinion – just like traditional religions.

But there was a downside. At the yoga center, there were times one could imagine one was back in high school; with its abundant supply of personalities, cliques, pecking orders, and egos one had to deal with. Inevitably one could come face-to-face with that nominal percentage of the population that had never progressed beyond the high school mentality, and never would. That meant they basically worshipped personality and wanted to attach themselves to who was perceived to be the most popular and/or wielded the most power and influence over the group. In this case, the fundamentally insecure gravitated toward the perceived subject matter experts. Naturally they were looking for someone, anyone who qualified, to show them *the way*. At the start it was a natural inclination, but eventually one should grow out of that dependency.

In situations where one was open to suggestion and asking for guidance from those perceived to be *in the know*, the potential for abuse was apparent. It was incumbent upon the seeker to be perceptive enough to avoid those who would take advantage of the situation. But many were not so discriminating. This was not to say that *the good, bad, and the ugly* couldn't be found in any venue if one cared to look. Nevertheless the fact remained some people could not tell them apart. Clearly the inability to look beyond the personality to discern the character of an individual was a human failing. And it was one all human beings at some time in their respective lives were subject to. The hangers-on and opportunists looking for someone on whose coattails they could ride were easy to spot however. They were the people with their hands out, willing to lend a helping hand if there was some spare change in it. The widest smiles of those who took were reserved for those who gave. Those who didn't give unconditionally weren't offered a second glance. There was an old aphorism, '*no good deed goes unpunished*'. Undoubtedly politician and playwright, Claire Boothe Luce had said it tongue-in-cheek. After a few months at the yoga center, one understood how it applied there. And it spoke to a common human experience – disappointment in what was offered as compensation for one's loyalty and dutiful observance of protocol.

When it came to social interaction, egos inevitably got in the way. All of the other complications inherent in social situations like the he said, she said rigmarole spoiled the entire experience; so as to make it ultimately unproductive and dissatisfying. But it was impossible to avoid where people were involved. If one could separate the emotional trials and tribulations of dealing with people from the technical details of the practice of meditation itself, one could easily see it through to its natural conclusion. If the entire exercise could have been kept on a technical level it might have worked, but personalities intervened and soon there were walls that couldn't be breached. Everything was reduced to a weekly soap-opera mentality. Often the topic of conversation devolved into who was mad at whom, who did what to whom, and how people rated on the popularity scale. For the serious student, all of extra-curricular activities were not desired anyway. High school was a distant memory; an unpleasant one at that. My desire was only to escape it with my sanity intact. The intent was not to repeat the experience – no matter how it was disguised. It was demeaning and degrading for anyone who imagined there was something valuable to be gained from it.

Since the yoga center was comparable to the high school experience, it labored under the misconception all this was the evidence of growing pains. The subject matter experts functioned like teachers, but they just couldn't keep the ideology focused, clear, and pure. People being true to form could pervert any noble purpose they chose to without even trying. The whole experience was diluted by personality because by and large that's what people responded to – the personal touch. The administrators of the yoga center strove to be customer-focused, but the personal touch they applied was the curse of a consumer-oriented enterprise. When one was doling out services of any kind, human interaction took precedence over the product. One liked who they liked and disliked who they disliked, and it was for the reasons they chose. But people being people it proved to be ultimately dissatisfying. When the topic of day became the resident yogi's pocketbook fetish, it signaled a crossover into ludicrous celebrity gossip. When it was followed by a cascade of giggles from the women who acted like school girls in a clique, it indicated for me a wall couldn't be breached. But instead of confronting the foolishness one could only take the high road and maintain a stoic silence; thinking to oneself – this too shall pass. Unfortunately it was a signal of what was to come.

Also the teachings were dumbed-down to the lowest common denominator so it had the widest appeal possible to the masses. When you did that something got lost in the translation, and you ended up with a dilution of pure principle; like offering a fruit punch concoction in which no fruit taste was distinct enough to recognize. It was no longer a *juice*. Now it was just a *drink*. The lesson was: when you tried to please everyone, you often ended up pleasing no one. So a watered-down version of spirituality was offered to allay one's thirst without quenching it. When the techniques were mastered, the group dynamic had nothing more to offer. Perhaps patience wore thin because more was expected out of it. When the one expert practitioner who commanded some respect for his professionalism decided to move on to a Buddhist temple some six hundred miles away, it was a sign changes had to be made. As he explained, it was time for a *"reformation of his own"*. He didn't like what was going on either and he was separating from his wife of 15 years who ran the Yoga Center for his own peace of mind. One could imagine Martin Luther thinking in a similar fashion when he tacked his NINETY-FIVE THESES (Luther, 1517) on the door of Castle Church in Wittenberg, Germany.

Moving on to private practice was a welcome relief. Meditation being an entirely subjective activity, one had to be flexible with one's expectations. My intent was to focus on the purpose provided in the deep trance session with Elwood Babbitt. That was to make contact. With whom or with what one couldn't be certain. Whether or not it was even possible would be my determination, not anyone else's. No one else was in a position to make that call anyway. The required social interactions with people one didn't really want to be associated with in the first place just got in the way of making progress. It diverted attention away from what the actual goals should be. Certainly it wasn't to genuflect before the resident yogi to score points with the Yoga Center. The aura of pomp and circumstance that had engulfed the Yoga Center hadn't made me long for the churchgoing experience. It had in fact pushed me further away from it.

Using the mantra Spirit had provided, my experimentation with meditation continued intermittently. Being afflicted however with the disease of modern man, the craving for instant gratification, made it short-lived. When it didn't bear immediate fruit, impatience only made success more elusive. On the back burner always was the desire to connect. The continuous intrusion of white noise made it near impossible to concentrate on the practice. Due to the static, every mundane task seemed more important to do instead. Growing increasingly disenchanted, it was difficult to adhere to the practice. With the fits and starts, impatience grew into frustration and the practice ground to a halt. Despite the best of intentions, it didn't take. *'The spirit was willing but the flesh was weak'* would be the traditional rationalization, but people often have the flimsiest of excuses for their failures; especially when a little effort was required. The resolve to keep it going couldn't be mustered. Patience was never one of my strong suits, but in this case it had to be. In the practice of meditation, the harder one pressed, the more impossible it became to relax into the flow. It was like crushing the bird in one's hand, when instead it should be cradled.

Instinctively knowing what the cause was didn't mean the problem was easily solved. It only indicated there was more work to do. A significant effort was required to let go of the bad habits of smoking and drinking to excess. Before new beneficial ones could take root, it was time to let go of an old identity. This wasn't going to happen without considerable effort. The urge to continually lapse back into those bad habits was a constant struggle. After being pulled in that direction for so long, a path had been worn to that feeding trough. The seductive lure of the *high* dwarfed every other motive. That's precisely what addiction did to you. Anyone who had suffered the throes of addiction knew exactly what that meant and how strong the attraction became. Anyone else could only imagine being in the pull of a giant magnet. The urge to *get a buzz on* too often outweighed the desire to progress in a meaningful way. It even overrode common sense, even though it may not be recognized as such at the time. Addiction not only got in the way, it became the way. One even made justifications for it. As a direct result of our animal instinct to seek pleasure and avoid pain, it overwhelmed every other purpose one could imagine.

Regarding substance abuse, human beings were prone to taking it to absurd extremes. By and large, human Society was trapped in an addiction to excess. The obsession with matter seemed to be all that mattered. The desire for bigger paychecks and more playthings surely dominated the public mind. In a word, desire ultimately would be our downfall if it was not brought under control. Surely it was a lesson one should take to heart. Ironically a Society that strove to get you hooked on every substance possible, at the same time strove to cure you of every addiction that plagued you. But perhaps that was the way to get you coming and going – covering all bases at the same time. Certainly it was disingenuous but effective in separating you from what many love most – their money and their ego gratifications. Self-esteem was often a casualty along the way. But perhaps that was only the quality of self-esteem offered by attending to one's physical and emotional needs while neglecting the spiritual ones. In my estimation with each succeeding decade, from the 1970's onward, the condition had gotten progressively worse.

But in order to deal with the enormity of the problem the user must recognize he or she was a cause of it, rather than just a victim of it. One was both. Lest one be labeled a hypocrite, the effort should always begin with the attempt to rein in one's own desires. In truth the test case for substance abuse rested in one's own hands. And if you wanted to make a difference, temperance was the course you must follow. You could not expect others to follow a course if you were not willing to follow it yourself. Most learned this lesson the hard way because they often neglected to see their human frailty as the cause of their dilemma. They preferred to identify some external force as the cause of their misery like the government, family relations, other people, or in extreme cases of dysfunction, even the devil. Most often however the causes were internal, and were shaped by attitudes and fears. The easy way was to accept their habit for what it was, an addiction, and resign oneself to it. The hard way was to recognize they had a problem, and submit to the treatment. That meant facing up to one's challenges and addressing them. Ultimately changing your ways was the most difficult task to accomplish because it got personal.

Quite frankly any substance qualified for substance abuse when it soothed the mind and body. If any substance was not taken in moderation, that's when it presented a problem. Substance abuse included everything from sugar to Heroin. At the core of the addictive urge comparable pressures were exerted upon every substance abuser from glutton to heroin addict. Of course the respective physical, mental, and emotional penalties exacted varied a great deal. The substance abuser may be quick to point out how his or her *problem* was not as severe as another's, that he or she was able to control it, and that its relative impact was under control. That was a clue one had a much more severe problem than one realized. But a fix was a fix; no matter how one sliced it. Sensory deprivation was the only way to address it. In the vernacular, the cure used to be called *cold turkey*. When you were free and clear, then you could judge the torment suffered by another to be comparable. But if you had empathy for another who suffered through the throes of addiction as you did, you should find it more difficult to judge them. If you didn't, there was something definitely wrong with you. There was really no point in belittling the substance abusers. And often those that did were projecting their human frailty upon them to deflect attention away from their own shortcomings. In particular it was that feeling of superiority that ego provided to make one believe one was somehow better than another. The reason was immaterial, and the results, counterintuitive.

Substance abuse had a way of making all serious spiritual pursuits null and void. Until you decided that was more important than the substance you were abusing, you were stuck in neutral. Actually each individual case was comparable to any other. Addiction at its lowest common denominator was all the same. Once this was realized it changed one's perspective. It was exceedingly difficult to concentrate when the mind continually wandered. In order for your meditation to be proficient, the mind could not wander. That was the first hurdle in the practice, and constituted a book by itself to explain the ramifications. Time and space did not permit that here. Suffice it to say a little diligence applied to control one's habits was enough so that the effort to meditate wasn't entirely wasted. It wasn't entirely satisfactory either. But until the habits could be terminated once and for all, the heights of spiritual expression were out of reach. In order to achieve a state of altered consciousness which meditation offered, one could not always reside in an altered state. It defeated the purpose of meditating. Much time and effort was spent convincing myself that something other than the substance mattered more. Like a car that needed to be pushed down a hill to get the *engine to turn over*, my effort was focused upon overcoming the addictive urge. In reality, it proved to be more expedient to just fix the car. But humanity possessed a fondest for its roundabout ways of remediation; particularly in how we continually addressed the symptoms of illness instead of its causes. It was always proven to be pointedly half-hearted, but that didn't change much if one was left to their own devices. However with the help of the ones that loved me, reason overcame compulsion. Partly because of this effort, and partly because of the moral support that was provided, a measure of success was achieved. That was what was needed to get me started on the path, but the actual breakthrough did not occur until much later. Nonetheless it was satisfying that for at least fifteen minutes the mind could be quieted without having it continually wander off the reservation. That was enough to lay the foundation. The sanctuary still had to be constructed upon it.

It took a shock to the senses on August 17th, 1989 to really motivate me. That was the day my 16 year old son was taken from me in an automobile accident. Words could not express the feelings of loss, so no time will be wasted here expressing them. It should just be noted it was absolutely the worst feeling one could experience bar none. No physical pain or emotional trauma could compare. Sedatives took the edge off, but they could not erase the memories. Nothing could do that. They could only provide a short-lived buffer zone while the healing process was engaged. However using a buffer zone merely delayed the inevitable. It prolonged the agony because one avoided facing loss head-on. At some point, one had to face it head-on to reconcile the loss. When one finally did, one was positioned for recovery. Until one did, one could easily wallow in it for a lifetime. In that frame of mind no one was served, neither the mourner nor the mourned. The danger posed was a life dominated by remorse and regret, and that was not even the worst that could happen. Falling into that trap was only the preface for a wasted life. Being unable to climb out of the emotional doldrums sealed one's fate.

During that period, a book by Steven Levine, entitled WHO DIES? (Levine, 1986), provided a small measure of consolation. It concerned coping with sudden and untimely death. Being written to assist those who were in the process of mourning the loss of a loved one, the author shared his experience with loss. It had a lot of good advice for mourners, but really most of it was common sense. Aside from the emotional aspects presented that eased the pain of the passing of a loved one, the essential point presented was that the key to recovery was to let the feelings go. As emoting was a way to release them, reconciling was easier said than done. But until one could reconcile the loss, the grieving process could not take its natural course. The purpose was for it to end, so one could go on with one's life. If one could philosophize instead of emote, they were better for it in the long run. Every traditional religion used this method. They would say so and so was in heaven, or with Jesus now (fill in the blank with your favorite savior), or offer a myriad of platitudes that inferred one had gone to a better place. It was all for the purpose of providing closure for the mourner.

Until one was struck by the stark reality that such an event was irretrievable, the inclination was to hang to the faint hope that the impossible could happen. But there were no do-overs. Thus one had to be sensible about it – their loved one wasn't coming back under any circumstances; at least not in the same form or to the same circumstance. No amount of prayer, affirmation, or heartfelt, grief-stricken promises-to-be-good-in-the-future was going to make any difference, but yet this was what people most often got hung-up on. All of that served to relieve one's emotional stress, but it was not going to change history. What's done was done. It was what it was and always would be. The finality of it all was sobering and irreversible. It was best to just accept it, and move on as best as one could. What death was really timely? Everyone who lived would die. It was just a matter of how, where and when. No one would ever be immune from the pain it caused to those left behind so it was best to permit it to wash over you, and move on. This was something no human being could ever change.

Considering the untimely death of his 33 year old wife, Thomas Jefferson, our third president, was not insulated from personal loss. He made a critical observation in a letter to a friend in 1813 which indicated a choice he had made in his younger days. He wrote *"The earth belongs to the living, not to the dead"*, and that he used as justification for letting the feelings go. He lived his remaining life accordingly; not looking backward but rather forward. There was nothing to be gained through acrimony and recrimination, he reasoned, except an early death for him if he held onto it. He went so far as to burn all letters between him and his wife after her death. Perhaps it was an extreme measure to divorce him from the past, but *burning bridges* did necessitate moving in a different direction. It was a reminder that one couldn't go that way any longer. Even if the *bridge* was a mental one, crossing it was no longer appropriate. It posed a danger for one to languish in memories. One could prefer their memories to living in the present, and use it to justify living that way for the duration. But they never would achieve anything of substance again if they did.

Each individual dealt with grief in their own way, but Jefferson's solution seemed to be born of reason and was consistent with how he approached life, intellectualizing loss more than most would. Intellectualizing a tragic event served to take some of the sting out of it. Relieving it of its emotional content also permitted him to take stock of himself. He used that to affect his recovery. Ultimately a heavy dose of introspection was what leads to the cure. The balm of forgetfulness could be a blessing in disguise because *letting go* had its merits. Not only was it an effective self-defense mechanism, it made good sense because the alternative of clinging to remorse dug an emotional fissure from which few could escape. Like a black hole of despair, it sucked you in. From it, light could not even escape much less sluggish remorse and regret brought on by grief. Healing could only be initiated as one progressed onward. That was if one was able to take the steps to proceed. Come what may thereafter, it was how one survived the emotional trauma of untimely death. It was not a cure because they were none, but an accommodation.

As a healing mechanism, meditation proved to be a god-send. From the depths of despair, the long climb to the light began one step at a time. Soon meditation was a regular practice, and the prospect of settling into a groove presented itself. As the practice progressed, the benefits to be gained from it began to evidence themselves as peace of mind and a quiet confidence in the results gained. The clarity of mind it offered dispelled any suffocating clouds of doubt. That didn't mean doubt never again entered the mind. Rather it meant it no longer lingered there. The strength of spirit it engendered gave me hope again. That didn't mean despair was never felt again. Rather it meant it no longer took up residence in the heart. That didn't mean no negative emotion would ever be felt again. But that no matter what negative emotion emerged; the prospect was it would eventually evolve in a positive direction. In other words, the road to recovery was laid out before me like the fabled road less traveled. It had peaks and valleys, steep inclines and precipitous drops. There were still potholes to avoid. It wound around corners the traveler couldn't see beyond, and it had many twists and turns. However it was navigable. That was what had to be proven to the one who traveled it. Even though *clear sailing* was never promised, confidence was high it could be negotiated. Far off in the distance, the ultimate goal looked to be attainable. It just seemed like such a long way to go. "*A journey of a thousand miles begins with a single step*", the Chinese philosopher Lao-tzu once said. Without fail, one began it from where one was. Visualizing the path in this way was a reminder that patience was a virtue not extolled often enough. But to persevere one had to summon the will to move forward.

Until one began meditating in earnest one could not even imagine what wisdom may arise from the well of soul. Traditional Christian religion had a catch phrase for these situations – "*ask and you shall receive*".[xxxiii] It had been my experience, however, that it was not even necessary to ask. When you were in a receptive frame of mind, you received what you needed to receive whether you intended to or not. The higher mind knew already what you needed to hear. It was you who chose whether or not to listen. With practice meditation made you a magnet for transcendental inspiration. Rather than it be considered an accident, it should be considered a beneficial side-effect, resulting from a receptive frame of mind. In reality there were no accidents only unanticipated effects. Until one opened a channel, one could not even begin to imagine what it was possible to receive. It was the reflection of the posture one took, and the quality of the reception. Feelings surfaced for which there was no logical explanation, but the thoughts came nonetheless. They resonated with the recognition of a complementary impression that already resided in the soul.

Until one quieted the mind one will never hear the small, still voice that had wisdom to offer from the higher mind. It was for your own benefit you must pay heed. In the silence were the depths of feelings unexplored. They rose to the surface like bubbles full of oxygenated wisdom drawn forth by a willingness to sample the fresh air of good judgment. They burst into thoughts that cause one to wonder where they came from. But where they came from wasn't as important as where they led. The ability to wonder was a human trait, but it was shackled in each of us until the *bard* was given free reign. One could not understand the phrase '*to be as little children*' until it was seen in this light. Thus feelings would not line-up until the simple, straightforward wonderment of a child invaded the adult intellect. It was then an occasional '*why not*' was introduced into the mix.

Whether or not this experiment was begun to clear a channel to the Atlantean Masters as Spirit had suggested was a matter of debate. There was a conscious decision made only to experiment with meditation to see if it would pan out. Trying to be practical, the effort was focused more upon lifting me out of the emotional doldrums. Full-blown enlightenment really wasn't anticipated as an end result, but still one harbored a hope it could conceivably happen. Well aware that these things could take time and effort the expectations weren't too high. Muddling along was the best one could hope for until that fateful day one was struck by the lightning bolt of illumination. When and if that was going to happen was strictly a matter of conjecture. As for the child who continually asked *"are we there yet?"* the answer would always be – *"you will know when you get there"*.

Languishing for years with a half-baked notion communication with the Other Side was possible; the thought crept in occasionally that notion would never be fully-baked. A modicum of healthy doubt served to keep one honest by keeping things in perspective. As long as it didn't cause one to quit in frustration, it had served its stated purpose. When the *why* mattered more than the *what* or the *how*, one better understood the need for the process. Without that knowledge, seeing it through to the end was problematic. One could only take life as it came and hope for something better. Or one could maneuver oneself into position for something better. It was decided that being a maker of circumstance was infinitively better than being a victim of it. Thus the search commenced for a reason to believe in the process. What else should one do with their allotted time? In all likelihood, the alternative would be to concentrate upon one's instinctual needs if one did not have a hunch there just might be a more noble purpose to life itself.

Michael L. Kilday

Truth Never Changes: The Genesis of the Path

Kubrick's Interpretation of Genesis

Stanley Kubrick in his landmark epic film, 2001: A SPACE ODYSSEY[xxxiv] (Kubrick, 1968), presented both an intriguing possibility for human origin as well as a potential course for human evolution. In the opening scenes of the film, a jet-black monolith of exacting proportions but with no markings to be seen stood on the edge of a prehistoric waterhole. Since it was not a natural outgrowth of rock or stone protruding from the soil, the implication was it was placed there. The natural question to ask would be by whom or what, but the inhabitants of the land weren't ones to question, not yet anyway. Huddled around the monolith was a troupe of apes who paid little attention to it until it began to *hum*. The humming sounded like a machine warming up, at once eerily familiar, but also possessing a quality of foreboding. With each second there was a barely perceptible increase in pitch and intensity. This was another implication that the event was timed or staged, and the humming was not a chance occurrence. Someone or something turned it on, and it certainly wasn't the apes.

One by one they cautiously approached it, and the surface of the monolith was caressed by individual apes. From their reaction, it appeared *the light of understanding* turned on in their eyes. Perhaps that light was a vague reference to a revelation simply because traditionally the eyes had long been considered to be the windows of the soul. Clearly this was an allegory of the Creation myth. Like Adam and Eve became conscious of their nakedness when they ate the apple from the Tree of Knowledge, it was indicative of one becoming conscious of the circumstances of one's existence. It was another way of saying they became *conscious of self* which was symbolic of the attainment of self-knowledge. No one really could attest to the fact animals were *conscious of self*, but rightly or wrongly it was assumed they were not. The monolith was a symbol for the Tree of Knowledge. When the tribe encountered it, they were awakened to knowledge previously unknown to them. They recognized their separateness from the Whole; meaning their individuality. It started them on the course of human evolution.

Michael L. Kilday

After that experience the tribe evolved. In other words, they became aware of their needs. They began to use tools, hunted and killed tapirs to sustain themselves, and formulated a new methodology for survival. They also brawled with a local troupe over ownership of the local watering hole. The evolving troupe became omnivorous now that they could utilize tools to enhance their existence. In other words they began to exhibit human traits. The film made this point by showing that they learned how to use a femur as a universal tool. The viewer could come to no other reasonable conclusion from their behavior that they killed for profit; whether that be for pride, power, or bloodlust. No other animal did that. Normally they killed out of necessity, for sustenance, or in self-defense. Man was the only animal that had designs upon a purpose other than meeting its instinctual needs. Operating upon pride, a lust for power, or bloodlust was one of the marks of being human. When the skirmish over the waterhole escalated to the murder of a peer with a weapon a threshold had been crossed; like when Cain slew Abel. From that moment forward the ape had evolved into a human being.

The film fast-forwarded to the present. A spaceship, outfitted as a commercial airliner, glided gracefully to a landing on the moon. The grace and beauty of the scene was set to classical music to provide an elegant flair. Inside the craft, a stewardess doted on the passengers as if this was merely a commercial flight on a routine excursion. Its connotation was business as usual in the 21st century. By honing his technological skills, Man had mastered the art of making and using machinery to augment his existence. He had come a long way from being a primitive hunting on the grasslands of Africa with his newly acquired tool, but there was further to go. One of the pivotal scenes of the film featured a second monolith uncovered on the moon which emitted a piercing tone the result of which was left to the imagination. However, the 21st century human beings who encountered the moon monolith reacted to it in a similar fashion to the way the prehistoric ape-men did. One could only infer another leap of consciousness in the human being was in the offing. Reportedly a signal was beamed to the planet Jupiter. That launched the Discovery, a spaceship, on its secret mission to Jupiter to find the source of the signal. On a mysterious quest for knowledge, the main plot unfolded from that point.

Truth Never Changes: The Genesis of the Path

The HAL 9000, the thinking, talking computer of the Discovery, appeared to represent that leap in human intelligence. This computer had intelligence, the ability to reason, and even expressed emotions, but that really was artificial intelligence because it was man-made. It was merely the offspring of human intelligence because HAL couldn't have existed without it. HAL showed that it could modify its own programming but it proved to be a ruse. It could also be turned off, and brought back to life. No living being could be unless it consented to it. Technically the HAL 9000 did not qualify as a living thing because it wasn't self-sustaining, mobile, and could not procreate. It had *spirit* in the form of electricity that powered it, but that wasn't enough to be classified as a living entity. It needed something more that humanity could not provide. HAL of course was not perceptive enough to realize the implications of its limitations even though it was a *thinking machine*. It imagined it had achieved consciousness because it could reason. What it could not imagine was that it only had a left-side to its *brain*, and because of that it was incapable of insight, intuition, or imagination. While it possessed a memory, it could not visualize its actions before they were taken or truly link its thoughts to its emotions. These were noteworthy attributes of living beings, effortlessly applied.

While one of the Discovery astronauts, Dave Bowman, was in the process of shutting down HAL's higher brain functions, HAL asked Dave "*will I dream?*" Dave didn't understand the question or the reason for it, so he replied "*I don't know, HAL*". Dreaming was distinctly a function of the right-side of the brain, and signified the dreamer was a higher life form. Visualization was the active process it employed in the waking state. The right-side of the brain provided one with a sense of wonder, and a playground for the emotions. Over this terrain feelings reined that visualized and extrapolated upon intuitions of faith, hope and compassion; being fed by a thought process that formulated beliefs. Until humanity could create a machine that had a soul implanted in it, the right-side of its brain would not function. Without a soul, one could not have beliefs, or have faith in them. Neither could one divine a purpose for oneself. These attributes were reserved for beings that possessed souls, housing a motivating energy within it. It was the Spirit within.

The fact that human beings were in line for a leap of consciousness was confirmed in the climax of the film. As the main character, Dave

Michael L. Kilday

Bowman, *entered* the third monolith near Io, one of Jupiter's moons, he went on a trip through the time/space continuum. His only audible comment, *"My God, it's full of stars"*, signified that sense of wonder human beings possessed. In large part, it was that sense of wonder that caused one to reach for the stars even if one could not touch them. Dave saw himself at various stages of development, from life to death, co-existing in a single space. The scenes shifted through Time literally with the blink of an eye. This indicated the transitions between them were controlled by thought. On his deathbed, he reached out to touch the fourth monolith that appeared in the film, and was transformed into a star child in-utero floating in the vastness of space.

The last lines of the Arthur C. Clarke's book (Clarke, 1968) truly expressed the conundrum in which the human soul found itself at the end of life. Typically the quandary was expressed in an eternal question – is there nothing more? One might think it was strictly human intellectual property, but to wonder could be the natural state of every living thing; especially when the transition was imminent. Primarily one postulated what came next. Two ancient civilizations the Tibetans and Egyptians thought the subjects to be so intriguing books were written on the subject, the Tibetan Book of the Dead and the Egyptian Book of the Dead respectively. It was required reading for those who awaited transition. Essentially it was the question HAL had in mind -- *is this all there is? Am I nothing more?* In the culminating paragraph of his novel, the author's contribution to the age-old query was as follows:

> *Then he waited, marshalling his thoughts and brooding over his untested powers. For though he was master of the world; he was not quite sure what to do next. But he would think of something.*

As the author implied, the end was nothing more than a new beginning. At the close of each phase of existence a new purpose is divined. In the Universe, choice reigned supreme. Physical life restarted each time in uncertainty with the potential that a purpose can be accomplished. From that uncertainty was derived a formulation of purpose. The prospectus of his novel offered that the next phase of human evolution would see the creation of a being that consciously cohabitated in all time sequences at the same moment in the same space.

Truth Never Changes: The Genesis of the Path

To this being, reason was the same as insight, and the past, present, and future were indistinguishable from each other. Until then the only thing one could know for certain was what they experienced in present time. In accordance with the continuance of life principle, taught by Eastern religions, the present was all that ever existed. But they also taught that all instances of Time inhabited the same space. Should this be true, then theoretically an entity could experience past, present, and future at the same moment in Time.

The inference was human life began with a blank slate because there was no conscious carry-over from one life to the next. However underlying consciousness there was bedrock composed of accumulated knowledge and experience waiting to be drilled down into. If one ascribed to a belief in reincarnation, that storehouse was the substance of the subconscious mind. The information to be drawn upon had to be stored somewhere. To think every frame of remembrance was not recorded somewhere was beyond the pale of reasonability. Where then would the substance of dreams and visions be stored? Such a thing as creative visualization would not be possible without a source of information to extrapolate upon. Beyond an individual's storehouse of knowledge, there was a shared storehouse where the sum total of humanity's knowledge and experience was stored. Edgar Cayce had a name for it, the Akashic Record. Carl Jung had a name for it as well. He called it the collective unconscious. If only one knew how to tap into that, all questions would have answers.

The end of one road was not a dead end but the start of another. Since a progression was implied, one had to wonder if humanity was evolving toward something. And at each stage of progression one groped for the same thing -- a reason to believe. In essence, that was purpose; otherwise why embark upon the journey at all? Even though the cycle of life repeated itself, the meaning of life was still not explained. Man was still searching for it; ever hopeful an epiphany was in the offing that would lead to him finding it. The clues were spread across God's Creation, but a human being still must interpret their meaning. By all accounts, it appeared to be incumbent upon a human being to fill-in-the-blanks for him or herself. Grace alone would not supply the answer. One had to delve into the so-called secrets of the ages and painstakingly grok[xxxv] (Heinlein, 1961) each one for oneself.

Michael L. Kilday

It was Sir Isaac Newton who postulated energy was neither created nor destroyed; declaring it merely changed form. That meant energy as such always existed, and would always exist. It was eternal. Energy transmigrated from one form to another. Albert Einstein expanded upon Newton's first law of thermodynamics with his formula, E=MC squared. That suggested energy and matter were the same thing or more appropriately matter was a form of condensed energy. Therefore the Universe itself was envisioned to be a vast, interstellar recycling engine. Matter was assembled and disassembled to be the container of energy. With purpose energy was transmuted from one form to another. By definition the human being was simply another form of animated matter. Or was this manifestation of energy something else more significant as religion would have us believe?

A definitive statement on purpose was the one thing left out of Kubrick's and Clarke's equation, but it was implied. It appeared it was a variable to be calculated in the living formula. And whether one ascribed a value that was religious or scientific or philosophical to that variable, it was required to bring the formula to life. That inferred an *invisible hand* at work substituted the variable. Whether this was by chance or by design and some saw it either way, that variable got applied. In a Universe ruled by mathematics it could be no other way because cause and effect was the rule. However debate raged over the intent behind it, and whether cause and effect had purpose beyond the mere substitution of a variable. It would ever be the substance of the debate until the issue was resolved.

Truth Never Changes: The Genesis of the Path

Darwinism Unveiled

Since the Renaissance a battle had raged between Science and Religion for ideological supremacy. The battleground was Genesis; specifically separating the fact from the fiction. An accurate depiction of the creation of the Universe and it's multiplicity of living things was the trophy. The questions to be answered were: where did we come from, why are we here, and was there a purpose behind it? As in any conflict, to the victor go the spoils. In this case, the spoils of victory were the triumph of faith or reason. Traditional allegiances offered a choice between Religion and Science respectively. Some said it was faith that opened the door to Truth. Others maintained it was reason. In either case one had to delve into the store of information available to them and arrive at their own conclusion.

In 1926 with the famed Scopes monkey trial that battle went to the courts. It featured a legal case that tested the Butler act passed in Tennessee which made it unlawful in any state-funded educational institution to teach the theory of evolution[xxxvi]. The trial pitted two noted celebrities in the legal field against each other, defense attorney Clarence Darrow and prosecutor William Jennings Bryan. Darrow billed himself as the quintessential agnostic, while Bryan presented himself as a man of God. On display was a tense courtroom drama between ideological heavyweights, featuring time-honored religious dogma, defender of the faith, versus modern science, the upstart challenger of the faith. Equal and opposite views were argued before the bench each earnestly believing, never the twain shall meet. And with each foray into character assassination of each opponent's belief system, certainly no compromise could be reached. Few court arguments got more personal and contentious. All of the angst, wrath, and frustration built up over the years by both sides spewed forth, and the Press were only too happy to comply. For them it simply was good theater.

Ironically the case was ruled one way then the ruling was overturned. Neither side could have been satisfied that Scopes was convicted of teaching evolution, and then had the conviction overturned on a legal technicality. That technicality was that the judge instead of the jury had decided the fine of $100. It showed that the issue was too hot to handle, and the trial settled nothing. During the course of the trial, both sides made their share of inane comments confirming that belief, no matter what it was, was a matter of personal preference as opposed to being proven fact. Because of the ambiguous results neither religious doctrine nor scientific theory won the day. In this showdown both proved to be equally flawed. The champions of each side, Darrow and Bryan, revealed themselves to be equally misguided in their intransient views. An impartial observer would have to wonder what all the fuss was really about. Could it simply be a case of misguided zealotry, bluster, and one-dimensional thinking – the left side of the brain pitted against the right side? Ultimately where did that leave humanity, having to choose between one and the other?

If one were to be brutally honest, all of the anthropological investigation invested in finding the missing link of evolution [xxxvii] could have been better spent on finding a cure for cancer, aids, or the common cold. If it was legitimate, however, no scientific inquiry was really wasted. Delving into the mysteries of celestial mechanics or the biology of living things was certainly worth the effort – just to have the satisfaction of knowing. According to religious dogma and specifically those who interpreted it, however, knowing extended only as far as comprehending what was written. Supposedly that was enough to satisfy any inquiry into the nature of things. Theoretically faith would supply any answer there was a question about, and humanity should just simply accept it for it was. No investigation was necessary because God had *spoken* through Scripture. And while there wasn't necessarily a prohibition against inquiry, there was an assumption that those that questioned were deficient in their faith.

To the contrary, the expressed purpose of Science was never to discredit the contributions of the Creator, but rather to reveal them. The proposition was if they were revealed one could better understand them. It would appear some religious zealots took exception to scientific inquiry as if human beings weren't supposed to know. They were simply supposed to accept IT for what IT was and leave it at that. One must wonder if the biblical tale of the forbidden fruit of the Tree of Knowledge had profound philosophical undertones or simply was a story with a moral – not to disobey the will of God. But why would God demand HIS subjects be fat, dumb, and happy for all time? It was curious that humanity was never to partake of knowledge by the command of God. In essence that would leave humanity in the same relative position as an animal; living instinctually instead of intellectually, meetings its needs and never questioning its origin or lot in life.

Nonetheless was the enmity of the Evolutionists toward Creationism to prove a point or an exercise in one-upmanship aimed at the Creationists? Was it payback for centuries of dogmatic self-righteousness like Galileo's revenge or was it simply legitimate scientific endeavor? One supposed that it was merely a matter of perspective and preference; as to whether one would choose to draw back a curtain to reveal what was behind it; or just leave it be. However considering the mythological implications, one could suppose that a pervasive tone of anti-intellectualism was set in the Garden of Eden. And it continued into modern times under the guise of issues and concerns pitting faith against reason. Hence throughout history the conflict had always been with us. Sometimes it was in the forefront, while at others in the background; ever behind the scenes directing the ideological fortunes of humanity in one direction or the other.

For a sincere seeker, it was difficult to imagine how the theory of Natural Selection substituted for Genesis. Nor was it ever intended to by Darwin anyway. Despite the hype, Natural Selection did not necessarily describe how life began, but rather how living things adapted to their environment. Inferences were made based upon observation, unlike the opening verses of Genesis which were an allegorical rendition of cosmic generation. If one was not deluded by their ideological preference they were able to discern that Natural Selection and Genesis did not describe the same thing. It was like calling an apple an orange because one arbitrarily decided to do it. Depending upon the question, each provided a different explanation; Genesis for Creation, and Natural Selection for Change. They didn't necessarily cancel each other out; unless one was so stubborn and dogmatic one could not comprehend the fundamental difference between the birth of an organism and the growth of an organism.

In their ignorance just because some chose to interpret Genesis literally, it wasn't just cause to invalidate its basic premise. That was simply that something set the wheel of life in motion. The Hebrews said it was

Michael L. Kilday

Light. The Hindus said it was *Vibration*. The Greeks said it was *Thought*. In each case, the primary action was attributed to a Supreme Being. However how anyone interpreted what that something was didn't negate the fact it happened. Creation had occurred. The Universe came to life and at that point evolution took over. When it did, all living things came under its influence and began to change. There may be a dispute over how many *days* Creation took, but no one doubted it happened. The physical manifestations of Nature were the evidence it did. And if one studied Nature there was no dispute evidence of cyclical change was manifested in its operation.

The main point of contention between Religion and Science may turn out to be how long a *day* was. Reasonable people on both sides of the argument were willing to concede it was an allegorical measurement of time, not a literal one. If the literalists would just admit a *day* could represent a billion years, the argument would die there. If only they relied upon the information contained in the Book of Enoch instead of calculating biblical lineages, it wouldn't be a hard pill to swallow. Even Jewish tradition didn't take this time measurement literally. A typical rabbi understood and accepted the use of metaphor in calculating Time in the context of the Torah. Only the Christian evangelicals seemed to have a problem with it, and one must wonder why? It only required one expanded their intellectual horizon beyond memorizing biblical verses, and stopped to think about their esoteric rather than literal meanings. Perhaps also they would benefit from expanding their library with other reading material from time to time. They violated the first rule of intellectual investigation by narrowing the field of inquiry to a single source of information. In the scope of geological time Man's contribution to it constituted a trickle.

For a rational person, that made it difficult to take the argument of the Evangelicals seriously in the first place. Surely there was enough space in the vast universe for a dissenting opinion no matter who held it. Unfortunately the field of vision was limited by choice to supporting Darwin's research or the content of the Bible as if it was impossible for one to do both. One could make the case that enforcing the dictates of THE ORIGIN OF SPECIES [xxxviii] (Darwin, 1859) left a bad taste in one's mouth like they were forced to drink gallons of castor oil to cure an illness they didn't have. Furthermore Darwin's research had been misappropriated to make inferences about the origin of species that didn't answer the fundamental uncertainties of human origin. These were embodied in the questions: who am I and how did I get here? What does it mean to be a human being? What is the meaning of life? Admittedly the answers indicated were more philosophical ones rather than biological ones. Yet it seemed modern science presumed to provide answers to philosophical questions by using Biology and Anthropology. While these were the prerogative of Nature, philosophy was the summary view one adhered to as a response to one's inquiry into the nature of things. These were questions that scientists shouldn't try to answer because presumably the answers could only be found within the province of reasoned philosophical debate. In the absence of reasoning, religious belief was adopted in place of it. It was the default value one assumed when one didn't have a clue like the star child of 2001: A SPACE ODYSSEY (Clarke, 1968). Nonetheless they were the questions human beings wanted answered above all others. Because of this the questions remain unanswered whereas humanity yearned for one.

Many have read into Darwin's theories implications that were untenable. Being a botanist, Darwin's theories pertained mainly to his field of expertise -- plant life. He never made any claims he was also a zoologist. Even if his theory of natural selection was taken out of context and applied to human life, it was not done necessarily to inflame debate over the origin of life. That was never his intent. It was the natural result of intellectual curiosity. Primarily his efforts were geared toward showcasing the diversity of life and describing how it evolved on Earth. No attempt was made to rewrite Genesis, or preclude its assertions. In his day, that would have been a pointless exercise that had no tangible benefit; only a detriment in making him a social pariah. Nonetheless his theories put him at the center of controversy. On Darwin's part there was no malice of forethought in seeking answers, just faulty reasoning applied in answering the questions it raised by those who followed him. For lack of a better explanation, his theories were adopted. In the scientific community, Natural Selection was endorsed as a stand-in for Creation. One may rightfully assume that was done to break free of the dogma of pre-determination.

Since Man had always been primarily concerned with Man, the natural inclination of human beings was to be preoccupied with the origin of human life. Ethnocentrism was an age-old affliction, and no one was attempting to cure it. In fact, the problem had worsened over the ensuing years, and both Creationists and Evolutionists were at fault. The proof was that in contemporary times the theory that man evolved from the ape was still anathema to too many. It should have been put to rest long ago for no other reason than one's biological ancestry was less important than one's spiritual heritage. If biology mattered in the case of ancestry, it only mattered to the ethno centrists who could not stomach the idea that a creature created in God's image could be the offspring of an ape. To the Creationists it implied God was an ape also. Conversely scientists rushed to dispel the notion of anything being created in *God's image* because there was no inherent scientific basis to it. It was therefore hearsay evidence. Were it not for that ingrained streak of ethnocentrism the issue wouldn't raise the temperature of the Creationists every time a new discovery was made in the fossil record. It was abundantly clear to all free-thinking, rational people for some time now that the universal purpose and design of Creation had not ever been Man-centric. It was DNA-centric if anything. Human beings were left to interpret the findings, and they disagreed. The rational on both sides of the issue must concede that. The idea itself was a leftover from a bygone era when Faith ruled the thought-waves. The concept of a Man-centric universe should have been laid to rest with the flat-earth and terra-centric theories when they were disproven during the Renaissance.

The following examples illustrate how Man's reasoning power had been misused to prove the hypothesis that biblical doctrine was infallible; for no other reason than the pious wanted desperately to fit the scenario it proposed. Therefore in the absence of reason, logic, and investigation, they simply accepted what was written as absolute truth. Divorcing themselves from the realm of scientific fact, the fathers of the Church toiled in a twilight realm where piety reigned supreme. In such a frame of mind, the pious could justify a belief that the Earth was flat because by casual observation it appeared to be. In spite of the fact, Euclid, a pagan Egyptian, invented a value called *pi* which was used to calculate the circumference of round objects, the pious adhered to an erroneous belief. Euclid did so because he had an intuition that the Earth was a round object. As every school child knows, flat surfaces were measured in linear units. One may draw one's own conclusion. Pythagoras had already proposed the notion that the Earth was spherical in shape if for no other reason than a sphere was representative of perfect form. Aristotle maintained a belief that the Universe also was spherical in shape. By observation the Earth's surface he conceived to be a flat plane within it. The revival of classical study in Europe brought these ideas to the forefront again. The scientists and theologians of the day sorted it out through their investigations. In 1492, Columbus proved the Earth was round to the Christian world. But the pagans were never really exonerated for being correct in many of their assertions.

Secondly Church officials endorsed the notion that the Earth was roughly 6000 years old because by calculating the lineages of all of the patriarchs in Genesis and adding the time that had ensued since the Bible was written, it approximated that total. Since Man was pronounced to be a direct descendant of God, such a calculation was deemed appropriate. It mattered not to the pious men of the day that using the Bible to calculate the age of the Earth was a violation of every known principle of logic known to the Greeks, Persians, or Egyptians. In this instance, the application of logic was irrelevant because the source of the information, the Bible, was sacrosanct. Without a means to refute it, the belief stood unchallenged. Until the birth of the science of Geology during the Age of Enlightenment, reason could not overtake religious assumptions. But it finally did. Now every school-age child knows the age of the Earth is approximately 4.65 billion years old (except for the home-schooled children of evangelicals naturally).

Thirdly pious men accepted the belief the Earth sat at the center of the universe, reasoning it must because Man was the centerpiece of God's Creation. It did not occur to the pious men of yesteryear that the universe could have existed for any other purpose than to provide lodging for God's favorite creation. Evidently the pious were not capable of thinking in anything but ethnocentric terms. When Copernicus dared to propose the theory of a heliocentric solar system, he was excommunicated from the Church, and castigated by medieval society. Under the threat of eternal damnation, he recanted his heresy on his deathbed. His fear was not the truth, but avoiding eternal damnation. Even educated pagans held the identical belief but no one was persecuted because they adopted a differing opinion. It only seemed that way because from Man's perspective it appeared that way. A terra-centric view was the direct result of selective perception. Man was the center of the Universe because he put himself at it. As the song said, *"a man hears what he wants to hear and disregards the rest"*. xxxix

Only in the twilight realm of faith could such arbitrary gross miscalculations go unchallenged for hundreds of years, primarily because the pretentious men of faith intentionally discarded a prodigious legacy of pagan science and cosmology. Merely because the ideas were the product of pagan cultures, they were discarded out-of-hand. Until Christians came of age during the Renaissance and began to question, they could not have conceived how wrong their Church had been. Without the Renaissance the tyranny of belief may have never been challenged. The Age of Reason that followed cemented the notion that one had natural rights; one of them being the right to choose. This the philosophers of the age extended to one's right to believe what they chose to believe and deny what they didn't without the threat of eternal damnation hanging over them. If they could prove it more power to them, but they didn't need to be bound by choices made by the written word of generations' dead and buried. While one would assume that the Age of Reason signaled the death knell of pre-determination, ethnocentrism lived on in our prejudicial faiths today.

The Biblical assertion of Man's creation in God's image assumed that it didn't apply to every other creature on the face of the Earth. If not in the image of that half-clothed, silver-haired, elderly gentleman Michelangelo painted on the ceiling of the Sistine Chapel, then in whose image would it be? Once labeled as the crown of Creation in biblical lore, the natural inclination of the human being was to exhibit that feeling of superiority one enjoyed as lord and master. As such other so-designated inferior life forms were at one's disposal to dispense with at one's discretion. If one ascribed to the notion that historical precedents were significant, then the image of Napoleon putting the emperor's crown (Holy Roman emperor at that) on his own head was accurate in its perversity. He did it because no one else was fit to do it in his estimation. It should give one pause to reflect that their estimation may not be infallible truth. What the interpreters of the Bible suggested was not appreciably different. It made Napoleon's act possible, and that should be sufficient to send a shiver up one's spine.

The belief that Man had dominion over the Earth had led to the idea that manifest destiny was a God-given right. Thus as Man surveyed the width and breadth of Creation he claimed ownership of all that he surveyed. It seemed Man wanted control of all things natural, but was unwilling to assume the responsibility for stewardship of the *system* in which they operated. While he was results-oriented, he remained sadly lacking in being process-conscious of the procedures of that system. Thus care was not taken in extracting the bounty of his domain. With control came responsibility. It was perfectly logical that as one sowed, so shall one reap. Neither lord nor serf was absolved of that responsibility. Being that the Universe operated upon cause and effect relationships, it seemed very likely that was precisely the case. It would also apply to all of the manifestations of Creation.

The as above, so below methodology fit like a glove. As the model was rendered by the Grand Architect, so it was made manifest. With each slight variation in the DNA strand, a new species appeared. Each time it was reassembled, there was a possibility of mutation, and so it went weaving its way on the strands of Time, finding a Place for everything in Creation. While everything had a place, the place of nothing was more prominent than any other. It was simply a set of coordinates positioned in space. It stood to reason this perception was in conflict with the human being's supposed exalted place in Creation. Only the words written in a single book ever put human beings in that exalted position. And understandably it was a position many didn't want to relinquish. Hence a problem arose when Science wanted to knock them down a peg or two; informing them they were but an insignificant speck of dust on the plane of the elliptic. Naturally the religionists objected because they coveted the position they imagined themselves to be in -- that of the favorite son and daughter of a Father God. And they didn't even acknowledge HIS consort – Mother Earth.

Although there was only a 3% difference in the DNA sequence between Man and ape (approximately 1.5 % if you were a bonobo) that gap in sequencing appeared to be enormous when manifested. If the natural process of evolution could cause a shift in that 3% it would be observable. The methodologies of modern scientific practice were competent enough to notice a deviation. Theoretically natural selection took millions of years to affect changes in species. Evolution was a slow, arduous process that operated over countless generations. It moved at a snail's pace. But did it ever cause one species to change into another? A recent archeological finding in Africa, dubbed Ardipithicus[xl], may have answered that question.

Formerly according to interpretations of the fossil record, the primate line split into prosimian and simian 47 million years ago. From that point, the evolutionary progression was thought to be ape to Homo sapiens along the simian line. After the recent discovery of Ardipithicus, a creature that exhibited hominid as well as simian traits, it suggested simian and hominid species had developed along parallel lines from a common ancestor. What that ancestor was, was yet to be determined, but it was now theorized that hominid was always its own branch. The hominid and simian strains of primate evolved on parallel lines. Some 4.4 million years ago, the creature nicknamed *ardi* roamed the savannahs of the African continent. Some 3.5 million years ago the line split again into the varieties of types of simians, namely apes and chimpanzees as end points. With each branch in the primate strain, the theory was a more proficient being was created, but no one could actually explain why; except to testify that a mutation had occurred. What the anthropologists could only do was suggest there had been mutations. A reason for them was another leap of understanding; few if any were capable of postulating. But now at least it was recognized that it was probable that Man did not evolve from the ape. Both hominids and simians shared a common ancestor. As for the evolutionary progression of the hominid line, the jury was out until more evidence was available.

Nonetheless evolution had to have a *why*. Until a *why* can be divulged, it will always be a matter of speculation as to *who* or *what* ordered the entree. Is there more reason to believe it was a roll of the genetic dice or a purposeful action by a superior being who manipulated the codes? If it was natural selection that caused Man to be created, what made Man a more efficient life form than an ape -- that 3% difference in DNA? Or was it the size of the cranium? It would be difficult to argue human beings lived more efficiently and were more proficient in their daily routines than apes were. The routines weren't necessarily comparable. What was the manner of comparison? Natural selection inferred changes in species happened to enhance the prospects for survival of that species. Assuming that was the case why would an upgrade be required for the ape? Apes prospered quite nicely without one. Logically there didn't seem to be a persuasive reason Nature would take this turn. According to scientific theory, Evolution made adaptations to species when the *need* arose. Apes were perfectly fitted to their respective environments.

The evidence seemed to show that the larger brained variety of creature (Homo sapiens) was more trouble than he was worth. Typically he showed no respect for Nature, it's Creator, and did his best to enforce his will upon it to the detriment of every other living creature. While professing to love the Creator, he systemically destroyed HIS creation whenever his need took precedence over that supposed reverence. The only explanation could be that he loved himself more. Man's need was paramount to his love of the Creator. If the actions of humanity superseded Natural Law was it the Creator's will? Was this a violation of the first commandment (*thou shalt not put any strange gods before me*) or was it a subliminal recognition that one had a kernel of the Creator within them? A large percentage of humanity simply didn't know how to live without cutting a swath of destruction through Nature. The evidence showed it.

If one diligently scanned the fossil record (one could safely presume competent scientists were doing so at this very moment) there was a persuasive reason for every evolutionary turn Nature took. Whether it was caused by external celestial forces, climatic, topographical, or shifts in the balance of Nature, there were logical reasons for it. The rise and fall of the giant fishes of the Cambrian period, dinosaurs of the Cretaceous, followed by the mammals of the Tertiary period were due to radical changes in the Earth. Their relative extinctions were the result of natural occurrences, albeit catastrophic ones. With the exception of Man's appearance on Earth, the idea that a dominant species ruled the planet in its stead made sense. The rest of the animal kingdom was faring quite well without human beings. Furthermore there was no evidence to show that any other species of mammals had evolved into a new genus for a very long time if ever. That suggested the process of natural selection stopped or slowed down to an imperceptible crawl. Unless there was a good reason for it to accelerate, why would it? A persuasive reason had not been offered to suggest this was true. By all accounts it seemed evolution went into hibernate mode like a computer when the user stopped typing on the keys for a pre-determined period of time. Had Mother Nature walked away from her celestial computer? There had to be another reason then why human beings existed at all.

Michael L. Kilday

On the other hand, if the theory of natural selection could not account for the creation of a new species, there were other possibilities. It was conceivable that there was an *intervention* that caused a change in evolution, a cosmic hiccup that was not repeatable. Centuries ago many scientists embraced the notion of a catastrophic root cause that affected life on a global scale. Because of it concepts like Panspermia, Spontaneous Generation, and Catastrophism were once considered valid scientific principles. That didn't appear to be the case now, at least in the scientific community. At present, these ideas fell more into the category of science fiction than science fact. If apes could evolve into human beings and it was part of the natural process, the theory of natural selection dictated it would be happening right now. It was common sense. It could be observed, measured, and quantified. No scientist had produced any conclusive evidence to show it was. One obvious conclusion was there wasn't any to provide. Did evolution just stop or were unseen forces at work building momentum for a momentous evolutionary event?

Since the laws of Nature had never been known to be any different than they were now, what was the actual reason the theory of the missing link had gained prominence? Perhaps it was because the scientific community could not accept a possibility that wasn't logically deduced. Furthermore if human beings could actually claim ancestry from the ape, then it still could be the result of cosmic intervention, rather than the result of evolution. Maybe the Earth was seeded by alien life forms who found it suitable to be colonized. Or perhaps aliens who visited Earth in prehistoric times found female apes to be very desirable (a twist on *angels lusting after the daughters of men*)[xli]. The historical precedents for believing these events occurred was found in the mythologies of the Sumerians, Hebrews, Egyptians, Hindus, and Greeks. While mythology wasn't actually part of the historical record, there was a thread of truth that always ran through it. Very few human beings were that creative that they could just make it all up without appropriating a more ancient tradition and building upon it. Maybe it was slightly altered to fit new circumstances and the names were changed to accommodate a new cultural dynamic. However the basic plotline remained the same.

For the past 40 years, the Danish researcher, Erik Von Dainigan, of THE CHARIOTS OF THE GODS (Dainigan, 1968) fame had been saying that the Earth had been visited by alien astronauts. Whether or not Von

Dainigan was correct, the facts on the ground still did not point to Evolution as being the sole cause of human development on Earth. To merely chalk change up to a chance mutation on the DNA roulette wheel really didn't compute as the determining factor. In actuality, as an explanation for human evolution, natural selection was really as far-fetched as the proposition of *alien visitation*. To make that assumption was counterintuitive to everything human beings had learned about the principles of Natural Law. Moreover Natural Law did not preclude terrestrial catastrophic change nor accounted for the intervention of celestial forces as being motivating forces for planetary change.

In so far as Man thought he was, so he was. Truly he was the product of his ideas and actions. As the scope of one's intellect expanded, one's domain extended. One would have imagined if Columbus and Copernicus in their own way could have stepped up to the plate as pioneers, a philosopher of comparable stature could have proposed that Man must relinquish his vaunted place as the crown of Creation. After all he did put the crown upon his own head. In a Universe teeming with life, why was the human being accorded a special place? One wondered what will happen when that fateful day came that we found out we were not alone in the Universe. Undoubtedly that day will arrive, and what excuse will we have for our injurious techniques of survival? The devil made me do it? Our technology had proven to be both a blessing and a curse. It depended upon how it was used. It was not yet sufficient to take us where we needed to be, but it was only a matter of time before it was. The only question was: will we afford ourselves that time?

As a counterpoint to the scientific viewpoint, the Creationists clung to a version of Creation that was equally untenable. The epic poetry of Genesis was proof of nothing except that ancient man had an artistic flair. As a piece of literature, its literary symbolism echoed the sacred writings of every civilization that preceded it. This included the Hindu, Sumerian, Chinese, Egyptian, Persian, and countless other mystery religions. These so-called mystery religions were deemed inscrutable because their conclusions challenged the rational mind. Humanity had a way to go in the development of scientific understanding in order to comprehend them in the correct context. Each mystery religion had creation myths and in substance they were remarkably similar. Their similarities inferred a big bang as the instance of Creation. It was followed by vibration wave multiplication, cell division, multiplication and differentiation, hints at the existence of atoms and molecules, and most importantly of all, explanations for the diversification of the species of biological life on Earth.

The origin of human life was still a mystery only because the answer wasn't recognized as yet to be one. But the answer was buried in the manifestations of life, and the key to it had already been found in the discovery of DNA. It was the set of instructions matter required to manifest itself. The very fact DNA existed implied Intelligence coded it. The Grand Architect was thought to be the Universal Mind. To believe that intricate patterns of DNA were arranged by happenstance was a stretch of the imagination, but no other explanation seemed plausible to the scientific-minded. That didn't mean one wouldn't be found at a future date. It meant humanity didn't know yet where to look for it. Perhaps the answer was not even found on Earth. It may literally be in the stars. It was conceivable that chance figured into the arrangement of DNA patterns, but chance didn't create the set of instructions by itself. Nor did chance run the clockwork of the Universe. Scientists were in agreement mathematics did. Nor was chance responsible for the institution of the laws of attraction and repulsion, gravity, light, electromagnetism, thermodynamics, or electricity. These were the effects the laws of physics produced. All of this implied Intelligence, and certainly it pointed to Intelligence greater than human intelligence. Human beings had discovered these forces existed but they did not invent them.

In a universal mechanism that operated upon the laws of cause and effect, what was the probability that anything happened by chance – slim to none? The existence of chance in universal design principles was counterintuitive to Natural Law. Matter moved like clockwork through the Universe. It displayed purpose, a life span, maintained spatial relationships and provided a means to measure all of these. Mathematics was the basis for the movement of celestial objects and the music of the spheres. In the Cosmos there was an essence of Order, a Balance of substance, and Harmony of motion in all aspects of the Natural world. Therefore on the metaphysical side of the equation wouldn't all of these same laws apply as well? It was logical they would and their interaction would be the creator, preserver, and destroyer of matter as well. The glue that bound it all together was the same as the substance of Nous; that the

Truth Never Changes: The Genesis of the Path

Greeks first postulated was the fabric that held the Universe together. Recently modern science had taken to calling that substance dark matter; perhaps for lack of a better term and understanding of its constitution. But it was analogous to what the Greeks imagined because it represented the same thing the Greeks sought to represent -- the space between particles of matter. In conjunction with dark matter, another mysterious force had been discovered, termed dark energy. The supposition was it was the force that caused the spaces between particles of matter to expand or contract. Even empty space was not equivalent to nothingness.

If the origin of the Universe was an application of force and intelligence, why was the origin of Man any different? The literal truth of Creation was somewhere between its scientific and mythological renderings. Admittedly the tale of Adam and Eve was just a story, an allegory to be more precise that inferred spirit's descension to flesh was embodied in original sin. The tale had no literal meaning; unless one catered to notion they were ancient astronauts stranded on an alien world. The allegorical meaning of Creation was that the human individual became conscious of his or her separateness from the Whole. There was no blame attached to the manifestation of matter like religion inferred. The blame (or error as the Gnostics termed it) came from neglecting the spiritual self and subsequently favoring the material self. The assumption that one or the other could exist in a vacuum would mean one believed there was no connection between them. The Creation myth suggested human beings were created by a spiritual process of *cell mitosis*; that being a deliberate separation from the One Consciousness. It was represented by a migration of spirit essence from the One into separate realities; units of the One that operated autonomously[xlii]. If any state of *sin* could be implied, it was in not realizing separateness was an illusion. Therefore it followed that original sin was a belief in the illusion of separateness. The philosophy of the Children of the Law of One stated as much. They didn't refer to it as *sin* per se, but there were numerous references in their literature (the Essene and Gnostics as well) of *errors* being made, and the consequences of them being the illusion of separateness permeated the thought waves. Presumably separation from the One was chief among them; perhaps the beginning of them. Where thoughts of separateness exist, certainly feelings of superiority and inferiority follow. Then imaginations of good and evil followed them. From it ideologies were formulated.

As for what the Bible said literally, there was no challenge presented in debunking claims that were the product of literary analysis. Anyone who didn't adhere to a literal reading of the Bible knew it. It was only those who viewed its epic poetry as something other than literature that didn't. The Creationists really had no philosophical ground to stand upon when the crux of their argument was merely *'it is written here by the hand of God, therefore we know it to be true'*. What did one say in response? Probably the only point left to contest was authorship of the Bible because it certainly wasn't God. That proposition was riddled with assumptions; ending with a final admission authorship could not be resolved. The author's name was anonymous. When biblical scholars offered their hypotheses should anonymous be listed as another name for God? As soon as a rational person heard that fateful statement *'the hands that wrote the Bible were inspired by God'*, the argument completely fell apart. What was there to argue about?

As soon as one heard a proponent of Creationism give credit to God for the works of human beings, it was a clue that the entire left-side of the brain of that individual was bordering on dysfunctional. That brain was in atrophy, and it could not continue the argument because reason didn't support it. When the argument relied upon the legitimacy of unseen forces, the argument became untenable – unless one supplied reasons for their existence. Faith could not be argued. There was nothing to argue when it came to belief systems except the legitimacy of the conclusions drawn. That argument quickly escalated into a heated dispute; one that usually could not be resolved amicably.

To be honest there were bits of Truth in both scientific and religious propositions regarding Genesis but not the whole Truth because that was not known for a certainty by any human being. Both were a swag taken at approximating the Truth. All one could do was to painstakingly piece it together from the evidence at-hand. That evidence was literally anything the human mind was capable of conceiving. Undoubtedly the question of how human life began on Earth was one of those eternal conundrums that defied explanation. Primarily that was because no *created* being was presumably in a position to observe the process of Creation. One needed to observe the Creation process from outside of it to grasp its meaning.

Truth Never Changes: The Genesis of the Path

If God was One, as proposed by the teachings of The Children of the Law of One, all of Creation had to be manifested in God's image. It logically followed that this had to be the case. It could be no other way. One could make the case that was the real meaning of Genesis. And mistranslation and ideas *lost in translation* were really to blame for an age-old misunderstanding; singling out the human being as the only living thing created in HIS image. The idea was patently absurd. It was quite illogical for one to believe that the Creator would not create every single thing in ITS own image. Logic dictated that must be the case. What other image would be the model? However if one replaced the word *image* with the phrase *modeled after* wouldn't that shed more light on its true meaning? And the model that would be used would naturally be drawn by DNA. It was the artist's brush wielded by the Supreme Being crafting a physical manifestation as a self-portrait.

The information offered would not answer the eternal questions definitively but it would provide intriguing possibilities that ultimately contributed to the recognition that a greater understanding existed. The need for a greater understanding was why Man created religion, but it fell far short of accomplishing it because those that took ownership of dogma could not abide it being questioned. Inside the box no questions were permitted. That inevitably led to a situation that forced one to take the argument outside the box the faithful put it in. One thing was for certain: until the question of human origin was answered humanity would keep asking it. The search would go on because it was a question worth answering. But it wasn't likely to ever be solved until Man stopped trying to take things apart to understand them. He would be better served to start looking for the answers to his many questions in an integrated, functioning whole. It was only through observing the process-in-motion that any understanding of cosmic significance could ever be achieved.

Studying the Universe while in motion had yielded scientists insights into its operation. Intellectual inquiry could yield the understanding human beings sought if one dared to wonder. But intellect did have its limits. One needed to bridge the hemispheric limits of brain function to answer the question from all angles. That was to bridge the gap between thought and feeling. If humanity didn't choose that route, then maybe it would never know. Certainly a mind that was closed to the possibilities of the right hemisphere of the brain could not ever fathom the depths of the unknown. Conversely one that was locked into the logic of the left hemisphere had difficulty in wondering. One type of brain was better suited to bookmarking selected passages from Scripture, and asserting that one's chosen doctrine was infallible. Another was content to lock itself in a laboratory to run endless tests of its hypotheses. Neither brain would ever lead with intuition. Theologians and scientists will be forever hamstrung by their assumptions until they dared to venture outside of them. They had to leave their respective comfort zones if they expected to realize perhaps there was another explanation. One they had not thought of.

Be assured it was neither one that scientific research or religion could fathom at the present time. Whether or not that explanation emanated from a psychic source was an issue with some who found intuition to be an unreliable source; failing to realize that was exactly where the bulk of religious doctrine originally came from – as dreams, visions, and intuitions. If the pious disagreed with this assessment, they didn't comprehend the origins of their own respective faiths. They began with the imaginings of men; even that God was communing with them. This included extrapolations that delved into the natures of God, the Universe, and human beings. But the truth of the matter was none of it came from God directly. All of it was filtered through the human mind. By some the myth and metaphor of their ideas was taken to be literal fact. This they labeled *divine inspiration* and turned it into dogma. Not understanding the origins of their faith how could they be taken seriously when they argued the merits of its veracity? And when would they realize they short-changed their own understanding by stifling the inquiring mind? Where did one imagine inspiration came from? What actually made it divine? Furthermore what would Sir Isaac Newton have accomplished if he hadn't taken a stroll into his garden to unwind?

Truth Never Changes: The Genesis of the Path

An Encounter of the Most Unnerving Kind

As Spirit had intimated many years ago that the Atlantean wise men would enter and introduce themselves, they had made themselves known.[xliii] No audio-visual hallucinations, encounters of a metaphysical kind, or lucid dreams had been experienced. Perhaps because the unseen communicated over the inward concourse through thought and feeling nothing out of the ordinary was evident, but they had made their mark. Merely listening to the echo of my own thoughts had revealed an undercurrent within it like a signal hidden in the carrier wave. Without fanfare they had been felt in my thoughts which had been recorded for posterity with a minimum of editorial comment. Spirit had suggested they had been offering their counsel for some time but that could neither be confirmed nor denied. However if masked by the constant stream of conscious thought, one could rest assured their input would not have been recognized as such. Furthermore the idea would have never occurred to me their influence was seeping in through the subconscious, had it not been introduced as a possibility. And the residual thought was that the ideas presented were too profound to be mine alone.

It was doubtful the suggestion would have been accepted at face value. That presented both an opportunity and a challenge. At what point did suggestion overrule the workings of the objective mind, or was it the subjective mind that tagged the input? Therefore a predicament arose whereby the skeptic in me would say this could not be happening as it appeared to be and the cynic in me was anxious to agree. Perhaps it was illogical to make these assumptions on the off chance they were true. Nonetheless the believer in me still yearned to believe in something, larger than myself -- something which could not be seen, heard, touched, tasted or smelled. Each individual who professed a belief in a Supreme Being came to a similar conclusion; that something endured after the personality they knew as 'I' exited the stage.

There was a spiritual essence in every living thing. Essentially, it was the *real me* - the *I AM* presence. Whether or not it was recognized as that was another matter, but one who was spiritually-inclined chose to believe in the existence of the soul. Because the human being had an ethereal essence encased in a husk of flesh, its existence implied purpose. If so it followed that each individual was here for a reason, even though one may not be consciously aware of what it was at any given moment. Every heartfelt question had an answer although it may be perceived to be rhetorical. Yet there was a part of each human being that always knew the answer to the heartfelt question as soon as it was asked. One could know the answer if one chose to listen to the small, still voice of the higher mind.

When the stream of conscious thought was quieted through the practice of meditation, a presence was clearly evident. But to provide positive proof it was present, and a reason why it was present, was decidedly problematic. There existed an impression that what was perceived to be, actually was. One must marvel at the prospect that the consummate rational man should be visited by an influence from the Other Side. Being the fact-based pragmatist a rational man knew himself to be, made it all the more difficult to yield wholeheartedly to the notion of communication from the Other Side. Since the rule of reason had never been displaced entirely by the power of suggestion, it was difficult to accept at face value. A modicum of healthy doubt must remain if only to protect oneself from self-deception.

Even though it could be rationalized going with the flow was beneficial, vigilance in monitoring the communication was mandatory. Although a communication came from Spirit through the higher mind didn't automatically mean it should be acted upon. For that there was an entirely different litmus test which could only be applied over the course of time. The test was a simple one. The harm in believing only occurred when one took leave of one's common sense. However if the communications were free of the scourge of self-interest and didn't conflict with the dictates of one's Conscience, only then may it be witness to what Truth there was to tell.

Therefore the remainder of this manuscript contained the counsel of the Atlantean masters regardless of whether or not it was requested because their operating principle was to collaborate as the spirit moved them. It ebbed and flowed like a rush of wind or a wave lapping the shore. Whether or not one could believe that such communications were even possible, regarded them as fantasy or evidence of a mental aberration, they existed nonetheless. However what mattered were the ideas which were conveyed and whether or not they vibrated with a tone of forthrightness and sincerity. That was the issue more than where they came from. If accepted at face value, they were just thoughts bobbing up and down in the stream of consciousness transcribed into words on paper with no substance behind them. If one delved deeper into the purpose for which they were relayed, the truthfulness of these communications was denied at one's peril. Words may appear taken out of context until they were applied to the human condition. That was what gave them context so that one could assess their worth in terms of the Law of One.

Regardless of however this communication presented itself, clarity of mind was now being experienced that a fog of miscomprehension would never permit before. The fog had lifted and the path of the sincere seeker was laid out before me. Where it actually led was yet to be determined. Whether or not that could really be attributed to influence from the Other Side was frankly beside the point. The communications had a beneficial effect on the thought processes, and it was strictly a matter of interpretation as to what the reason might be. It may be that meditation had cleared the cobwebs out of the mind, but if it had not been freed from the throes of addiction that would have never happened. Despite what anyone else may want to make out of it that may be the most logical explanation for the phenomenon. Nevertheless for one who had always labored in a cloud of doubt and suspicion over one's feelings, a connection with them was now made of remarkable precision. The thoughts were crystal-clear. A clear channel was presented. That was a new experience for me. Depending upon how one may interpret it, it had altered the course of my life in ways that defied explanation.

Though compelled to convey a perspective one had to share, the product of a life-changing event, or life-awakening event, no ownership was claimed. It was only understood to be an integral part of the higher mind -- that timeless kernel of sublime consciousness that was seeking an outlet. Giving it voice while understanding it was a private opinion offered for public consumption provided enough satisfaction for the giver. One could take it or leave it, solely on the basis of what was offered, disregarding who offered it. That was the objective of every statement from the higher mind. Free will was the rule and guide of all manifestation. A testimony to what Truth there was to tell was the only motivation for telling it. By comparison the wagging of the preacher's tongue was like a hand at the back of the object of affection. It caused a forced march to the beat of ideology. The communicant had his or her own measure of control to keep sermonizing at bay. When the communication came from the heart, there was no need to censor it.

The masters' communications may at times read like a text book, and at other times sound like life-lessons offered for the faint of heart. It was never really intended to be that way. Due to the mechanics of automatic writing, it just came out that way. In actuality, this personality had little to do with the manner in which the ideas were expressed. The material had merely been organized so that the statements were arranged in an intelligible fashion that showed purpose. Therefore for the major portion of the manuscript, the masters commandeered the narrative. Consequently the reader should exercise patience, and be judicious in his or her opinions. It may be necessary to read between the lines to get the full impact of the content. When there was an opportunity to reveal information that served to enlighten or educate, it should be taken. Any effort made to provoke an open-minded dialogue was worth the effort if it served to lighten the load.

Though impressed to provide the following message by those who shall remain anonymous (other than myself), the message was meant for the living. Spirit commented on a world in which they no longer lived. Their interest was only to prep humanity for its fight for survival. It was the living who must rise to the occasion and pull their bacon out of the fire before it was burned to a crisp. Spirit could only serve in an advisory capacity. Their purpose was simply to tell what Truth they knew as it appeared from their vantage point. The result of not revealing it perpetuated the fiction human beings told each other when they were at a loss for something productive to say. Like the ocean tide, it rushed in to fill the vacuum in the absence of Truth. To satisfy the vested interest of Spirit was to adopt the Wisdom of Solomon in the judgment of human conflict.

After reading this account, the question one must ask oneself was: did the content resonate with the crystal-clear ring of Truth? Was there an ulterior motive, hidden agenda, or duplicitous need in evidence? Furthermore did it potentially do harm to me specifically or to the human race in general? Would it do more harm than good if one dared to believe in it? If one could answer "*no*" to all of these questions, then obviously

Truth Never Changes: The Genesis of the Path

the motivation was pure no matter what the source was. And one must trust in the fact that no one profited from it who did not envision truth-telling to be a selfless act. If one removed the ego from consideration, then what was left was a selfless offering of service to humanity. In the final analysis it was pureness of heart and the selfless motive that accompanied it that rang true. One didn't need a bell in a steeple to call one to worship. One's way was one's own to find.

In a moment of silent reflection, an epiphany dawned upon one who as an observer was telling the tale. Gradually one found oneself immersed in the tale, interwoven into the plot as it unfolded. And from that moment forward it was no longer possible to separate oneself from the tale because one was fused with it. What truth there was to tell was the core of one's being. One was a carrier of the message that needed to be delivered. To bring it forth, one needed to recognize it as such. When the light broke over the horizon in the splendor of a golden dawn, it streamed forth in crystalline clarity. It was appropriate any climb toward the Light began with the individual feeling his or her way through the maze erected by those who wished to keep knowledge under lock and key. Its retrieval was not predicated upon fulfilling ideological prerequisites or maintaining filial associations. The ability to retrieve it was directly proportional to the effort one was willing to make to mine it from the depths of one's soul. That mining expedition to find the precious gem of Truth was central to one's life purpose. Once cutting and polishing the stone, you fixed the gem in a setting that accentuated its beauty. And so the reader could see the author's motivation in putting his labors on display; not so they could be admired, but that they could be taken to heart. The purpose for revelation of any kind was not to take pride in one's accomplishment but to foster awareness. In actuality, there was much to be aware of as well as much for which to prepare.

Michael L. Kilday

Truth Never Changes: The Genesis of the Path

Atlantean Genesis

A final remnant of the deep-trance session in 1979 was revisited by a single word, Krophron, which unleashed a torrent of memories. Pictures flashed upon the mental canvas and thereafter they were transferred to paper. The following intimation was received by tapping into the historical record of the race memory. It was the same thing Carl Jung called the collective unconsciousness, and Edgar Cayce called the Akashic record. Skeptics denied such a thing could ever exist; mainly because they could not conceive of it themselves (evidence of atrophy in the right-side of the brain coupled with hubris). But if radio and TV waves could fly through the air and be picked up by electronic devices sensitive to selective electromagnetic wavelengths, why couldn't the human brain also function as a receiver? If 500 gigabytes (a gigabyte is one billion characters) of data could reside on a hard drive, it would seem the human brain could hold infinitely more. Probably we couldn't calculate that high. If memories could be stored in cells of the human brain, then why could not a race memory be stored in *cells* in the Universal Mind? If data could be resident in the memory chips of a computer, why couldn't it be resident in the ether? The storehouse in the ether just wouldn't be silicon-based. Quite possibly it would be composed of whatever dark matter was. As outer space appeared to be infinite, it would seem inner space could be infinite as well. It gave one pause to think what actually was possible. If one didn't set limits upon the mind's eye, the possibilities were limitless.

The subject of this intimation was how the Children of the Law of One came to be on Earth. It provided a counterpoint to the biblical story of Genesis the reader will not find in any Bible. In it, there were analogies to the Book of Enoch[xliv] which was officially removed from the canon at the council of Nicaea in 325 C.E. One could only suspect that the questions of human origin it raised were problematic to the early orthodox Christians. There was much more to the story than that, but to know it one had to comprehend what Enoch purportedly wrote. Few actually did for what it was. The reader was encouraged to give it a read, but it only served as deep background reference material for the account that followed. This intimation stepped a bit further back in time to explain who the *watchers* actually were and why they were watching.

Before the question was asked, this bit of information was not elicited from the writings of Erik Von Dainigan, nor did it strictly adhere to the legacy of alien astronauts. While most of those sources were the ancient scriptures of the Tibetans, Hindus, or Egyptians, their beliefs were their own. That was not to imply anyone was more right than anyone else, nor had vested rights to the Truth. All were searching in their own way and should not be faulted for that. The proponents of the ancient astronaut theories made coherent points in their argument. However the piece that followed was over and above most of these theories. It sought to explain where the so-called ancient astronauts came from as much as it was to explain what they did here after they arrived.

The intimation began with an abridged history of the Krophronites and ended with a dissertation on The Children of the Law of One. Their histories were intertwined suggesting they were one and the same. Where the individual mind was concerned there were no absolute certainties, only relative ones. The proof was in the mind of the beholder. It had a window that opened into the ether which supposedly was the Mind of the All-in-All because one could envision it as nothing else. It did not belong to any single mind but was theoretically available to any individual mind which could commune with it. Memory was always a mysterious stranger to those who didn't have an inkling of where they came from, while it was a welcome friend of those who had a perspective on their origins.

The material that followed was an example of automatic writing. Though it came from the higher mind to be placed on paper, the ego found it difficult to believe it was nothing more than an instrument of transmission. But that may be nothing more than the willfulness of ego to play a role that maneuvered the conversation toward an objective; a last ditch attempt to be in control. Ego was not the creator, but the receiver; merely an actor learning its lines. The interpretation of Genesis that followed was a clear indication that one could access the teachings of the Law of One if one was attuned to the inner stream of dialogue. The hope was the expression of these thoughts had been translated in a coherent way so that the reader could comprehend the feelings which spawned them. There was no hidden agenda except to share knowledge that was available to anyone who would listen to the small, still voice of the higher mind. The information was available if and when one was dialed into the proper wavelength. The following script described how a cosmic hiccup could account for changes of evolutionary scale and dimension. It begins.

In the far reaches of pre-historic time, a cosmic event occurred that dramatically altered the course of human evolution on Earth. An alien incursion of epic proportions was instigated by a dying race trapped on a dying world. Initially the incursion was not intended to be menacing, but as time passed the perpetuators succumbed to the temptation to dominate and manipulate the human being. It altered the course of human history, and ultimately usurped and forever dominated the destiny of the human race. Nothing that was done could ever be undone, but understanding why it happened was worth the effort because it did have a bearing on the future course of human evolution. A benefit was derived from understanding errors in judgment so that they could be avoided in the future. As in all stories with a moral, it came with a warning label that could read – no being was above Universal Law. This one was no exception, and it had a profound influence upon all involved.

The Krophronite civilization had reached its pinnacle eons ago on a distant planet that evolved much earlier in the time sequence of the creative life cycle of The Milky Way galaxy. The Krophronites were a highly-evolved race of humanoid beings which had already passed through the adult phase of their civilization which was dying as the red sun they lived under waned. To the human being little could be comprehensible of the planet, Krophron, its history and evolution as a world. In comparison to Earth, it was less dense and humanoid life there was of a lighter shade. The density could be described as the ethereal quality of substance generally ascribed to manifestations of Spirit. It appeared as a translucent substance that made beings who resided there appear to be of *angelic* constitution. Due to Krophron's proximity to the Central Sun of the galaxy, light exerted more of an attractive force upon the inhabitants than it does on Earth. Beings virtually translucent once lived on Krophron where night was a gentle gray haze of a few hours duration. Hence *living in the Light* had a dramatic effect upon the inhabitants that translated into a physical state of being. Whereas upon Earth this statement had a metaphysical meaning, on Krophron it had a physical meaning. The Krophronites lived in a state where thought dominated their entire lives to the degree that it was the motivating force of their existence.

On Krophron the polarities of light and dark did not exist as such. The balance struck between them was replaced by the metaphysical properties of light and dark. That resulted in highly-developed metaphysical senses of insight, intuition, and sense-vibration. Replacing the physical senses was the ability to sense the auras and frequencies of vibrations of objects that human beings would have difficulty in comprehending. These auras and frequencies identified Krophronite individuals like biological characteristics identify human beings. They were a signature, signifying the thoughts and feelings of the essence of one's character. From them they took their names which were not pronounceable in a material language, being largely symbolic of state and being. And it was not meant to be because one's identity was sensed intuitively. All expressions of communication passing from one being to another were felt as vibrations. Since musical notes and colors were vibrational patterns as well, they were manifested differently on Krophron in sensory wavelengths, the tonal quality of which could not be described by language. There were no words for it. Because the entire planet vibrated at a higher frequency than Earth, sight, sound and taste existed in ranges beyond human perception. Where physical form was irrelevant even touch was reduced to sensory vibration like the intersecting circles of ripples on a pond. Intuitive perceptions and visualizations that could not be verbalized was the best way to describe how Krophronites communicated with each other. When tones were beyond the audible range of the human ear, and sight was beyond the visual range of the human eyes, they existed primarily in creative visualizations that passed between them. Crude expressions of material language were not required to communicate. It was accomplished by thought instantaneously.

There were no clear analogies that could compare Krophron with Earth as a place in a time sequence. These were concepts foreign to Krophronite existence for they required manifestations of solid matter. If etheric matter took shape and form then it could be said to exist in time and space, but its actual state was timeless and not bound by dimension. It took up no space. Matter flowed like streams of consciousness. If one were to imagine that Krophron was a gas giant the size of Uranus or Neptune that would be an apt comparison of it. However unlike Uranus or Neptune which were cold enough to support rivers and oceans of liquefied gas, the gas on Krophron did not congeal into a solid substance. Due to its proximity to the Central Sun of the galaxy, the planet was more a hot ball of swirling gases. No land or oceans graced the surface. Plant and animal life was virtually non-existent as human beings would understand it. The conditions were too different for there to be a basis for comparison; for example, where Earth held solid images of form and substance, translucent images were projected on Krophron. These translucent or astral images appeared as holograms to the human comprehension. That would be the closest of representation of matter to be made as a manner of comparison. Having ethereal bodies the Krophronites had developed telepathic skills of communication as well as life habits and mannerisms that suited their bodily frame. Thought-forms were materialized quite easily in the Krophronite atmosphere. These meandered through the atmosphere like clouds do on Earth.

Time and spatial relationships were quite different mainly because of the planet's position in the galaxy. In the etheric substance of which the atmosphere was composed, objects were transported effortlessly by electromagnetic means. There was no resistance offered to the physical movement of matter. Thought instantly produced astral matter. Living in such an atmosphere was effortless due to a much higher rate of vibration. It gave physical labor or physical substance an entirely different meaning than they had on Earth. Physical representations of substance, as human beings would know it, did not exist because it required a representation of a gaseous, liquid, or solid substance. None could actually be found on Krophron. Neither could bodily organisms. The mental lives of the Krophronites (if one could call it that) were lived in the astral plane. Here etheric substance predominated; so truly as a Krophronite *thought*, so he or she is, was, and would always be. And his or her entire existence was enveloped by the expression of that *thought* as long as their energy was focused upon it.

Life on the surface of Krophron, however, was coming to an end. Because the Krophronites were well-versed in Cosmology and sensitive to its creative cycles of life knew the end was near. Their sun would be extinguished and their planet along with it (somewhere in the vicinity of the Orion Nebula). It would mean the Krophronites themselves would be returning to the One. Their dispersal into the One meant a return to homogeneous spirit essence. Many Krophronites desired to live on in heterogeneous form. In other words, be separate from each other. Many favored *discorporation*[xlv] into the biosphere of another world to begin anew. Others found this end to separate'life acceptable and offered no resistance. Since colonization efforts had always preceded outward from the Central Sun, many Krophronites looked outward to quench their thirst for a physical life. Because of the spiritual station of their civilization, they appealed to the supreme council of the universal command for permission to *discorporate* into an under-developed world for the purposes of continuing their advanced civilization. They were on the verge of perfecting the scientific-spiritual phases of life into perfect harmony which would have permitted their transcendence into a state of immortality. Thus death as such would not have existed at all. As in all cases of all such progression, it was a time of flux and danger that imperiled the stability of all consciousness involved in the process. Hence the propensity for disaster increased exponentially. Whenever stability was breached on a cosmic scale, great calamity could follow. Calamities had already occurred on Krophron where the production of psycho-spiritual mechanisms and their output hastened the end of that world. In doing so, it drained too much energy from their star.

Members of the supreme universal command council were well aware of this fact. They expressed fear the same would happen elsewhere if the Krophronites were turned loose on other worlds. As they put it, Krophronite ingenuity could pose an unwarranted risk for the Universe as a whole. The argument as presented was echoed by a majority of the members of the council. The Krophronites did have a reputation for being loose cannons at times. They were known to be risk-takers and experimenters, beings who would overstep their bounds. Sometimes innovations worked to perfection. Sometimes they didn't. The greatest concern of the Krophronite leadership was that their race would have the opportunity to pursue their innovations from a base of operations. Self-governance was the eternal rule of Law. The council merely existed as a vehicle for collaboration, rather than as a court of adjudication. Representation served the need of the One to maintain balance and harmony within the Universe, and the operation of its Process proceeding in accordance with Universal Law.

Truth Never Changes: The Genesis of the Path

Having a seat on the supreme universal command council, conditions on Krophron were common knowledge amongst the races. In the spirit of goodwill and harmony, the Mennenites which were closer in their development cycle offered the Krophronites safe haven. It would have been more of a lateral move to Mennen where conditions on that planet resembled Krophron. Their self-esteem and adventurous spirit, an evidence of ego, was considered by many an undeniable Krophronite trait. It posed potential danger but at the same time if properly focused held great promise for all races because the Krophronites were a race of innovators. They were very much admired for their steadfast faith and persistence in the accomplishment of universal ideals. They had produced many lawgivers, seers, and prophets which were revered as well as scientific inventions which were used in many parts of the galaxy to great effect. Krophronite wisdom was outlined in the pale moons of the Pleiades system – a collection of bright memories of past glory. The pioneer spirit exhibited by the Krophronite race was emulated by all colonizing races, but was unsurpassed in its inventiveness. But what they proposed posed a danger to all because it circumvented natural process, and assumed that the wisdom of the Krophronite high-command was sacrosanct and inviolate. When they proposed a step-down to the physical plane, it was deemed to be an inordinate challenge. That was a migration to a planet on the outer rim of the Milky Way galaxy known as Earth.

A suitable tract of land was deemed to be a newly-risen island spanning one of the Earth's two oceans. This land mass stretched horizontally between land masses surrounding that ocean with the 30 degree latitude at its center, and the 45 degree latitude at its northern extremity, and equator at its southern extremity (from the American continents to European and Africa continents but touched no other continent). That meant it sat entirely within temperate and tropic climate zones, and its geographical situation was also symbolic of the non-interference edict. The Krophronites were cautioned that an incursion because it was occurring in an untraditional fashion, not through birth and rebirth in the physical plane, would disrupt the natural order. Also because of their lighter bodies, Krophronites were not of the same corporal constitution as the human inhabitants which were much denser. In order to exist on Earth, the Krophronites had to *descend* into a denser material. Many council members were opposed to this regression of substance because of the moral and ethical standards that would be violated. The argument was that the Krophronites could not manage the transformation without a similar reversion in their mental attitudes, and subsequent dulling of their spiritual natures. It was believed a denser body would eventually be paired with a denser mind.

Many of the council elders maintained the *descension* could not be managed without disrupting the natural order. They added the Krophronites could not manage such a transition without violating the standing edict of non-interference with under-developed civilizations. Such a civilization was developing upon the Earth, and it needed to be left to its own devices. The interlopers would succumb to the temptation of making the Earth their own. Moreover no intermixing of the Krophronite and the human race could be permitted since the natural environment would be perverted by a new source of vibration, alien to its existing planetary cycles. The gap between Krophronite and human development was so wide that the Krophronites by natural selection would easily dominate any relationship. Krophronite and human collaboration could only result in a master/slave relationship whereby the Krophronites would be revered as gods because of their intellectual and spiritual superiority. It so far exceeded the development of the human being at that time; it could not be conceived any other way by the human inhabitants. It would produce undo strain upon the cycle of planetary development because the doctrine of free will could not be observed in its fullness as was the case throughout the universe. The incursion would elevate the vibrations of the Earth itself prematurely, and generate developmental activity before its time sequence had arrived. The geo-physical, bio-magnetic, and environmental strain created would eventually warp the planetary forces, and disfigure those living on it. Mutants would arise as a result of this alien stress, and Nature would be forced into an intense period of re-adjustment. The stress could be controlled to a degree and equilibrium would eventually be achieved but there would be casualties on both sides of the equation. But over time new pathways for evolution would be devised. Planetary rotations though altered would eventually find their point of equilibrium. And natural elements which had their constitutions altered even the slightest bit would find a way to adapt to changing causes and effects. No one knew to what extent the incursion would alter the time/space continuum, but they also knew as in all cases Nature would find a way its way back to balance.

As a result of this debate, many Krophronites were dissuaded from participating in the planned incursion. These remained in Spirit until a time sequence could be arranged for their *natural* re-entry into physical life. At this time, they could be incorporated into another world closer in the development scheme to their dearly departed world of Krophron like Mennen. Overall, the council maintained that *discorporation* was risky business and would not sanction such an incursion. Even though they would not approve it, because of the doctrine of free will they could not stop it. Directives were cited which forbade the disruption of terrestrial evolutionary processes on alien worlds, and encroaching upon the free will of their inhabitants. Child worlds such as Earth was at that time were protected by laws which forbade unauthorized contact and cultural intervention by adult civilizations. Understandably, they were easy prey for the desires of manifest destiny harbored by less than benevolent civilizations scattered amongst the stars. The vested interest of those who could not protect themselves against domination was then safeguarded. Evidences of transgression and interference by the adult civilizations were recorded by the council. These were presented to try to convince the Krophronites that their incursion had historical precedents. They were informed of cases where alien worlds were scouted for habitation, colonized, and the indigent populations put under the sway of a ruling class. Even if the subjects were treated benignly that was not in keeping with Universal Law that stressed free will, even-handedness, and compassion for all living beings no matter what level of development they were at.

The ruling class on Krophron had planned an incursion into Earth's denser plane since they became aware of their planet's imminent demise. Well aware that certain biological changes would be required, they plotted a course to win council approval that would endorse colonizing a world; that being Earth. The council demanded a reversion to the karmic principles of cause and effect required of all beings living on the denser planes of existence. The Krophronites because of the advanced nature of their civilization had already passed through that stage of development. They felt a reversion was not necessary due to the advanced mental and emotional state of Krophronite society. What may been appropriate for the human inhabitants were not appropriate for them. In other words, a simple *'trust us we will abide by the dictates of Universal Law'* was considered to be insufficient. From their standpoint, highly-evolved beings would not succumb to the temptations that beings lower on the evolutionary scale did. The Krophronites had been through it all before and thus considered themselves to be immune to the ravages of an ego-driven life. While the pride of the Krophronites resisted a *descension* into the gross substance of the Earth, they realized it was doable if not desirable. What they did not fully consider were the potential consequences to all concerned. What was an incursion to them could be more importantly described as a cosmic disturbance to everyone else involved; even if it was sugar-coated to the council as merely a transplant operation – characterized as exchanging worlds, an old for a new.

A continuance was requested by the Krophronites to deliberate those consequences amongst themselves. At this time, they were split on the issue of incursion. Those in favor saw it as an opportunity to relive past glory. Those in opposition saw it as a return to material enslavement for no good reason. Thus the Krophronites argued amongst themselves. Nothing was resolved except an agreement to disagree. The council feared the Krophronites would go ahead with their incursion anyway. That they did, but in smaller numbers than was originally planned because a consensus could not be reached that was satisfactory to all. The hope was the damage would be local, and could be contained. Since the council was powerless to stop it, they prepared to deal with the consequences.

Initially what seemed like a simple case for the Krophronites really overlooked the human inhabitants of that planet. Those humanoids had an established evolutionary process operating which would be circumvented by a Krophronite incursion. Certainly the Krophronites were unconcerned about this, but many council members were. The Krophronites were aware of the human presence because the council had been observing them for millennia. Since the Krophronites knew of their inevitable demise for some time now, migrations had been occurring at time-ordered intervals to various suitable systems; where the worlds were adaptable to the Krophronite constitution. These worlds operated upon nearly the same wavelength and were at nearly the same developmental level. These migrations proceeded through the proper channels in accordance with Natural Law. The incursion into the Earth plane was considered a violation of universal statues for obvious reasons. It wasn't a matter of right or wrong. It was an issue of propriety. Thus when the council reconvened they made it known this was the preferred, endorsed solution.

The proposed incursion into the Earth plane violated several council directives prohibiting contact with a developing civilization and its subsequent contamination. The original colonizers currently residing on the Lemurian continent had migrated to Earth (from *Darma* and *Aerion*) before the planet were inhabited by humanoids. Thus the issue of incursion was not raised. Directives of the non-interference variety served to prevent overt contamination of spiritual, emotional, and physical environments with alien elements. Civilizations with an advantage were discouraged from interfering with those behind them on the evolutionary scale. This circumstance lent itself to the development of mythologies, legends of gods and men, supernatural interventions and a hint of spiritual hierarchies which did not really exist in fact. The Krophronites would be stepping into where they didn't belong. That would upset the equilibrium of Cosmic force and the Balance of Nature. Therefore the incursion was deemed *a crime against Nature*, more than it was considered a crime against humanity. Maintaining the Balance of Nature was inherent in the Seven Laws of Creation as defined by Vishnu. They were: Order, Balance, Harmony, God-Perception, Growth, Love, and Compassion. These were embodied in the operation of all of the variegated processes and expressions of Force and Intelligence through physical, mental, and spiritual energies. These have been disturbed ever since like muscles and bones moved aside by a chiropractor waiting to spring back to its original position. Before it could be stopped it was done. Such was free will. With control comes responsibility whether or not the chooser wished to accept it. So it was written. So it must be done.

As told in the ancient Book of Enoch, these titans as the Greeks referred to them, walked the Earth terrorizing its human inhabitants. Satanail, leader of the incursion forces, an elite group of Krophronites who were unwilling to submit to council authority, had been subsequently characterized as *Satan*. He was the leader of the *fallen angels*, (the Neophilm) who took up residence with the human female. Here the myths of half-human, half-animal beings like centaurs, pans, mermaids, griffins, the sphinx, and the nubus resonate with the tone of half-truth.

Michael L. Kilday

The animal and human natures were intermixed in horrific shapes which in reality reflected an astral representation of a content of character. The properties of human and animal natures were re-arranged by the effect of the Krophronite intervention. In the ensuing years, potential interchanges of energy between Krophronites and the human population led to a hybrid form of energy; a mutation of natural forces emanating from that union. A race of manipulative, egoist beings evolved of the union of Krophronite and human lineage; worse than even the Krophronite interloper could imagine. They were considered gods endowed with magically properties and mysterious abilities no human beings could understand. However the desire for sensual exploration had lured the first wave of Krophronite travelers into the Earth plane. To the lure of sensual delights they inevitably succumbed. The Krophronite race had survived but not without dilution of spirit or diffusion of energy that had befallen so many of their number.

Upon seeing the incursion had taken place, the Council reconvened. The Council members who represented all of the *adult* races studied the Krophronite situation and a devised potential solution. Due process was served in the diligent effort to prepare the argumentative briefs. It was argued that no intercourse with the human inhabitants of Lemurian descent could be permitted. As Earth was recovering from a period of traumatic shocks, environmental and cultural, during this time *darkness* threatened. It would be exacerbated when the Krophronite influence was introduced into the mix un-tethered. Thus it was ordained that a new order on Earth be formed, The Children of the Law of One, to provide moral, ethical, and spiritual guidance for any and all affected by the incursion. The Krophronites were obligated to teach The Law of One to all inhabitants to offset circumstances of the incursion. These Krophronites were branded with a designation of Elohim in opposition to the Neophilm that had already *descended* to the Earth plane.

A plan of rescue was formulated under Council leadership to lead the band of the first incursion back to the Light, or at least make the attempt. These were the Children of the Law of One whose high spiritual resonance would ensure they could not be perverted by the descent. The mission was undertaken out of compassion for their fallen comrades who they hoped would be inspired to find their way back to the Light. Thus the Children of the Law of One made their appearance on Earth on a rescue mission hopeful that their cause would be successful. Under the guidance of their master, Amelius, (who in a later incarnation was known as *Thoth*, and a still later incarnation known as *Jesus of Nazareth*), they smoothed the path for the man-animals. Once trapped in the flesh themselves, they decided to embrace the ways of the human beings so that all could eventually be led back to the Light. With the Law of One, they set the course and laid out the requirements. Since the path of the Krophronite and the human being were now intertwined, any and all could follow it, and achieve oneness. And it was an arduous path mainly because the lives of human beings were so much shorter than those of Krophronites. Much effort was required over the course of lifetimes to stabilize one's life purpose and focus it properly.

Since the descent to Earth, the Krophronites had adopted the ways of human beings with reservation, but not the temperament that demanded temperance and moderation. Ancient memories were held fast but distorted over the centuries by likes and dislikes. A new land drew out new expression. New experiences replaced old ones – gone but not entirely forgotten. Their influence had been felt over the entire planet as a frustrated ego that could not be satiated. It delved into all manner of sensual gratification to compensate for what had been lost spiritually. Pulled away from the Universal consciousness, many struggled to make sense of their separate selves – those they had not known for millennia on Krophron. Sensual appetites grew out of proportion to material need into gluttony and resulted in excess. The spiritual need was neglected. Images of Sodom and Gomorrah represented their preoccupation with emotional stimulation and perverse desires. The pursuit of pleasure through technological means dominated their attention now that their options were limited. It focused upon culture, art, and mechanical devices; all lending themselves to material abundance and spiritual lack. Earthly delights was small compensation for the waning of the Light; not a fair exchange from the doorstep to Elysium to the gateway to Hades. As the Light faded, the darkness overwhelmed; the length and breadth of which they were not accustomed to experiencing. Once enveloped in darkness, their thoughts turned to *darkness* as well. For many of them those thoughts sank into despair for what once was. And thus their impatience grew to make what happened with such little effort on Krophron, make happen on Earth with so much more effort.

Michael L. Kilday

When the Krophronites became opaque, their spiritual chemistry changed from that ethereal white luminescence they sported on Krophron to a bland oatmeal-like haze. Their esoteric remembrances of transcendent oneness were transformed to the ceremonial blandishments of Belial.[xlvi] Their singularity being accented meant that their unity was compromised. And underneath it all a duality was formed. In the process they forgot the subtle Truth; as they were separated from it unwittingly. The erstwhile aims of great civilization crumbled under the weight of misguided purposes. Not only were the Krophronites drawn into the web of deceit and deception but also were the human beings who mixed with them. Because they were no longer *excited* by the Spirit, emotionalism took its place. Sensationalism became their credo and they were caught in the web. Their human partners turned from their ways of simplicity to the pluralistic views of their Krophronite comrades. The Krophronites amazed their human counterparts with supernatural abilities left over from the descent. They were perceived as magicians and revered as gods for their mysterious operations which was little more than a mentalist's sleight of hand. For millennia these powers grew. Their lost abilities were those which could develop in the human being eventually if it followed the normal course of development, and be re-instilled if the Light was regained. But this was not their immediate concern. It was covering their tracks. The trail that led them back to Krophron was quietly erased. When all remembrance of the incursion had faded to the aged recesses of the sub-conscious mind, the transformation was complete.

At this point they had become Atlanteans for all intents and purposes. Their original intent was to inhabit this isolated section of Earth, now known as Atlantea. This continent had raised millennia before during the great cataclysms in the Pacific, and had previously been uninhabitable as a series of salt marshes and sand bars. When the land dried out, a great civilization was installed upon the Atlantean continent. The towers of Posideia and Aryan sparkled in the setting sun. All of the colors of the rainbow shone through the crystal pyramid of Eden focusing laser beams across the circular harbor like lighthouse fires. They all attested to a magnificent technological proficiency that had awakened in the descent to flesh; one that would have forever remained dormant because it was not needed to live the simple life on Krophron. Over the millennia their technology shown in ways that manipulated matter in innovative shapes and forms. Great machines they adored had replaced the great mechanism in the Cosmos they once served. What they were once able to do with their minds, they now had to resort to creating machinery to compensate for; perhaps even over-compensate. It precipitated their decline. Their spiritual proficiency kept everything focused on the soul, a beam moving outward toward the One. But it could not forestall their ultimate demise in new surroundings.

As the continent began to disintegrate, the vibrations moving from west to east in rhythmic patterns, the Krophronites knew their days were numbered again. Compared to the millions of years of residence on Krophron, their stay was relatively short on Atlantea, a nominal blink-of-an-eye in comparison. Three major catastrophes occurred which obliterated the three major provinces of the island. These in fact had the effect of splitting the continent into seven islands over a relatively short span of time. Vibrations resulting from the original incursion were reverberating through the Cosmos and returned with momentous force. Eden was the first province, to be severely affected. Its major city of the same name, home of the crystal pyramid, shook apart in a single day and night, as it is recorded, to its very foundations. All that survived were the island group known collectively as the West Indies; those peaks which were the highest mountain chain on the original continent. The second province, Aryan, bordering the mid-Atlantic ridge on the east, a region of volatile forces, crumbled to dust. It was shaken to its roots during the second catastrophe. Nothing remains but open sea. Survivors were few. The third province, Posideia, the northern most of the group, also affected by explosions along the mid-Atlantic ridge sank slowly in the ocean. This was the island that virtually touched the British Isles on the north; the center of which sat almost directly across from the so-called Pillars of Hercules. The Canary and Azores island group are all that remains today. The volcanically-active mid-Atlantic ridge was responsible for the final demise of the Atlantean island group, and was what caused the initial split of the continent into island groups, as well as its final demise. The northernmost island, Posideia, the largest and least seismically active, was spared until the final catastrophe. Explosions along the mid-Atlantic ridge caused by the alignment of extra-terrestrial forces caused huge tidal waves to spread toward both coasts of the Atlantic theater. Bordering the mid-Atlantic ridge on the east, the final land mass was swallowed by the sea in a moment.

While the bulk of the surviving inhabitants of Eden island-hopped to the Yucatan peninsula, a small minority ventured north to the marshy reaches and sand bars of the North American continent. Those that ventured south mixed with the indigent populations of Lemurian descent. The influx of the Atlantean influence blended with the Indian cultures and produced the Maya, Incan, Toltec, and Aztec civilizations. Remnants of Eden exist as the Caribbean archipelago and the islands of the Caribbean basin. Once the great fertile valleys of Aryan connected to North America via the Mississippi River channel, fed the Atlantean population. The island dropped 1000 feet during the monumental Lemurian volcanic eruptions. The force felt as far away as the city of Poseidia in the northern reaches of the continent, caused the dormant volcanoes along the mid-Atlantic ridge to explode in sequence. Pumice and ash rained upon Posideia and Aryan to the east. The crust creaked ominously but aside from the encroachment of the sea along the mid-Atlantic ridge, relatively little damage to the northernmost island was done at the time. The split in the crust effectively divided the continent in two because Eden expect for a group of islands had disappeared. The encroachment of sea formed a strait laced with volcanic islands between the cities of Posideia and Aryan. These were formerly joined by mountain passes through the mid-Atlantic ridge. All commerce between the major cities diminished to a trickle. Since there was no land traffic, it continued by boat and air. During this time a rift developed.

Symbolized by the rift of sea, this schism constituted a philosophic and conceptual break spearheaded by the prime minister of Posideia named Belial[xlvii]. Belial and his followers who numbered among them, Mordach who ascended to the religious leader of Posideia after the fall of Eden, launched a campaign against Aryan, subduing it in a short time. Those surviving inhabitants of Aryan who considered themselves followers of the Law of One escaped to the islands of the west or died trying. Converts to the new faith of self-love proposed by Belial soon forgot the lessons of the masters, and proceeded down the path of manifest destiny. They took what they wanted when they wanted it, and justified it with the doctrine of *only the strong survive*.

Spurred on by the urging of military conquest, an effort sallied forth against the Mediterranean theater of Atlantean colonies. As it is recorded in THE CRITAS AND TIMEAUS (Plato, 4th Century BCE) by Plato, they resolved to conquer the colonies through force if necessary. Belial contrived a grand scheme of conquest aimed at the Mediterranean theater. It became an imperative when their continent began to break-up. Using Posideia as their base, they invaded the seafaring civilizations of the Mediterranean theater. With the Children of the Law of One literally scattered to the four winds, the last obstacle to global conquest had been removed. Their moral authority had been vanquished by natural catastrophe. The master teachers of the Temple of the Living Spirit were gone with it, and their influence over the population was removed.

Colonies established in North Africa and Western Europe had flourished in the new lands as well as on the coasts of Asia Minor, Greece and Egypt. They were an example of earlier economic and cultural exchange which now was threatened by a desire for matricide, like a mother strangling her offspring while they slept. The opportunity to rule over the human beings overcame their sense of reason and propriety. They lusted after power. Desire drew the Atlanteans out into the wide world, at first to trade with the Phoenicians, but then to covet ownership of the known world. Atlantean model cities like Athens, Thebes and Cossonosos had sprung into the fullness of culture, philosophy, and artisanship with an Atlantean flavor. Architectural wonders resembling the great cultural centers of a majestic Posideia, picturesque and bountiful Aryan, and mystical Eden was evidenced in the structures of Athens, Alexandria, and Thebes, respectively. All manner of cultural achievement was emulated in the stately column design and temple fashioning. It was all put at risk with Posideia's new imperialistic venture which was interrupted by the rumblings of the Earth. The end came for Posideia before the conquest could be completed. All memory of it literally slid beneath the surface of the sea.

Michael L. Kilday

Truth Never Changes: The Genesis of the Path

The Coin is One

The Atlanteans who were later to be labeled the Watchers (ref: the Hebrew Book of Enoch, and the Sumerian epic of Gilgamesh) by those who they watched. The human beings were a race of adolescents by comparison; they being the ones that were being watched. Why they were being watched was not known to them; only that they were. The motives of the watchers were suspect because as these sources so crudely put it -- the watchers were also associated with the *giants who lusted after the daughters of men*. The word *giants* was an obvious mistranslation; a more appropriate word, inferring their stature as *the wise ones* should have been used. It noted their intellectual superiority, rather than their physical size. However as any explorers would be, the watchers had been sent on a mission to scope out the territory, investigate the indigenous tribes, and make a determination if colonization was a viable possibility. Lascivious intent was not their primary motivation. It was only what it resulted in from the perspective of those who were being watched. Due to their limited intelligence, the human beings could not conceive of any other motivation that did not relate directly to them. Except for the education of Enoch by an *angel* named Uriel, no other motivation was known, or even hinted at by their association. So it was a matter of perspective that came across in the historical record.

Thoth was an Atlantean who survived the destruction of Atlantis by escaping to a colony founded in Egypt. It might also be inferred it was unlikely he traveled there alone. The ancient wisdom of the Children of the Law of One traveled to Egypt with him, as well as an entourage from the Temple of the Living Spirit. There was little to add except to say that if Atlantis was as advanced a civilization as it was said to be, anything was possible. Advanced civilizations tended to expand their domain at will. It's called manifest destiny in contemporary times. Colonization and commerce tended to go hand-in-hand. Their technology was said to employ lasers, crystals, magnetism, and electricity. If they could harness the atom, store data in crystals, or travel on electrical impulses through a magnetic field, they could certainly build ships that could travel great distances on water or through the air; perhaps even into outer space. If so, no one should doubt they had access to the entire planet by air or sea. And having this capability it was perfectly reasonable they would use it. No more compelling reason could there be but to flee to safety while their continent was being destroyed by natural disasters. As mystically-conversant as they were, they no doubt had a premonition of the imminent series of calamities that would befall their continent. As scientifically advanced as they were it was likely they used their technology to ensure safe passage for as many as possible. There was no esoteric meaning to be found here; just sound reasoning. It was logical to assume the Atlanteans believed that to save the best of their civilization, the best they could do was to transplant it somewhere else. Their pinnacle of accomplishment in philosophy was the teachings of the Children of the Law of One. Preserving them would be high on their list of priorities at least for the priests in the Temple of the Living Spirit. If it was appropriate to save anything from Atlantis one would assume that was it.

The concept of *as above, so below* was older than any civilization humanity possessed any records of. It predated known history, and because it did few lent any credence to this concept as being viable. As above, so below was the universal rule proposed by a man known as Hermes Trismegistus[xlviii] and was ultimately the product of the Hermetic school of philosophy that bore his name. He was considered to be the first Egyptian. That was to say his advent on the scene was the spark that ignited a cultural bang in Egypt. In Egyptian mythology, he was given credit for the rise of the Egyptian civilization. In terms of mythology it was believed there was always a thread of truth to it however slight. In a single generation a nation of hunters and gatherers were poised to ascend to the top rung of Mediterranean civilizations. A village of mud huts was transformed into a metropolis of magnificent temples within a century. Egypt's meteoric rise to prominence was due to a transplant of Atlantean culture and philosophy.

The indigent population (those who occupied the land when he arrived there) depicted him as coming from a land beyond the setting sun. One day he appeared among them. They named him a god, Thoth or Tehuti, a lord of wisdom and learning. It was because his genius surpassed theirs; not because he was an actual god. Because in every way his skills surpassed theirs, it was evident he knew and lived the Truth. Thoth governed over mystical wisdom, magic, writing, and other artistic disciplines and was associated with healing, while Hermes was credited with being the personification of universal wisdom and the patron of magic. It was only those who did not have clear understanding of the mandate of Universal Law that believed in magic. There was nothing in it that either defied logic or appeared inscrutable to one who had his or her finger upon the pulse of the heartbeat of universal force and intelligence. The level of mastery attained was due to achievement through learning and growing rather than endowment as if receiving a *gift of grace* from unseen forces. It was a perspective that had been intentionally lost over the millennia. His wisdom was hidden from the masses by those who wished to keep knowledge under lock and key. A priest class arose to jealously guard the secret wisdom lest it became common knowledge.

Some psychics maintained the entire catalog of Hermes' writings (notwithstanding the HERMETICA (Trismegistus, unknown)) was lost when the Library of Alexandria was burned to the ground in the second century of the Common Era (CE). The Roman emperor Diocletian razed it during his conquest of Egypt. Quite probably he didn't know or care it was a library or what it contained. Being a Roman he probably felt all the knowledge and culture the world needed Rome already had (perhaps not fully realizing much of the culture Rome did have was appropriated from Greek civilization which had appropriated much of it from Egyptian civilization). The loss to humankind was incalculable. If it had been known who Hermes was, where he came from, and what he knew, the mystery of human pre-history would have been exposed. The ravages of Time had claimed great civilizations so it was not unreasonable to believe that would include great ideas as well. Humanity could not even imagine what was lost because in order to know that would require knowledge it didn't have. The teachings of Hermes or what was known of them mirror the teachings of the Children of the Law of One. That stands to reason since he was one of their number.

Purportedly the Law of One constituted the main body of teachings of the elders of the Atlantean race. Hence it was reasonable to assume it was appropriate to draw a correlation between them because much of the terminology used was the same. To believe they were one and same without comparing texts might be a stretch of the imagination when it was primarily based on inference. However, much of humanity's biological history was pieced together by a fossil record, and gaps in the linear historical timelines were filled in by implication. Therefore who was to say what was contrived and what was not? Often what separated mythology from historical fact was the intellectual honesty of the historian. Some ancients had it; others did not because they were privy to esoteric teachings. Incorporating enough of the human element in one's mythology made it appealing to humanity, but didn't make it qualify as Truth.

It was said Hermes carried an emerald upon which was inscribed the essence of his philosophy with the caduceus, the symbol of mystical illumination. The reason the emerald tablet was known today was because knowledge of it survived as part of the HERMETICA.[xlix] The stone was inscribed in Phoenician, and purportedly revealed the secrets of the universe. The inscription was later translated in the Arabic languages and Greek. The inscription on the emerald tablet read: *"That which is above is like that which is below and that which is below is like that which is above, to achieve the wonders of the One Thing. This is the foundation of astrology and alchemy: that the microcosm of mankind and the earth is a reflection of the macrocosm of God and the heavens".* Reportedly the entire system of traditional and modern magic was inscribed upon the emerald tablet in cryptic wording. Whether it was the obscurity of the translation or the difficulty of deciphering it, there was little on it that appeared to make sense to contemporary thinkers. Classical esotericism theorized its true meaning must be found in every human's soul. Hence the meaning was elicited from the soul's remembrance, rather than the mind's thought process.

The message of the emerald tablet read as follows: *"True, without falsehood, certain and most true, that which is above is the same as that which is below, and that which is below is the same as that which is above, for the performance of miracles of the One Thing. And as all things have their birth from this One Thing by adaptation, the Sun is its Father, the Moon its Mother, the Wind carries it in its belly, its nurse is the Earth. This is the Father of all perfection, or consummation of the whole world. Its power is integrating, if it be turned into earth. You shall separate the earth from the fire, the subtle from the gross, suavely, and with great ingenuity and skill. Your skillful work ascends from earth to heaven and descends to the earth again, and receives the power of the superiors and of the inferiors. So thou hast the glory of the whole world – therefore let all obscurity flee from thee. This is the strong force of all forces, overcoming every subtle and penetrating every solid thing. So the world was created. Hence all were wonderful adaptations, of which this is the manner. Therefore I*

Truth Never Changes: The Genesis of the Path

am Hermes Trismegistus having the three parts of the philosophy of the whole world. What I have to tell is completed concerning the Operation of the Sun."

The conceptual meaning of the phrase, as above, so below, was summarized in the inscription on the emerald tablet that Hermes carried. It was believed to hold the key to all mysteries. It was said all systems of magic function on the basis of this formula: *"That which is above is the same as that which is below. Macrocosmos is the same as microcosmos. The universe is the same as God. God is the same as man. Man is the same as the cell; the cell is the same as the atom, and so forth ad infinitum."* The preceding statement theorized that man was the counterpart of God on Earth; as God was man's counterpart in heaven. Therefore it was a statement of an ancient belief (of Atlantean origin, it was proposed) that man's actions on Earth paralleled the actions of God in heaven. This belief pivoted upon the proposition that *"all things have their birth from this One Thing by adaptation"*. Mind and body, galaxy and atom, sensation and stimulus were intimately bound. The mystic quality in spiritualism strongly imbued the view that all things at once, were independent and interrelated, differentiated as well as integrated. These concepts pivoted upon the belief that all things came from the One Thing, or First Cause, and its power was integrating, if it be focused on spirit or matter.

The purpose of all rituals in ceremonial mysticism was to unite the microcosm with the macrocosm, to join the Universal consciousness with human consciousness. When such a union was achieved the subject and object became one. This was because the mystic felt he or she was consciously in touch with all elements of the universe. This feeling intensified the more the mystic successfully practiced his or her craft. Whenever failures occurred, one knew the ritual was not performed correctly. When feeling in unison with the universe the mystic knew he or she had reached his or her higher or true self because one had attained mastery of the connection between oneself and the universe. Thus one felt one's skillful work *"ascends from Earth to heaven and descends to Earth again, and receives the power of the superiors and of the inferiors"* as Hermes said. Therefore, one *"hast the glories of the whole world therefore let all obscurity flee from thee."* Now the miracles were possible.

No matter what the derivation was of the One Thing, the understanding of its composition could not be accomplished without significant effort. That effort was being trained upon the intersecting lines of force among God, Man and Nature. It was central to possessing a core of Idealism upon which to draw. For one to be able to produce that which was real one had to understand the Ideal from which it came. This was where the teachings of the Children of the Law of One came into play. They were as older than mankind itself; being delivered from the Other Side and being taught in an oral tradition since the dawn of Time. They had been carried through the Ages and delivered to humanity by every major religion and by every major prophet or Adept who received it directly from the Source. These teachings were the undercurrent of philosophy of force and intelligence of the ONE itself which manifested in the expression of the one commandment – Love. The prophet of preference had always carried the message of the One.

For our current age, this prophet, Jesus the Christ, taught the message to love your neighbor as yourself. No other precept of moral code preempted it. No other precept of ethics was required to enable it. It stood alone as the enabling rule of Natural Law. Universal Law worked in concert to manifest it. These included all laws of attraction and repulsion, cause and effect, and spiritual or material force and intelligence. They all melded into the One; being its expression. And if humanity were to follow this commandment with its full force of spirit in the spirit it was given, it wouldn't need to be saved. It was this sustaining and life-giving message to all humanity that provided salvation. It was the only edict to follow (Perish the thought all human beings would decide to follow it!) All of the perversions of faith, doctrine, and misguided ideology would inevitably fall away and the clear light of transcendental wisdom would prevail. But that would not happen without the human input to the equation. Therefore one must put one's shoulder to the Wheel to move the mountain or it will not move. It could not without the force behind it. Life was never intended to be a spectator sport. One must act. What was given was really earned. It was a function of cause and effect. One's body of work, their so-called karma, was the baggage one carried from womb to tomb. It was only the misgivings of the separate-but-equal philosophy that declared spiritualism and materialism inhabit distinctly different planes of existence. It was the imbalance between them that kept humanity in bondage. The belief that the twain-shall-never-meet ensured one would never be free from a life of toil and travail. There was always work to do, but if it was the work one loved to do it was not chore, but a blessing.

It was an undeniable fact that in the current age a rift existed between spiritualism and materialism. Over the ages, a duality had developed between satisfying the needs of body and soul. Primarily because conventional wisdom had always equated religion with spirituality, humanity anticipated that religious doctrine also equated to Universal Law. In so far as Webster's dictionary supported that misconception, religion had assumed the mantle of catering to the needs of the soul. But the fact was spiritualism and materialism were only opposite sides of the same coin. They came from the same Source. Since Universal Law had both physical and metaphysical components, by necessity human beings had a foot in both worlds. They saw the dichotomy, but viewed it as an effect of a preference for one or the other, and consequently had attempted to separate one from the other when no such division really existed. No wall could exist between them. They must collaborate or a physical world would not even exist. Furthermore the absence of physical manifestation would mean the metaphysical would exist as one thing where the parts were indistinguishable from each other. It was true human beings existed as separate entities, but they were also parts of the Whole, the One. The One subdivided itself so that individual souls could exist. It was also true human beings lived with a figment of imagination that set one apart from another so that a distinction could be made between separate consciousness and universal consciousness.

However if one believed the coin represented the One, the relationship between spiritualism and materialism was seen as collaborative, not in opposition. The rift must be straddled; meaning there was a point of reference where one side could communicate with the other. Plato believed that too, and it formed the base of his philosophical teachings. There was a symbiotic link between, the meaning of which was transparent to the beholder. That was why Hermetic philosophy coined the phrase, as above, so below. It was a concept embraced by Platonic philosophy as well. It represented the working formula of the connection between God, Man, and Nature – the unity of all things. While it implied that each individual was striving to reunite with the One, the soul's lesson plans were individualized. Each individual learned what they needed to learn at the appointed time. The spiritual meaning of *separate but equal* taught that each individual learned the lessons it needed to learn at its own pace as well. But the way was blocked by the selfishness of the separate self. When the way was cleared, another door opened. When this happened it did so when that unit of soul was enlightened; meaning it recognized it was an individual which found its place within the One. Were it not for the prospect of enlightenment no individual would ever find its way home. And the greatest accomplishment for any individual was to recognize Oneness while retaining recognition of his or her individuality. These individuals saw both the portal and panoramic views at the same moment in time, and understood that they were One.

While it might not seem logical to the human mind that change operates on different economies of scale, the Universal Mind understands that logic. That matters more than what any human being thinks. If one is to understand the true import of the as above, so below philosophy, this makes perfect sense. Generally the uninitiated don't see things as they are at a macrocosmic level. Normally one is bearing witness to their own narrow, portal view of how change affects them. That outlook is a slice of life that cuts across the grain and provides a cross-sectional view. While the *portal view* is the view an individual has, the *top view* is the panoramic view from the Universal Mind. That is the *big picture* of all the parts of the One Thing. Until one achieves *enlightenment*, one does not partake of that panoramic view. It is difficult to fathom what that actually means for one who has always see the world through that portal. Nonetheless it is what it is. If one sees things as disjointed and separated, reality will be viewed that way. However if one sees things as connected and interrelated, reality will be viewed that way instead. But again only an enlightened being can see it in the fullness of the interrelated moving parts and their relationships. Hence one only sees with clarity what the conscious mind can draw associations to. That is to say one can only view the cause and effect relationship of the connection, rather than the underlying causation. The fault lies only in not wanting to expand the view to encompass the Universal Mind; that which is the source of causation.

The panoramic view yields an entirely different image from the portal view. Because human perception has been made to serve the will of the portal views, selfishness has ruled the world and everything in it. Achieving salvation would not only entail a revamping of our philosophical and economic ways and means at their most fundamental

Truth Never Changes: The Genesis of the Path

level, but would also include a re-examination of our belief systems and philosophies to readjust our views of God, humanity, and Nature. This is all that a man or woman of true spiritual import could ever hope for. But the question remains: will reason prevail or will a dogged determination to preserve an imprudent ideology preside over our ultimate demise? Only the practice of agape[l] on a global scale enables the salvation of the race. But it is a door humanity must choose to walk through. It has never been any different nor will it ever be. Choice is the rule, rather than the exception to it. Humanity must recognize that observing any ideology must not preempt the health and welfare of humanity at large. The Will of the Universal Mind takes precedence over human beliefs of what is best for humanity and the natural world. But the course of human events is chosen rather than mandated. Thus a lifeline tossed to the drowning man could pull him to safety or provide enough rope for him to hang himself before he is dragged to shore. It's all in how that lifeline is used.

As light required darkness to complete the day, so the Children had their enemy. It was a small group of their number who had adopted a perversion of the Law of One. In their case, the *one* was the self. To use a Star Wars analogy, they were the dark side of the Force, the children of Belial[li]. They were just as powerful and just as dedicated to their cause. Furthermore they had deceived a multitude of human beings to follow them. What they had to offer was the same thing that the devil tempted Jesus with during his 40 days in the wilderness: pleasure, power, riches, and world domination. With their deceit and guile they were a formidable adversary, and then as now by all accounts they had won over a large percentage of the human population to their cause. They offered what the vainglorious craved: ego-lust and narcissism. Love of self with an appetite for destruction was the sum total of their credo. It appealed to those who desired carte blanche to feed their egos to the bursting point without any checks and balances to subdue the urge.

Underlying this also was the recognition of an eternal battle between the Children of the Law of One and the Children of Belial. It would be appropriate to view this as an analogy of the traditional conflict between Light and Darkness, or spiritualism and materialism. The writings of the Essene sect were filled with references to the sons of light and the sons of darkness, and the inevitable battle between them. They are now known as the Dead Sea scrolls, but they were the Bible of their day. All fables or myths had an element of truth in them; not because of who told them, but because of where they came from – a subconscious remembrance of days gone by. They often instilled a foreboding of days to come. Latent in the collective unconscious as a race memory was this battle which was carried down to us as a fable like that of the conflict between God and Satan. From that conflict the fallen angels or agents of Belial worked in earnest to separate humanity from the Law, while the children or agents of the One worked in earnest to rejoin humanity to the Law. Each side endeavored to swell its ranks; the objective being to control the destiny of the human race. Truly it was the battle of the ages, at the center of which was control of the human thought process, and subsequently the fate of the human individual. Ultimately this dovetailed into the fate of the human race as a whole, and Nature itself. One could imagine angels and demons casting lots for human souls; exchanging universal consciousness for separate consciousness respectively. But a game of chance it was not because as one heart was reclaimed at a time from the refuse pile, the balance shifted in the positive direction. Conversely the opposite was true. As the influence on the human mind meandered between these poles of influence, the magnetic pull of each registered in the human soul. While choice was the determining factor, the field of choices was pre-determined. They encompassed the full range of Creation, but light and darkness could not cohabitate the same space at the same time. In effect, the expression of each cancelled the other out if they cohabitated, null and void.

    In the Book of Revelation, the writer substituted another name for Belial, the force of ego, dubbing it The Beast. It came to power when it joined forces with The Harlot (the facilitator of ideology). That could be interpreted to be the backing The Beast got from the human expression of government, press, clergy, and economic interests because they each wanted a piece of what the strategies of manifest destiny offered. That was – you could keep what you claimed for your own. But it seemed the real meaning the Book of Revelation was lost on them because they were all distracted by the heavy-handed good versus evil scenario. That was not the issue at all. Good and evil were only value judgments. The issue was living one's life in accordance with the spirit of giving, versus living one's life in accordance with the spirit of taking. For this reason the Children of the Law of One had created the Path back to the Light of spiritual essence. Thus they taught principle and how to bring oneself into alignment with it. The Children of Belial wanted to keep humanity anchored in the darkness of matter. Thus they taught substance and how to manipulate it. Both meanings had been taken out of context and immersed in competing ideologies so that one must choose between them to be saved or damned. All that was really meant by it was a choice of returning to the One or remaining in separateness.

Consequently a magical, mystical meaning was sought that was couched in mystery so that only the initiated could understand it. Originally The Book of Revelation was a coded message for the faithful. It advised them to keep the faith, and know that divine retribution for the pain they suffered was at-hand if they kept to the Path. In essence, the message it provided was that the devil was a worthy adversary, but God would prevail in the end. In the lingo of the Law of One it meant that light would overwhelm darkness. Without light there would be no consciousness of life. Pure principle was the progenitor to its subordinate manifestations. Desire was relative while principle was constant. Attraction and repulsion, electricity, and electromagnetism were physical manifestations of universal force. Universal Law was derived from an understanding of the operation of these forces, both spiritually and materially.

By contrast the message provided by the Children of the Law of One had deeper significance than that a simple outline of the battle of good versus evil. It clearly defined the aspects of Christ Consciousness and anti-Christ Consciousness and inferred how to recognize each. The difference could be demonstrated in the simple phrase: The anti-Christ was merely the opposite of the Christ. It could be delineated by saying: the Christ operated within the Law, and the anti-Christ operated outside of it. The Christ had no possessions. Conversely the anti-Christ wanted all of them. The Christ strove for unity. Conversely the anti-Christ strove for divisiveness. While the Christ preached the brotherhood of Man, the anti-Christ wanted men to seek dominance over each other. The Christ wanted you to share your abundance with everyone else. Conversely the anti-Christ wanted you to hoard everything for yourself. This was not a hard thing to figure out; at least for one who knew what the Christ Consciousness was really all about.

Michael L. Kilday

The task was to look at it as objectively as possible without getting caught up in the subjectivity of expressing likes and dislikes as human beings were wont to do. A preference for one ideology over the other was a pointless exercise in one-upmanship. Its purpose was to keep humanity arguing the fine points of faith amongst themselves so that they will never unite in a common purpose to observe the Law of One. Therefore the concept of ideologies competing for the favor of the Father meant not a single one of them would lead to the One. They would all lead away from it as was the plan of the Children of Belial.

One thing was for certain. It was no mean feat to walk the straight-and-narrow path of the Children of the Law of One. While it was easy for a human being to yield to the material desires of pleasure and pain, it was hard to transcend them. The path of spiritual endeavor was a long arduous one; the reward for which was not immediately evident or tangible. Selflessness often wasn't. The path offered by selfishness was a short-cut often showing immediate results. But it was a transitory gain. It ebbed and flowed with the tide of cause and effect given expression by the circumstances offered in lifetimes human beings must all endure. They chose their path from the smorgasbord laid out, and paid for it thereafter with every breath they took. It was much later in the process of life that one may experience buyer's remorse. But by then it was too late to undo the damage that one had wrought, but it was never too late to alter one's course. Until one stopped listening to the ego that was in a panic because whatever it got was never enough, one was ensnared in its grasp. The way was blocked by its desires. When one started listening to the higher mind which told you that the love in your heart was enough, the way was cleared. As Thoth suggested, *'now the miracles begin'*. And the first miracle came when one had the epiphany that each individual *'was one and the same'* even if they were physically separate. Each succeeding *miracle* depended upon how one applied that knowledge in the form of behavioral modifications. The true miracle of life was achieved when one comprehended the dichotomy of sameness and individuality, and manifested an appropriate change in behavior. That change in behavior revealed one *got it*. The path one took was revealed in the epiphany one received in a single moment of crystalline clarity. To see, however, one had to know where to look.

Truth Never Changes: The Genesis of the Path

Opening a Vista on The True Faith

The whispers of the secrets of the ages had become little more than a rumor of treasure. Mysticism of all kinds, being founded upon secrets, was jealously guarded. Secret societies arose for the expressed purpose of keeping knowledge hidden from those who would misuse it. Rituals were practiced behind closed doors by the select few. Lest one be worthy one was not permitted on the path; in essence to find and express Truth. Not everyone was deemed worthy to find the Holy Grail of the secrets of the ages. The problem was who decided who was worthy and who was not. Often it was those who had ulterior motives for making those decisions. Most often the purpose was as much to retain an advantage over one's fellows, as it was to keep the knowledge from those who would pervert it. Civilizations had risen and fallen because too few were privy to the knowledge required to perpetuate them. They rotted from within out of fear of being conquered from without. The faiths of these civilizations were all founded upon a false premise that knowledge should not be freely given to whoever asked for it.

No ruler was needed when any human being was capable of ruling. The only qualification should be that one was a sincere seeker of high moral fiber. But instead the qualifications enforced were piety, obedience, and loyalty. Throughout the ages, these prerequisites were cited as virtues when they were not virtues at all. They were assurances that hierarchical allegiances were observed and the walls of the holy of holies of any faith were not breached by the unworthy. However the truth of the matter was no one was truly unworthy of receiving one's birthright provided one was pure of heart. That should be the only qualification. Even then, that test of character was not always predicated upon an honest appraisal. Human beings driven by emotion more than principle caused likes and dislikes too often to get in the way. Their vision was clouded by prerequisites that preferred filial association and ideological concurrence to merit and character. It was based upon an assumption that one's worth was predicated upon how one measured up in the eyes of others. That assumed the assessment was always unbiased and sincere, but it rarely was.

Michael L. Kilday

Being a case in point, the concept of attaining Christ Consciousness was thought to be reserved for the Elect (anointed ones); when in fact by universal law it was the path each soul was destined to travel. The path was available to all who requested it. As the masters had always said: *"ask and you shall receive"*, but one was free to ask for whatever they desired whenever they desired. No qualifications were ever placed upon the requestors that were not within reach by choice. No knowledge was hidden unless one made the effort to hide it. The key to unlock knowledge was turned by one's understanding, and the effort one made to attain it. Barricades had been erected that exacted demands from the seeker before he or she was allowed to turn the key. First and foremost was the oath one may be obligated to swear before the Idol of mystery – that the knowledge be kept from those who were deemed unworthy to receive it.

Once one became familiar with the teachings of the Children of the Law of One, one understood how wise the Atlanteans were to preserve these teachings. Whenever Earth Changes were imminent, it would be wise to put their preservation high on the list of priorities. Thoth made the effort to preserve them once before when he carried them to Egypt. As scribe for the *gods*, Thoth was credited with authorship of all the sacred books of the Egyptians. The hope was wise individuals were already making preparations to do the same. If it was appropriate to save anything for the rebirth of civilization that was it. Their entire teaching could be boiled down into one commandment. It was one everyone knew. Many had referred to it over the years as the Golden Rule, and it probably had the distinction of being the commandment that had been broken the most. Perhaps the correct terminology was never obeyed. It was the single commandment Jesus gave to his disciples that bore repeating. He said *"Love the lord your God with your whole heart, soul and mind, and love your neighbor as yourself"*. If one equated the term *"God"* to *"Self"* like Thoth did within the as above, so below methodology, then that means that '*God*' was equal to '*you*'. Thus you were commanded to love yourself, and love your neighbor as much as you love yourself. If you obeyed this commandment with the fervor and resolve that you committed to observing your ideology, there would already be a paradise on Earth. If you failed to do so, the opposite was true. And that negative experience which humanity shared at present where a man loved neither himself nor his neighbor was because of the free will to follow the dictates of ego. And the calamity would be repeated until the lesson was learned.

The annals of the Children of the Law of One were an open book provided one understood the language. Anyone was capable of reading it, but to understand one had to be open to the process. Unfortunately most individuals had been stunted in their growth. Apparently they never learned to question why not. Where the fault lies was a matter of debate. But often one opened the doors they chose to open, and left those closed they chose to leave closed. Whether fear or negligence was the culprit, there was no good reason to fear. As for negligence, that was an individual choice. An individual chose it or was advised to choose it. In either scenario fear or negligence were tools used to keep one from attaining knowledge. Those that used it equated imagination with fancy and considered insight and intuition to be inferior to reason. In many ways the free-thinkers who thought outside-of-the-box posed a danger to those straight-laced thinkers whose thinking was limited to the dimensions of their box. Consequently the Children of Belial strove to keep a lid on that box. Such had been their objective throughout recorded history – stilling the inquiring mind. The word history literally meant *his story*, but it was not a single individual's property. It belonged to all human beings. An individual was entitled to find their own place in it. To decode it one started by *feeling their way* through their internal dialogue.

Over time the practice of meditation had yielded intimations which could be considered as a postscript to the Earth changes information detailed in the first book of the series. Bits and pieces of it bubbled up intermittently until it congealed into a solution statement. Some may question the reliability of the delivery method, but if the communications were free of ideology and self-interest that was the acid test. Even though it took an inordinate amount of time to get these communications down on paper, it was worth the effort. It languished for decades unattended until it could be properly framed. The vision offered was at the very least worthy of a dialogue that men and women must have if they wished to persevere through the Earth changes which were on the threshold. It was an interchange that must be held forthwith because the shadows were lengthening. Were it not for the urgency of the times, the message probably wouldn't have been revealed at all.

Michael L. Kilday

It would have been unconscionable to receive these intuitions without disclosing them. They were offered now; not because of the desire for a pulpit, but because of a desire to yank the pulpit out from under those using it to line their pockets. Some may say what was offered here was a figment of imagination written to serve an agenda. A case could be made to support that view, but every idea formulated served some agenda, or it would lead nowhere. Each seeker must decide where it led; for he or she was the one traveling the path. Every idea expressed was connected to another if it had a purpose. The motivation behind this one was an appeal for peace and harmony on Earth. The consequences for not achieving it were dire. Perhaps it was more critical now because of the cosmic threshold humanity approached, a watershed moment in human history by the reckoning of cosmic time. By Hopi reckoning, the fifth age of Man was on the threshold and the human race was behind the eight ball as the cosmic pool shark lined up the next shot. Humanity was behind the eight ball because it had strayed so far from its root belief system.

What was presented next served as an introduction to the Law of One, the root of human belief systems. It was not intended to replace the wisdom or guidance that could be offered by a true teacher. It was being offered in lieu of one. Among other things their instructions indicated was that one must will to be one's own messiah. The salvation offered by religious ideology may provide temporary emotional relief, but in reality it was merely an attempt at mind-control perpetuated by those who had something to gain. Be it material abundance or the warm feeling inside you got when you perceived you were helping someone else *see the light*, it's value was in stimulating the spirit within to move. In the long run, no one was being helped for long if they were taken by the hand. This type of selfless service was an indulgence for failure to comprehend the Universal Mind offered by those who were not necessarily empowered to provide it. Its effectiveness was directly proportional to one's propensity for self-delusion. It was never going to supplant the need for purposeful action on the seeker's part. That action you had to supply of your own volition. If you didn't speak for yourself, who would speak for you? If you didn't act for yourself, who would act on your behalf? Life was a continuous stream of action and reaction within a river that flowed. Therefore one was not ever absolved of the responsibility for the choices they had made.

Feeling Your Way

The individual chooses whether to pursue an understanding of his or her soul, his or her higher mind, and the spiritual link between, or to yield to the desires of the material self. The individual chooses how one's quest will be performed, over what avenues it will traverse, and what will be collected along the way. One is free to choose from whatever options are available to one. One is a full-partner in the decision-making process with the impulses of reason, conscience, intuition, and insight. The individual defines his or her own values out of the storehouse of life experience which reflect benevolent or malicious intent. One always knows which is which provided one chooses to listen to the source which always knows the difference, rather than the desires of the ego.

The individual's choices are multiform and multi-dimensional, and emanate from the region of self called the mind. The body merely performs those tasks which it is instructed to perform. Beyond sensing the physical world, it is mute. The driving force of the body is the mind. It is the only part of self that can be faulty; for it has limitations of consciousness, and with it, illusions of time and space. When the mind presupposes its autonomy, it is in fault. The arrogance of intellect knows no bounds, but those it can reason. It processes the input which it is presented by the physical senses of sight, taste, touch, smell, and hearing. Through thought, it extrapolates upon concepts from the storehouse of information at its disposal. Beyond that it knows not what to think, but there is little to stop it from using the imagination to fill in the blanks.

All sense of value, form, and substance come from the mind. Unless imagination is kept under tight rein, the possibility of fantastical thought is ever present. The mind has a penchant for tangents from real purpose which it will opt for at every opportunity. Since it is void of purpose without the input to operate upon, it is a blank slate. Liken it to a computer which of itself has no life without electricity (spirit), no processing power without the hardware (body) and software (mind) to operate it, and no purpose of process without the micro code instructions (soul) to guide its functioning. Without the interplay of all of these components, the human being would be as lifeless as the computer detached from its power supply.

The mind is a poor ruler; for it judges without wisdom, making decisions based solely upon articulated fact. The mind deals in concepts and engraves patterns of thought. It functions as the transmigrator of impulses from Spirit to matter. This is accomplished through the mental processes of identification and interpretation that serve as an alternator of a multitude of vibratory rates. Thinking is continuous analysis and definition. The mind creates associations between thoughts and feelings; to which are attached templates of metadata characterizations which construct a memory of everything to which it is witness. Through this process the spherical ripples spread or cease. The further the circles travel like ripples on still water, the greater the scope of intellect. The greater the scope of intellect, the more power and influence it generates over the self. And the more it desires to command.

Feeling drives the mind to which it provides form and dimension. Without the programmer of Spirit to instruct, the mental processes would be chaotic. Feeling is the primary process of sensing vibration. Since thought is a secondary process, it requires the input to operate upon. That input can be impressions of *feeling* rising up from the well of soul, sensory perceptions derived from the physical world, or extrapolations upon existing thoughts. Spirit is the source of the primary process. While its depth, breadth, and width cannot be measured by conventional means, it is known to exist by inference because its byproduct is animated matter. Subsequently meaning is provided through thought, emotion, and the expression of material language. All perception originates as feeling, rather than thinking; for vibration is the common denominator of the life impulse. In the absence of feeling the processing engine would grind to a halt. Furthermore like any processing engine it will run until it exhausts its fuel. That fuel is the essence of the Spirit in any living thing.

When a feeling enters the organism through the abdominal brain in the solar plexus, it is first realized subconsciously, and instantly passed to the mental brain where it is provided associative meaning. Here the thought processes of the conscious mind perceives the feeling again, and assigns to it a form of self-expression. The only thought that lives forever resides in the soul as a feeling. When compiled into images memories result. All thoughts generated by the conscious mind through the processes of reason and imagination are founded upon those impressions which reside in the subconscious mind. Thoughts not originating in the soul dissipate with the passage of time unless they are stored in the vast cellular storehouse of memory. This information warehouse serves the individual as the repository of thought, word, and deed. Every entry is logged for future reference, tagged, and indexed with associative feeling or images, so that it can be called into the present moment instantaneously. Thus one may consider that the sum total of their memories is a vast cellular warehouse of multimedia presentations that can be assessed in their waking moments or in their dreams.

Cognition and personality is the province of the mind. Voluntary impulses come from the mind gleaned from sensory perception and sensory response. The subjective mind drives the nerve center for the body as the force which moves the individual in the physical world. The objective mind operates the faculties of intellect, reason and imagination. While there is no doubt that the mind exists because it has had life breathed into it. The existence of the soul has been questioned throughout the ages because there is no objective proof of its existence. Its existence can only be inferred by the circumstances of human existence. But consider that if one had no soul, one would have to think to breathe, to pump blood, and to operate the internal organs. One would have to *think* to think. If one had no soul, the conscious mind would logically be the only source of thought. How could thoughts not born of the reasoning process or the physical senses be explained? If circulation and respiration were functions of the conscious mind, one would have to put maximum effort into these functions to survive. Wouldn't that leave little time for abstract thought? For all intents and purposes would it then make conceptual thinking impossible? If one lived solely to keep the body alive, this would be the natural order of things, but doesn't that seem a slightly limiting proposition? In a universe teeming with life, with so much to learn and so much to know, wouldn't the existence of that handicap cast doubt upon the wisdom of a Supreme Being?

There are a multitude of words to use to describe feeling. The mental image one conjures when a feeling is described can take a myriad of thought-forms. They span the width and breadth of creative impulse. And the vocabulary one employs to describe it accounts for the range of human experience. How the human mind associates words with feelings is solely dependent upon experience. Could you describe the taste of an apple to one who has never eaten one, or the smell of a sea breeze to one who had never been to the seashore? Could you explain the sound of the pitter-patter of raindrops on a windowpane to an Eskimo who spent his life in an igloo? The true test of effective communication is the precise and accurate conveyance of feeling. Ironically for a being which has been bred upon the internal processing of feelings, and the association of words to describe them, the conveyance of feeling has always been the main stumbling block for human communication. Being able to communicate one's innermost thoughts and desires then is the touchstone of all human endeavors. It is the benchmark by which one's effectiveness as a human being is measured. That may not be entirely fair to those who are not adept at it. Nonetheless it is the way the individual is made. Any limitations evident are self-imposed. Generally they come from the fear to express one's feelings.

As the individual delimits his senses with a narrow mental view of communication, much of what is open to him is perceived as closed. Then communication is recognized primarily in the material vein of thought, word, and deed, and little attention is given to the recognition of the feeling underlying its expression. That is the conveyance of words. Consequently the image of the human being as an economic and social unit overshadows any consideration of the needs of the inner man, and forms the basis of what is considered to be a quality life. It causes a persistent failure to capture the essence of one's feelings and hampers the ability to translate them into a coherent expression. Furthermore the inability to communicate feeling stunts one's awareness; for the conveyance of one's innermost feelings largely consist of the only opportunities for the meaningful growth of one's awareness. And if for one reason or another one chooses to keep that hidden, the inability to share those feelings isolates one from one's fellows. Because of this, the full potential of the human being can never be realized in a spiritual way. Sporadic starts and stops more aptly describe the course of an individual's development, and can explain why he has developed just so far and then stagnated. The continuous stream of data into the subconscious may never go anywhere but into the storehouse of memory. It is being filtered out by the process of selective perception because it does not meet the criteria of the outer man. That can only serve to stunt the growth of one's awareness which in the end is the reason one lives a physical life. Meeting the challenge of material stress and strain offers the greatest opportunity for growth. If there were no trial or tribulation to experience, there would be no badges to earn. Testing the organism is the only way to determine if it is functioning properly.

Soul is a threshold to another plane of existence that has indescribable boundaries. On these planes, dimensions are unknown. All that exists does so in an array of causal effects. All that moves does so in accordance with the Seven Laws of spiritual cause and effect. The understanding of these laws promotes clarity of vision, pureness of emotion, and efficacy of the expression of these concepts in their common and unique terms. Order, Balance, and Harmony are expressed through the objective mind, while Growth, and God-Perception, and Compassion are expressed through the subjective mind. Harmony provides for the unity of all Creation and its interrelationships, while Balance defines the role of every bit of creative force in the Cosmos. The result is the essence of Order. The harmonious interaction of objective and subjective minds produces a Love for all creation, and an understanding of the interrelationships of soul and Spirit operating within the Mind of God. This is the comprehension of the divine self, Divine Whole, and how they are meshed into a cohesive unit. It provides the foundation for the Law of One.

Soul is the doorway to the spiritual dimension; the vehicle by which the individual *feels* his way. Though it seems to be centered in the mind, it is centered in the heart. Thought emanates from the mind, but not before it's originally felt in the soul. From its depths emerge thought-forms of what the mind perceives and inventories. The soul is eternally conscious and willful. Not a moment passes when a feeling is not realized, and submitted to the mind for inspection, dissection, or disinfection. As if originating from nothingness, feelings are filtered through the coarse sand of astral consciousness into reality. The soul cannot disregard any feeling like a farmer cannot disregard the weather. The climate of the soul is as constant as the atmosphere of Earth, evidencing itself in alternating periods of turmoil and calm like the weather. Until you are able to predict the *weather* in your internal climate, you will never know why you feel the way you do. Until you know why, it is impossible to know what to do with it. The forecast will be intelligible until you understand the framework in which it is cast.

When you have questions seek answers from within. Settle with the explanations that feel right even if they do not seem to make sense to the mind. One only fears sharing one's knowledge when it does not fit comfortably with one's expectations. Logic determines what fits in the mind. It is the plane that shaves the board until it fits in the opening. Logic is not tolerant to a fault because it relies upon the principle of reasonable doubt. It is the analyzer and debater, the scientist who experiments with causes to forecast the effects. Be mindful of its limitations. Analyze without getting lost in the analysis. Scrutinize every detail without being blinded by the design. Recognize in your heart rather than ponder in your mind. Do not entrust your feelings to the analyzer; for it will always find something wrong with them. Do not be confused about what the function of the mind is. Know that it is not the transmitter, but the receiver. Its role is to calculate and disseminate information, and deliberate options for its deployment. It cannot make decisions in a vacuum; for it needs the input to operate upon.

Whereas the physical life stimulates coherent and realistic thought patterns centered upon sensory input, the spiritual life thrives in quite a different mental climate. One must still the mind so that the Spirit may operate. In that stillness the metaphysical senses of insight and intuition carry the message into the corporal zone. It fuels the notion that subtle acumen is the province of the wise, as much as blunt literalism is the domain of the fool. However snap decisions no more serve your purpose, than carefully considered ones if you don't listen to your heart. Either way it can tie you in knots if you are not flexible enough to adapt and grow. Show me a man or woman who prides themselves on never changing their minds, and I'll show you someone who is afraid they will lose their way. Show me a man or woman who isn't afraid to change their mind, and I'll show you someone who is confident they can find their way regardless. Being consistent is not a virtue if it results in being consistently wrong. Being decisive is a virtue if one has the self-confidence to know the right way to turn. On the other hand, indecisiveness is a symptom of doubt. Between them is a happy medium if one takes the time to reason it out.

Truth Never Changes: The Genesis of the Path

The mind is what must be purified; for it is the source of conflicts, traumas, and crises. From here ego derives its strength of purpose, and if one strives to reduce its potency, the ego can be conquered. Harnessing the force of will generated by the ego will place your feet on the threshold to eternity. This task is easier said than done, and the proof lies all around you. The mind's penchant for ego-gratification can be witnessed in every twist and turn of fate, in every fortification raised to protect it, and in every course of action except one. And it is that destination that all humanity ultimately seeks knowingly or unwittingly: to know oneself, to know Spirit, and to know why. All other earthly purposes are tributaries leading to this one, but even this course can become grid-locked with the insincere and vain-glorious jockeying for position. Hence the care and feeding of one's quest for knowledge ultimately rests in one's own hands. Agility of mind is a goal worth achieving so you can turn on a dime. Take care in your interpretations; someday soon it will meet your need.

The lesson to be learned is: you could not leave it to chance, or place it at the doorstep of anyone else, and expect your questions to be answered. The quest for knowledge is not a spectator sport. While selfless service is its own reward, one must also realize at some point the collar must be removed. At that point what ensues – a herd of lost sheep looking for a Shepherd? The words that roll off the tongues of the faint of heart fall upon deaf ears. The Word is in your heart. It is not spoken or written. It is lived. The Truth that matters is in your heart. Your task is to find it. At best the words from the pages of any book could only point one in the right direction. It is from the heart that they derive their power. The limitations of language will not always do justice to the feelings in your heart. One could only hope it is an accurate approximation. That is why learning at the foot of the master is preferable to reading a book. One cannot question a book. If there is an object lesson to be taught, one can be shown the answer. In the classroom of life a teacher is required if one is to reach the heights of spiritual expression. However there is much one could do on one's own; the least of which is to watch, listen, and learn -- in a word, prepare.

Michael L. Kilday

Independence of Mind

Independence of mind sets the stage for meaningful self-expression. If one does not lay the groundwork for a firm foundation, the house built upon it cannot stand. It will be blown off its foundation by the stiff wind of doubt. This is true for any belief system that cannot produce the answers one craves. At issue is the dependence upon traditional means to find answers, or be the answer of all the questions that individuals really want answered. Your thoughts, words, and actions are not yours if they are dedicated to adopting an acquired faith. They belong in the archives of that Cause. Yours is only the effort made. No effort is really wasted, however, because no matter what one happens to be doing, on some level it is appropriate at the time.

If one wishes to be an independent thinker, one cannot depend entirely upon external sources for the wisdom one needs. This dependence interrupts one's growth because one is busy studying someone else's definitions, and abiding by someone else's rules. For better or worse, you can at best make them your own, but you cannot have full attention focused upon your own development if you are following a script written for you. At some time, all pass through a stage of intellectual or emotional dependency upon external resources because it is a necessary step in the growth process. The information gleaned from them may be necessary to get one started upon a spiritual path, but the time will come to venture forth on one's own. Unfortunately for most individuals, they may become so intent upon achieving an objective they neglect to realize it is an objective laid out for them by someone else. The true genius of religion is in making you believe it is your objective, and the choice is yours to carry it out. Thus you are obligated to fulfill it. As a result, one rarely considers a change in course, and it becomes virtually impossible to break free until one summons the courage to cut the cord. Until then like an addictive personality one who worships at the throne of another, the desire to please the master takes precedence over the desire to uplift oneself. Of itself, striving for selflessness may be a noteworthy goal, but only if the master is not someone other than you. Until one realizes all the tools required to renovate the self are located within oneself, the cycle of dependency will remain unbroken. Until such time you awaken to the realization that God is within you, you will seek HIM anywhere but in yourself.

Independence of mind is a critical factor in attuning the outer-self to the inner-self, but developing the inner resolve necessary to accomplish this is the most difficult task imaginable; for you must trust your own intuition. This is no trivial feat if you have been continually reminded how sinful you are, and you have come to believe it. That is just a device to keep you dependent upon the wisdom and guidance of your superiors. Your expertise alone can guide you if you have taken the time to acquire and fine-tune it and have been encouraged to do so. But this expertise must be founded upon an inner resolve; the core of which is a process of acquiring bits and pieces of wisdom from a variety of sources, and congealing them into a coherent expression. No one's wisdom is appreciably better than another's, just different. What set one's wisdom apart from another's are its respective credentials. No matter what one's angle of perspective is you should always cross-check acquired knowledge with the code of the heart; for it will catch the errors made in translation before they become entrenched in the mind. No one is saying we cannot learn from each other, but that it should stop short of worship.

Be advised that the first rule of spiritual code-breaking is: *think for yourself*. No one else is obligated to keep your best interests in mind. Only the higher mind can be trusted implicitly. No human being should be. As trust in your inner self grows, the need for reinforcement and consensus proportionately decreases. The more you trust the feelings of your innermost self, the more your bounty will grow. But it will likely die on the vine if you entrust its care to another. The second is to look before you leap to see where you'll land. Eagerness is a praiseworthy quality, but it can too easily be used against you. The master senses the servant's anxiety because he or she is attuned to it. Withhold the keys to your kingdom until you can trust the person you give them to. If they had no value, they wouldn't be in demand. But yet that does not mean human beings always choose wisely either. The third is to prove to yourself there is a reason to believe. Do not assume your association with the spiritual profiteers will profit you. They cannot guarantee you anything but the same things you can have without them. Whatever you get out of the relationship depends solely upon you. Be wary of the hard sell. What they should be selling, sells itself. If their wisdom has true value, you will feel it in your heart. You will not have to be told, nor coaxed into realization. When the master becomes consumed with your welfare, be advised there is more at stake than your enlightenment.

Fortitude is born of independence of mind and self-confidence. It is enacted by the placing of trust in the inner self, and is nurtured by the active pursuit of wisdom. When trust is placed in the inner source, fortitude will stand watch over one's contemplations. Cowardice then evaporates in the light and heat of this commitment. Forged by the internal combustion of conflict, it is measured by how well one can withstand the tremors of life without shaking apart. When karmically-derived the tremors are eternal and inescapable. Thus it is imperative to make as few waves as possible while steering one's course which is easier said than done when one does not know what circumstances to embrace or what circumstances to avoid. Until the cause is known, one can only react to the effects. Therefore one must cast an introspective gaze upon one's spiritual situation, and proactively come to grips with it before any real progress can be made.

Fortitude is derived from the trust one has invested in one's belief system, material or spiritual, that forms the nucleus of one's living will. From it are constituted a core set of values which are used to mold a character that provide a framework for that will. One is propelled forward by the will to pursue the Truth and wherever that may lead. Pursuing the vestiges of the outer self which are superficial and impermanent, produces a lower grade of fortitude like pig iron. It is insufficient to withstand the high temperatures of material stress and strain that one is certain to encounter over the course of one's life. It melts into listless pools of sludge or cracks under the weight of a heavy volume of traffic. The vestiges of materialism will be forever changing, requiring a re-examination of values. This provides a persistent challenge that need not be persistent, a challenge of ego by definition.

Having an inner fortress of fortitude means one is self-reliant. Thus one is not pre-disposed to cracking under the pressure of eternal influences. In the midst of chaos and confusion, the way is clear when one looks inward for guidance. This is not say one will shun the counsel of the wise when it is offered, but that one will not come to depend upon it. Truly one will be able to discern the way of the sage from the way of the fool. When one is self-reliant, one will not blame others for his or her situation, but rather be able to focus upon one's purpose in spite of the obstacles placed before one. One will not falter even when alone in the wilderness of the outer self.

Jesus the Christ is the premier example of a man of fortitude; for he persevered under the severest of negative influences, and did not seek to blame anyone for his disappointments nor seek retribution. For all of the punishment he endured, his spirit was never broken. He never recanted a spoken word, or compromised his principles, or lied to save himself any pain, or gave up when all his disciples had forsaken him. His 40 day trial in the wilderness of temptation is a message of fortitude for each man or woman who probes that wilderness themselves to test their mettle. One must rely upon that private stock of personal conviction when tested by the temptations they face. However building a firm foundation of fortitude on the tenets of Truth is the chore; for you must recognize wisdom when it enters, and apply it correctly. Recognizing the false fortitude of ego is the challenge of soul.

The courage to stand alone is forged from independence of mind and self-confidence, and it is essential for embarking upon the journey to self-realization. Each human being wanders through a wilderness of his or her design, relying upon a reserve of inner strength to persevere. Fortifying this reserve with the tenets of the sage is the chore; for one must recognize wisdom when it is encountered. A positive mental attitude must always be maintained, for a lapse into negativity forms karmic entanglements. The more positive one can be fewer are the steps that need to be taken. First and foremost understand that the Truth never changes. It is only the misconceptions of selective perception that undergo periodic renewal and revision because it fulfills the human need for clarity. It need not be that way if one recognizes the wisdom of the God within, and adheres to the dictates of the simple truth it offers.

You have an ethical responsibility to be fair-minded, honest and sincere. However how you do it is up to you. It can be difficult or it can be easy. The guideline to follow is: *Let your Conscience be your guide*. You must incorporate the rules of ideal human behavior as you have been taught into your own daily guide for living. You must complete the equation to bring forth the Light. Although you may be constantly reminded you need to be shown the way, I assure you no one knows better than you how to make yourself shine. Do not fit yourself into another's scheme for lack of one of your own. You are not absolved from having one or required to acquiesce to the plan of another. Free will must be exercised by each individual to make that effort for oneself to fill in the blanks. To express the divine right to know, however, one must first realize there is something to know. And it is not laid out in black and white. One may have to dig deep into the recesses of the subconscious mind to draw it out. Furthermore one must come to this conclusion of one's own volition.

To meet your responsibility, you should follow these simple guidelines. Do not believe the information you receive unless you know the source from whence it came beyond a reasonable doubt. Before you believe anything, investigate and experiment with the knowledge you gain. Prove to yourself there is a reason to believe. You are not required to have blind faith. It leads to dis-ease. You are required to investigate, and to make your own effort. There exists a multitude of ways to accomplish your goals. Individuals live with the self-imposed limitations of their thinking processes, and must abide by them. These limitations are caused when individuals misinterpret the feeling they get from concepts.

The way of the heart will know which way is for you. You need only follow it. Carelessness arises from an unwarranted fear, while courage is born of recognizing your fears and overcoming them. Do not fear the unknown without just cause. Remember what you seek is the unknown part of you. It remains hidden until you open yourself to the knowledge that God resides within you. HE is close. HE is not far away. HE is the essence of breath that resides within you.

Do not listen too closely to perceived experts; for they cannot do for you. You must do for yourself. Do not expect to be carried along to enlightenment on the wings of a demigod's thoughts, words, or deeds. No matter how holy a being might appear to be; one should realize that is a perception of holiness. That being cannot save you with words. No one has that power. The power vested in words really resides in the feelings they elicit. No one can give you their feelings. You must have your own. Invest in your feelings. They are more precious than a first folio of Shakespeare's works. Take care in what you believe for it gives you a focus. If you are in the tow of a self-proclaimed master, exercise caution for his or her first concern is likely to be the care and feeding of his or her own ego. Your welfare is likely to be an afterthought, the belated result perhaps of a twinge of conscience. Realize one's first responsibility is to oneself. No one can take your steps for you because one must take them for oneself. The more time you spend following in another's footsteps, the less time you have to walk your own. If you walk for another, serve and revere his or her needs to the neglect of your own, you will have to walk until you can walk alone. No one is meant to be dependent once they have the will to walk alone.

Be cautious of organizations, particularly religious and political ones, because they have their own agendas. They will dissipate your energy under the guise of offering you empowerment, and enforce their will in its place. They may claim their aims are altruistic, however, the fruit of their labors would indicate otherwise. If organizations should put their benefit before the benefit of individuals in their care divest yourself of them. Organizations cannot exist without individuals, and it is individuals who either pervert or champion their aims. It can be a balanced give-and-take relationship, but it seldom is not because some feel a compulsory need to control the thoughts, words, or deeds of others to maintain control over them. Thus there will always be some who cannot help but take advantage in any way they can. All of the energy generated in observing the values and beliefs of the philosophy handed to you detracts from the care and feeding of a philosophy of your own.

If you are a mimic, you risk losing your sense of identity. You are vulnerable to the whims of the multitude of false prophets who play a persuasive confidence game but the *insurance policy* they offer is not worth the premium you pay. You cannot be a mimic and reach the *promised land* no matter who has informed you that you can. No one is meant to mold himself or herself into the shape of the holy man. No molding is required. Rather it is changes from within that bring your line of sight into focus and connects with the spirit that moves you. It is the *moving* that is required. You must change your mental conditioning to become your true self, the reflection of the God within. A full realization of self cannot be achieved until the self is accepted unconditionally for what it is, rather than what it is imagined to be.

Faith is a personal issue, not conceived or instilled by congregation. It cannot be legislated by rule or regulation. Simply stated, one's beliefs are what are known to be true, derived from reasoning or intuition. All thoughts or feelings one sanctifies satisfy the reason to believe. When that reason is contradicted by the friction of differing philosophies, the mind searches the soul for the Truth. Self-examination affords an opportunity for verification that otherwise would not be considered because the self is not examined upon a whim. One has always a choice in selecting beliefs, and the freedom to change them at will. Choice cannot be avoided because it is necessary for growth. A sense of commitment must come from within the individual of his or her own volition. A dependence upon congregation serves those who need to be herded into a corral by those who feel compelled to herd them. The outdated analogy of a Sheppard and his flock is surely one archetype which needs to be abandoned; for it harkens back to a time when men were ruled by kings, princes, and potentates. The image presents an antithetical view of a freedom-loving, democratic society, and any values which a society of this kind should hold in high esteem; that being honor, integrity, and liberty, enabled from a personal standpoint.

But the simple truth is too often the truth people tend to ignore. If it seems to be what everyone appears to know intuitively it is often judged to be inconsequential. If independence is your goal, you would be wise to follow these simple guidelines. Learn to do for yourself and you will never want for a thing. Learn to think your own thoughts and you will never be at a loss for words. Learn how to follow your innermost feelings and you will never be lost. Challenge to know your universe completely. Take charge of your emotions and use them opportunely; for they will provide an accent for your intellect. Give vent to the inner self; for it has much to impart to the personality that has a window on the world. The ocean of consciousness has depths that cannot be imagined. When you wander through your daydreams think on the fathoms not explored. Think on what you do not know. Knock and the door will be opened unto to you. Fear will keep it closed.

What you do with your talent is your own affair, but you must accept the consequences. It is called responsibility. If you can accept responsibility for your actions the way is clear for you to accomplish anything you desire. The end result will depend only upon the effort you are willing to expend in pursuit of your goals. However you have to know where you are coming from to know where to go. You have to be secure in your wisdom to continue to grow. Remember there is no escape from any part of yourself. Give up trying. There is no metamorphosis in the offing that will transform you into something you are not. The transformation is to unveil your true self. You must stand in the midst of the hurricane; let it pass over and through you to be at peace. As the horizon retreats as one approaches it, thus the Wheel of Life proceeds unbroken while one walks the edge. It is only when one gravitates to the center that the turbulence ceases, and then one can find calm in the eye of the storm.

Really all that is required to set one on the right path is the effort it takes for one to remove the cultural programming they have been imbued with since birth. In other words reprogram yourself using the axiom '*I require a reason to believe*'. The chore is to find out what that belief should be. The only place it can be found is within the self. It can only be felt in the soul. The true teacher taps it and it vibrates like a tuning fork. When the student vibrates like that tuning fork upon hearing the Word; that is when one knows the Truth. The Children of the Law of One operated upon this paradigm. Essentially their approach is a process by which an entity undergoes a growth of awareness. That awareness centers upon an understanding of Universal Law, and its operation upon all things material and immaterial. It is consummated by the recognition that all manifestation is One, and follows the as above, so below design. Being a prerogative of free will, one must ask to receive.

To foster the growth of the wisdom of the ages within the human soul does not circumvent free will as does the preacher's words. If the words were measured to instill a seed of Truth, cause it to take root, and cause it to grow, the effort would be better served. If the true teacher was able to tap into the source, the wondering of the human mind, and receptivity of the human soul, then the seed that had been implanted could grow on its own. And no one would be encouraged to exploit its period of gestation by fertilizing it with doctrines, rituals, and ceremonies; for other than the vessel in which it is planted, no one else should claim responsibility for it or benefit from its growth. All of the efforts of the evangelist could have been better spent if they were concentrated upon rejuvenating the human being at the source. When we've had enough of the misguided work of the missionary, then it will fade away because if no profit can be shown; no effort will be expended anymore. When you can say, "*I have my one commandment, and that is enough for me*", only then will you be free. Where will that leave the effort to educate the human race? The answer is: in the hands of the one it should always have been yours alone as a matter of individual choice. It is the prerogative of each individual whether or not to seek reunification with the One that explodes.

In good time, all questions are answered by the One. It bides its time waiting for one to ask so that you may receive it. What is left for you is to position yourself to receive it. The following are the set of instructions one is obligated to commit to memory for the purpose of leading a purposeful life. Nothing is out-of-place and nothing is extraneous. The One is an integrated whole. Your one obligation is to be receptive and use your god-given talent for its highest and best purpose. When you do, you will find and live the Truth you seek. So begins the journey to recapture your sense of wonder – the potential of Oneness. After the experience of Genesis, Evolution takes over. One must plan the journey back to the *womb*, their origin; in this case, the One. To reach the One, one must walk the Path. For this reason the Children of the Law of One created it.

Michael L. Kilday

The God-Concept

Because God has left it to you to be your own source of inspiration, the formulation of a God-Concept is incomplete without your input. God's purpose is not to punish the wicked, or reward the virtuous. All of the so-called filters which arbitrate an understanding of good and evil are located within the human mind, rather than outside of it. Thus no phenomena in Nature are inherently good or evil. It is human perception which assigns a value. It is the pious who have a vested interest in controlling human behavior thus ensuring that human beings treat each other justly. To this end, the pious have devised commandments to govern the rules of engagement, and set them in stone. All of the so-called laws of religious faith were devised by human beings who required an objective measuring stick to reward the observers of their law and punish the law-breakers. Consequently the obsession with right and wrong arose from one brother's need to judge another when he or she transgressed. On the contrary, God has no emotional stake in seeing justice done, nor a vested interest in assuring the laws of humankind are strictly observed by all. God has no rules or regulations other than those Laws which set the Universe in motion, and sustain it. HE requires no individual to kneel before HIM, nor a proliferation of religious ceremonies to remind HIMSELF of who HE is or extol HIS virtues. HE suffers no individual to worship HIM, nor judges those harshly who fail to do so. God makes no value judgments concerning human behavior. Those are needs of human beings. Throughout the ages, the pious have presumed to speak for HIM.

Despite the supposition of divine intervention in human affairs, one may be hard-pressed to identify a single religious concept or ideal that can be directly attributed to God. What concept or ideal has ever been delivered to humanity without human intervention? If one were to equate every biblical dialogue with God to a device of literary convention, then one must concede that God communicates with the individual through one's internal dialogue. Unfortunately those who adhere to a literal reading of the Bible naturally assume the patriarchs and prophets of old at opportune moments actually carried on a conversation with God. In our day and age those who hold to this belief would be advised to find themselves the nearest couch and psychiatrist to accompany it; for by modern standards, they are judged to be desperately in need of care. Whether it be metaphorical or literal, there is no evidence to suggest the person of God has revealed HIMSELF to any individual at any time, nor walked the Earth in bodily form and actively contributed to the affairs of human beings. The mere suggestion that this could be the case casts doubt upon the sanity of anyone who suggests it. Either these individuals who make this claim have an ulterior motive for *playing God* in which case they derive some benefit from it. Or they have so little confidence in their own perceptions they neglect to place any trust in them, and therefore need to attribute their ideas to God. Perhaps they suffer from such a low level of self-esteem they cannot convince themselves *they* are the source of their own ideas. Or they have a compulsive need for consensus that forces them to do so. It has to boil down to one of these three types; those who exploit, those who are exploited, and those who are clueless. Each of these conditions is treatable by some form of therapy. That therapy equates to the faith of one's choosing.

In reality there would be no need for God to make an appearance in the world since HE is revealed in HIS works on a daily basis. One has but to look at the wonders of Nature and biological intricacy that is the human being to see them. What need is there for HIM to make an appearance? HE is already present in every manifestation of the physical universe. A full frontal view of the person of God is likely to be more than any human being could tolerate, and maintain his or her sanity. No sane human being would invite his or her own demise. The human instinct for self-preservation would override such a desire because it protects the organism from incurring any fatal damage. The biblical patriarchs and prophets were fond of saying God told them this or that and they were compelled by conscience to convey HIS message to the unaware. As the self-proclaimed conduits of God's Word, they naturally viewed themselves as the instruments of God's Will. During biblical times, their teachings, condemnations, and premonitions were the basis for God's contact with humanity. But one must wonder how much human beliefs and perspectives colored these discourses, and how much was issued directly from God. Today it is recognized that it is human nature to interject one's own ideas into the discourse. Furthermore it is exceedingly difficult to know where one begins and the other ends. In good conscience how can any interpreter of the Bible, Torah, Quran, or any other *good book* assert that one can discern the difference? God is the silent partner in this form of communication, and HE remains forever mute on the subject of the veracity of HIS supposed communicants. Consequently it is left to the individual's discretion as to what comes from God as opposed to what comes from men.

Be assured God has no need for concepts because HIS divine action is the source of them. It is the human being who needs them to comprehend the works of God, not the other way around. God has no need to study HIMSELF. HE simply is. To attribute theological concepts to God as the giver negates the individual's contribution to his or her own destiny. It presupposes the individual has no free will. Self-determination, however, is the rule, rather than the exception. Consequently the concepts of heaven and hell are more the product of religious hysteria than they are true depictions of the ultimate fate of the human individual. They are concocted to apply consequence to human acts. In essence they are the stylized representations of capital reward and punishment as envisioned through an artist's rendering like Dante's inferno. In their fits of righteous indignation the pious of every persuasion presuppose God's will be done. But it is invented from their desire. It is their law they enforce to control human behavior.

The Law of Moses came from Moses insomuch as the law of Hammurabi came from Hammurabi. They chiseled it on stone tablets because human beings needed a rule of law to follow. The people were unable to think of it on their own. Therefore righteous men rightly assumed the people needed guidance. They could conveniently forget the law when the spirit moved them in the wrong direction. As such they were also told the laws were given to Moses by God on Mount Sinai. If the truth be known, however, men or women would never revere the laws the pious have written over the ages unless they were told for millennia they were commissioned by God. Despite the overwhelming evidence of biblical misinterpretation which the misinformed assume to be fact, God truly does seem to follow a prime directive. That is NOT to intervene in human affairs. But the human being yearns to know a Father and a Mother because one needs to believe one has an origin. A fantasy takes shape in the imagination, and life is breathed into it. It is the creation myth reborn. This truth changes with each new revelation. How can it be anymore than a desire?

God's purpose is simply to plant a seed and watch it grow. As a cosmic parent, HE has supplied the human being with a sample of ITS spiritual DNA from which each individual is obligated to evolve into a more perfect being by perfecting the execution of the instructions HE wrote. While the concept of a symbiotic connection to God yields a different meaning to individuals of indeterminate faiths, it depends upon one's individual perspective of God. But the essence of the idea is the same. The critical distinction lies in understanding how the connection is made; for the relative positions of God and human being seem to be misunderstood. Because HE is the source of spiritual DNA, God lives within each human being. HE is the source of all answers worth knowing because the way to know them is quite literally through HIM and because of HIM. Therefore if an answer is available, it must be known within one's own being because no one knows what you are feeling when you feel it. Only through that portal of self is the individual able to perceive the Universe. Not a single thing can be perceived without it, and it begs the question can a single thing exists outside the range of its perception? If the observer is removed from the act of observing, is there nothing to observe? If there is a Watcher, what is HE watching and why?

For the human being to perform as God intends, one should always strive to be God-loving as opposed to being God-fearing. But if one cannot love himself or herself, one cannot love God. Conversely if one fears oneself, one will inevitably fear God; for they are one and the same. If one cannot accept his brother or sister as an equal part of God, then one cannot love God either; for they are one and the same. The net result is that if one fears God then one fears being human; perhaps so much so one feels the need to apologize for it. That apology has evolved into a belief in original sin – the decension to flesh. It seems one must prove one's worth to remove the stain. One proves it by worshipping the Creator. Even though one has never met HIM, one imagines HE exists by inference. The existence of a Creator is inferred by Creation.

It is written that Jesus referred to God as being his Father, but he did not mean it in terms of flesh and blood, as Joseph was. He was careful to make a distinction whereby Joseph was identified as being his biological father, and God was identified as his spiritual father. His references speak to a metaphorical relationship whereby the essence of God lives in all of us by virtue of the fact we carry ITS spiritual DNA. And by our genetic make-up we constitute a community – a brotherhood of Man.

By all rights if one does not respect the natural wonders of HIS works, and does the utmost to safeguard them from harm, then one is truly wise to fear God. One cannot claim to love God without exercising due diligence to cherish all of HIS works without exception. The rational approach to loving God is to honor HIS works, and show the proper respect to them. If God did not create Man until the sixth day, are the first five days of Creation less important? Did Creation begin on the sixth day? Creation does not begin and end with a human perspective. That is the narrow view of the literalist. The literalist view is in conflict with Natural Law but they see it not, preferring instead to be apologetic for their sin before it is committed. They act as if it is only their sin that ever mattered. It may to them, but God has much more on HIS plate. HIS Creation encompasses all. Thus HE is called the All-in-All.

The essential tenet of the Law of One is that God cannot ever be divided against HIMSELF. HIS purpose can never be harnessed to serve personal gain at the expense of another's loss. HIS force and intelligence will not ever serve an individual purpose that does not coincide with HIS own. Hence the focus and intent of HIS Laws are diametrically opposed to the methodologies of personal gain unless one's striving for abundance serves the needs of all. If one enjoys a material or spiritual bounty, it is because one earned it. Conversely if one suffers from a lack of material or spiritual abundance, it is because one earned it. This does not take into account how that may have happened, but neither was it granted through the grace of God. This would circumvent the law of cause and effect, and throw the entire system out of balance. The belief is counterintuitive to the expression of Universal Law. Life is strictly an earned experience. It always was and always will be. Where humanity has failed in its perception of God and its obsession with religion, is in fabricating a belief system to serve a contrived need. It is incumbent upon one only to meet one's own need in a sincere, righteous fashion. Rather than trying to imagine what God wants you to do, lend credence to the God within. Be assured all God wants you to do is to be true to yourself, take responsibility for your thoughts, words, and deeds, and govern yourself accordingly. If you strictly observe Universal Law in the spirit of harmony and good will, it is the best you can do for yourself.

Even evangelism has its limits of personal commitment and endurance, and there comes a time when it no longer satisfies. The novelty wears off, and one is left with nests full of fledglings clamoring for mama to feed them their daily bread. Emotional extravaganzas are not meant to convey any message attributed to God. They are entertainment for the masses; a stimulus to hold one's interest while salvation is marketed. One has no inherent right to bias an expression of faith with scripted messages and contrived doctrine. The profiteers of religious faith discredit the solemn Word of God by putting themselves on a pedestal. Know that any tribute to God is cheapened by the *Hollywood treatment*. In HIS eyes, there are no stars or walks of fame. Anyone walking the same path is treated the same. The Law of One takes precedence in every case. The rules are not bent for celebrities, nor are rules made for them alone. The same rules apply to everyone. You cannot reserve a place in heaven or in hell. It is festival seating – come as you are.

There is no room for animosity in the expression of the Word, nor is there a place for self-righteous bigotry. When God's work is perceived to be more important than the people it is supposed to serve, the soul-searching should begin, but it often ends at the sacrificial altar. Any belief system that promotes the separation of individuals into ideological camps is the root of evil. The polarizing effect of antagonistic philosophies creates an *us versus them* mentality, a conflict without end, fostering anti-social behavior on all sides. It is counterproductive to individual growth along the true path; for no one prospers in the lapse of brotherhood. Any individual who imposes his or her views upon another in lieu of compassionate understanding should re-examine their motives. No one has been charged with the duty to direct the lives of others. If any individual feels the need to do so, he or she has empowered themselves. God does not ordain hierarchies of masters and servants in the corporal domain. That is Man's doing. No human soul is loved by HIM more than any other. It seems the human being wants there to be distinctions of class, stature, and station that only exist for one's time on Earth. If nothing else, this is only evidence of ego. Life in Spirit knows no such distinction. And if it did, the distinction would only be measured in pureness of heart; for one is judged by one's works.

The false axiom -- *'The Lord helps those who help themselves'*, only works in the context of self-governance, if that is what it is meant to convey. Those who are well-equipped for the practice of self-governance truly need no other help from the Almighty. Whether or not one wishes to immerse oneself in the practice of a religion, so be it, but a mandate should never exist for institutionalized faith, unless one wishes to make an investment in oneself. That is the only profitable return on investment that is available to you. The penalty you pay for burying your head in the sand in the limitations of ideology is that you have to continue doing it until you can prove your love for your enemy. However pinning your hopes and dreams on a wing and a prayer in lieu of the due process of leading a moral life, truly is casting one's fate to the wind. For whatever is done, there will always be an accounting. The Eternal Auditor waits patiently to balance the ledger sheet. Determining one's net worth is not as cut-and-dried as subtracting expenditures from income. The credit/debit mentality will not serve the purpose of adjusting one's self-image; for it is a dollars-and-cents view of one's net worth. The process of At-one-ment is more a matter of aligning one's real image with the idealized image of self contained within. Certainly perfect alignment is not achieved overnight. It is the product of a process of sorting the wheat from the chaff.

Though HE cannot say it in so many words, it implies God intends the individual to be emotionally and intellectually self-sufficient. The proposition is that one's philosophy would be the product of one's individual mental and spiritual awareness without the encroachment of doctrine or mythology to distract the focus of one's quest. The literalists and the self-appointed prophets have spoken for God and HIS intentions for so long now; they assume HIS silence lends credence to their propositions. They assume the *good book* they hold in the palm of their hands gives them license to claim HIS endorsement. However it means only there is no voice forthcoming from the heavens to correct them. In actuality God has designated each individual to correct his or her own misconceptions, and how one sets the record straight is of concern only to them. The results will not alter God's Law nor will it disrupt God's Plan. It will only affect each man and woman who adopts the individual change in course because it is a human prerogative to find God even though God is precisely where HE has always been.

Out of necessity, the revelations of pure essence have always been presented as allegories or parables to showcase an esoteric truth. Examples of Nature or human behavior have been used to express esoteric truths because that was understandable to humanity. But it is that limitation that requires the allegory to be preserved because many have not yet grown beyond it. Too many continue to be locked into a stage of spiritual development where they require the appropriate icons of authority to be in place to ensure their lives are on-course. They require universal archetypes to be on display for them to understand the universal truths they portray. But upon hearing the words, often they fail to make the connection if left to their own devices. Too few are prepared to grasp the meaning of God's spiritual principles without the accompaniment of story and song.

The lesson to be learned is that a song is not impressive unless it is sung, nor is a poem impressive unless it can elicit the sweetest or sourest of moods. The beauty of words or notes can be appreciated for their inspirational quality in the conveyance of feeling, but are worthless if not understood. The music of the spheres can stir the soul into awakening the spirit within or it can lead to an uneasy silence. The cacophony that could result can drown out the symphony and lead to confusion and despair; whereas a fine-tuned melody can lift the spirit to heights unimagined if one is attuned to the music of the soul. The self is a skeleton; bare limbs which are dressed with convictions. Once the self is stripped to its skeletal remains, you find what it is made of: clay for the shaping. Without forms, the self has no meaning, but the soul lives on.

No random course of events can account for the existence of life. It is illogical that life would occur as a result of them. A study of Nature reveals intricate details of biological interplay that infer a superior intelligence is responsible for its existence. This fact alone lends credence to a belief in a Supreme Being. Thus the existence of life implies a Plan has been put into action by a superior force of intelligence. Nothing exists which is contrary to the purpose of God. Therefore life must evolve according to a Plan, and each individual must find his or her place in that Plan through the execution of their own scripted role. Nature can do no wrong. Every one of its actions is right. It is therefore logically better for the human being to adapt to the laws of Nature, than to persist in his or her attempts to abridge them. Acknowledging there is a path to salvation is akin to a subliminal acquiescence to the Plan God has enacted in accordance with Universal Law. Once the human being becomes aware of and accepts that Plan, one will be on the path. What remains is for each individual to take the steps necessary to learn their role in the Plan. A full realization of self cannot be achieved until the self is accepted unconditionally for what it is, not what it is imagined to be. One does oneself no credit by clinging to a tradition that determines what one believes without the counsel of the believer. This is spiritual taxation without representation, an injustice to the son or daughter of man.

Thus far what you have gained are insight into who you are and where you have been placed. What you want still must be extracted from what you need. Your line of sight requires re-adjustment before it zeroes in on the knowledge you need to acquire. As yet you may not have realized how to get it, but on your present course that is only a matter of time.

Michael L. Kilday

Truth Never Changes: The Genesis of the Path

The Quest for Knowledge

The individual design is etched into a carefully-woven cellular fabric like a pearl-inlay in a sea of sequins and glitter-lust. When the design is perceived, it stands out in bold-face type upon the letter of Life, and is not mistaken for the texture of the fabric. When undetected, it appears as though it is only a contour in the grain, barely perceptible to the untrained eye. The design becomes merely one of the possibilities with which life is pregnant. One stands in the nexus of converging and diverging lines of force. What care can be given to nurture one possibility when there are so many from which to choose? The Grand Architect is not predisposed to explanations, unless the engineer poses the questions, and seeks the answers. The Grand Architect does not feel the urgency or inclination to reveal the design unless an explanation is sought by the engineer. Thus the individual is led to enlightenment by his or her own inquiries. Then one is shown the result; not in so many words or phrases but in frames captured in real time. Realization does not occur by miraculous accident or glorious mistake. One is carried on a tidal wave of enthusiasm and willful persistence. Nothing of value is gained unless it is earned because one does not stumble from the shadows into the sunlight; one steps. In moving the cloud that hides the sun, the wind blows by design.

Most look for answers in the bustle of thought, and leave home in search of the Truth to indulge in the many ways of experience. To set forth as a wanderer leaves one exposed to reckless endangerment. Wandering is the way many lose themselves among the causes and effects of the Creative Life. The result of which is many circumstances and many quests. All humanity can lay claim to this heritage without realizing its purpose which is to impress upon one that life in its base form is trial and error. The seeker is not a wanderer precisely because he or she is directed toward a goal. A seeker may approach knowledge from a variety of directions, but one logically employs two methods. All knowledge acquired from a variety of sources may be accumulated for the purpose of deducing the truth from the existing facts, or through the process of inductive reasoning the truth is assembled from the existing facts. In either case, knowledge is edited for integrity and probability to determine what bits are assimilated and which are discarded. The wisdom to make the right choice during the editing process requires a measure of insight that results from the proper alignment with the God within.

The choice of whether or not to trust external sources of information is the seekers alone. Though pressure is brought to bear upon this choice by well-meaning family or friends, it is the seeker alone that lives with the consequences. It should be the seeker alone that decides what to do with the knowledge gained. However, the seeker must realize that external sources are inherently imperfect because their effectiveness lies in the quality of interpretation. Just as any fault in knowledge lies in its interpretation, any fault in self is nestled in the mental processes of the conscious mind. At one time interpretations can be a blessing and at others can be a curse which can lead the individual to wisdom, or to the bastardization of the Truth. It is left for the seeker to know one from the other; for the individual mind is the test bed.

Do not confuse yourself with life's riddles and parlor games; for they will certainly sap your strength, and subsequently, the determination to find their underlying Truth. The more mind-games that are invented by humanity's ingenuity misguided, the more difficult it becomes to discern the thread of Truth in them. Like taffy, one becomes pulled in so many different directions fueled by the heat of moment that patience wears thin. With so many false starts and dead ends, the trails grow cold. When your frustrations are signaling a new course to follow, move into your soul, and you will never have to move again. Once you are centered in the totality of what is you, you will be at the place you seek. In this place, the manifestation of cause and effect from which all creation emanates, the nature of life will be made manifest. The concentric spheres of life coexist in the same place with the perceived intersection point being recognized without the context of time and space. However this is a narrow view of the creative life of the soul. In the broader sense, you are but a grain of sand on the shores of eternity cast out to dance in the ethylic wind until you reach your final resting place. Often one cannot imagine when a stiff wind will arise, so be flexible in your movements, and survey for a soft place to land.

Your inner place is where the products of cause and effect are realized and provided with meaning by the operating faculties of the mind. Since realization is facilitated by these faculties, it is critical that the mind be cleared of the waste of wanton thought-forms. The time-honored, traditional method of purifying the mind is meditation. It can do more to clear the way for understanding than any book or process of education; for it is the very essence of self-reliant realization. Every culture promoting self-consciousness has made allowances for the process of clearing the mind so the Spirit may operate to the fullness of its capabilities. It is in your best interest to acquire the skills that enable clarity of vision and formulate a single-minded purpose to make every deed accumulate toward one's ultimate goal. The silence of meditation provides a backdrop of tranquility against the turbulence of material life. Once moderation is recognized as the way to achieve Balance, then Harmony is tuned into the soul. Your mind is a radio tuned into static when you cannot hear the music of the soul. And when you have heard it, you will know when to be passive, and when to take charge of your destiny. Find the balance between giving and taking, and you will know when to talk and when to listen.

The ego has a role in your place as gatekeeper and protector of one's window on the world. It is a significant miscalculation to believe its obliteration will automatically launch one on the path to enlightenment. Its removal would be akin to steering a boat without a rudder; for one uses ego to steer a karmic course through the physical aspect of life. However fresh karmic conditions do not serve your best interests, and once this is realized you are on the right path. The ego may prevent you from realizing that Spirit is the prime-mover within thought, word, and deed, and is the root cause for their existence. Too much ego is the cause of all compulsions, delusions, and phobias that run you like an engineer operates a locomotive. While ego is at the controls, you will never rid yourself of mania or depression, or tighten the reins on your emotions. It will lead you away from the narrow path to Truth and Justice because its focus is upon carving out a destiny for itself. Ego's interest will not coincide with that of the soul. It is forever seeking new frontiers of cause and effect from which to erect a magnificent abode; for it fancies itself to be the Architect as well as the Engineer. The aim of the soul is to clear the path, rather than clutter it with material desires; for that will override the striving for one's spiritual goal.

All of humanity lays claim to a birthright of love, harmony, and peace in the Law of One, but learns fear, misunderstanding, and mistrust propagated by exposure to the Godless world of Belial (materialism). To be fully immersed into the Law of One, the individual must leave behind his or her fear and miscomprehension. A fully-functioning individual cannot be plagued by either, and if one is truly a fully-functioning individual, he or she is not yet under control. The seeker must also leave behind his or her selfish desires; for they cloud the judgment. Even when one desires the right things for the wrong reasons, it is accompanied by an insatiable thirst. Never make satisfying the insatiable thirst the object of the quest. The thirst for knowledge will never be quenched until one no longer possesses the longing for it. It will cause one to crush the bird in the hand; for wisdom is an exquisite delicacy that needs to be handled gently. Wisdom can never be grasped by a mind that is clenched. It requires a mind settled in the posture of an open palm. Wisdom needs to be cradled for it to be absorbed.

Plato taught that fear is the enemy of the seeker's climb into the Light. Thus every effort, conscious or unconscious, must be made to foster understanding instead of superstition to prevent one from falling back into the darkness. Once fear falls away with the evaporation of what the ego wants, you alone will remain: what you really are, and what you can become will be laid at your feet. Once free of trauma and frustration as well as the distorted images of spirit and soul propagated by *houses of worship*, it will be realized that religious authorities tend to manipulate concepts according to their respective agendas. The essence of soul and process of life are not dependent upon religious institutions, their needs or desires. They only confuse the issue with preconceived notions and vested interests. For your own peace of mind, it is important that the falsehoods of orthodox faiths are dispelled swiftly and gracefully because they reflect upon the stormy seas of delusional and illusionary opinions which serve the superego of pomp and circumstance. The historical record shows they foment conflict among men and women to enable an erection of minor ideological principalities of faith to establish dominion. They block the entry of any spiritual learning which may be in the offing if it conflicts with the institutionalized status quo. Making as few waves as possible so as not to rock the boat has its merits if one lives in a boat. If one stands on firm ground, the analogy makes little sense.

To find the Truth you need not leave home. You need not do anything but realize the core essence of yourself. If you are wandering,

Truth Never Changes: The Genesis of the Path

you may need to, and until this urge is satisfied you will not be at rest. New causes and effects are forever in the making, and the evolutionary process of mind and soul will be renewed for countless lifetimes. The process of evolution or devolution can be endless, or it can be ended, but not until the individual life cycle is complete. Ultimately the cycle is not complete until all of life's lessons are learned, and the equations of self, soul, and spirit are resolved to their lowest common denominator. When this occurs one's energy is transmuted to the next inner sphere of one's journey as one navigates toward the center of the circle of life.

To find the knowledge you seek, you must release your fear of the unknown. It will prevent you from taking the leap of faith that is necessary to find the Truth. You have knocked on that door when you put your feet on the path, but you need to be fearless to open it. Do not distort the message you are receiving with your own fine tuning. No one stumbles onto the Truth. It is found in the luster of finely-polished silver when one has made the effort to make it shine. No one has a patent on the Truth. Accessibility to it is an open invitation to any and all who find it. Be aware of the motives of your heroes, mentors, and confidants. Inevitably the time will come when you may need to know where someone stands. Conversely know the motives of your perceived enemies; for without this knowledge you could never call them friends.

Do not be overly impressed with the compilation of vast data banks and exercising mental gymnastics; for ultimately they are exercises in futility. Do not accumulate knowledge for the sake of knowledge for this ultimately leads to its perversion. Do not be overly-enamored with book-knowledge; for experience is its teacher. Knowledge doesn't provide a benefit if one does not know how to use it. The woods are full of individuals who cannot fathom the knowledge they do have. It may as well be gibberish. The passion to know is a motivation of all men and women, but it has been repressed by those who think they have already reached their objective. The thirst for knowledge will never be quenched by those who never opened their minds from the outset. The consequence of closed-mindedness is obsessive paranoia. Obsessions cause one to lose sight of the true goal which is the total awareness of mind-body, soul, and Spirit within the Spring of Creation. Obsessions assume the goals of their makers. Be deliberate in pursuing your goals. Do not allow an obsession with the cultural trappings of pomp and circumstance to deter you from the true goal of connecting with the Spirit that moves you.

    Avoid wild speculation because it can fuel the ego and create needless trials and tribulations. Imagination can be an enemy as well as a friend, so be wise in its usage and exercise control over it. When you find storm clouds gathering, pass through them and pay no heed; for this does not contribute to your enlightenment but to your confusion. Vent it into the void and return to a meditative posture. The mind does not always understand what ego lobbies for it to consider. Sometimes it needs a refuge from a nagging dream. At other times it needs to understand that dream. Do not be frantic. Live within the calming influence of your pure essence, and let it flow through you. Be rational but do not let rationality be the absolute ruler. Be intuitive but do not jump to conclusions that are unfounded. Exercise your intuitive faculties to know yourself without becoming obsessive over the knowledge attained. You must check and balance intuition with reason. Use your reasoning power to consider your choices, but do not let it make your choices. Listen to your heart and you will always make the right choice.

    When one gives up the quest for understanding, one relinquishes one's right to know. If one seals that chamber of mind that had been knocked upon, ignorance or fear will not open the door. In essence it will lock it. To bury one's talent is not a way to preserve it; for the yearning for knowledge is not satisfied by default. One must satisfy the yearning oneself, and the only way to do that is to convince oneself there is a reason to believe. Do not depend upon the voice of God to fill in the blank. God has no voice other than the seemingly endless variety of the sounds of Nature. What you may hear in your mind is the reverberation of your own thoughts echoing through the mental landscape. It is one's choice whether or not to listen to the echoes, but they are only that; imprints of feelings. Take care not to mistake your feelings for instructions from the Universal Mind, nor substitute the voice of God for the voice of Man. Pick and choose carefully if you wish to observe its commands. Be mindful that it is not the Universal Mind that demands. It is each subjective mind drawing from it. If you are careless in your governance, you may find yourself entrapped by its ramblings; for the whirlwind of its cacophony may never let you go.

You must confront yourself, and know yourself thoroughly because you cannot reach full-knowledge without fully understanding yourself; for the universe begins and ends through your portal. Be inner-directed until you have solved the puzzle of yourself before venturing outward on anyone else's behalf. Be wary of judging another's need. It is their need to find their own way. Being judgmental is another obstacle to overcome. Those that revel in their level of achievement have not progressed as far as they think they have. Don't revel in the level of knowledge you may have already acquired; learn more. It is the reason you embarked upon the path. Just when you think the path will end, another door opens on a new vista.

The mental landscape is boundless, and the energy derived is infinite in scope once one learns to tap it. Therefore the only real limits that exist are in what one believes and puts into practice. That means one should never stop learning. One should never reach a point in one's life when the belief is there is nothing more to learn. When one accepts that belief, one begins to move horizontally rather than vertically. It always will be a fallacy that the creative cycle of life comes to an end. Believing the fallacy, short-circuits the process of growth; for performing that process is a human prerogative. One chooses to be open to new growth opportunities, or chooses to avoid them. One opens another door or keeps it closed. When one is no longer growing the mind enters a state of deterioration. One could liken it to the preliminary stages of Alzheimer's disease where the memory begins to fail. One ceases to live dynamically, and merely awaits the inevitable transition to the next stage in the creative cycle of life.

When one is not growing then one is being poisoned by stagnancy; for the longer one remains motionless, greater is the opportunity for infection. Growth in a spiritual sense is an evolutionary process of becoming a better you. A revelation is not knowledge that will achieve this end. It is only a catalyst that will set the evolutionary process in motion. Rather than it being a notion that one is *born-again* as a new and different version of oneself, the fact is that one should always be in the process of becoming an improved version of oneself. It is a fact of one's biological, mental, and spiritual constitution. The task presents itself as making it one's life quest. For what other reason should you live?

Michael L. Kilday

Your charge is to know your Universe completely, and with that knowledge seek the meaning of your life. Plato taught that this is the reason to live, and the essence of coming out of the cave. Once you emerge the view is panoramic. You can open your mind to the possibilities, or you can keep it closed, but remember it is but the first step to Enlightenment. If you can count yourself among those who claim to follow the Golden Rule and the Ten Commandments, your foot is on the right path. However it is but a guideline for behavior. One must govern oneself accordingly in observance of the ideal they propose. Know that the requirement for living a virtuous life is to observe the spirit of these moral codes of your own volition, understanding that all things are connected. The character portrait one paints a brush stroke at a time is completed when the image is crystal clear. What one makes can never be undone, but yet the opportunity exists to try again. Plato instructed his students that there is nothing to learn if one remains in the Dark. In the absence of the Light, there truly would be nothing to know.

The whys are answered when you ask the right questions. Do not worry why you are here. Know where you are, where you want to go, and what you need to know to reach your destination. Live in the present, but be mindful of your past for it will shape your future. Even though time and space are an illusion, the observer requires a vantage point from which to observe. For one to make sense of the journey from darkness to light, there must of necessity be a point from which to start and a point at which the journey ends, and most important of all, a path to follow between them. The beginning, middle, and end of one's journey are different for each traveler, but the reason to embark upon the path is always the same -- to make the unknown, known.

If you let the current carry your vessel, you will be aimless. Take an oar and steer the vessel where you desire to go. The objective is to remove all wasted motion that would detour one from the straight-and-narrow path; for once one has determined one's target, the shortest distance between two points is a straight line. Any detours one takes, one takes at the peril of losing oneself at sea in the darkness. Every road not taken is an opportunity lost in validating the correct path to take. Every road taken is an opportunity gained in validating the path one is on is the correct path to take. The challenge one faces is in recognizing one has taken the correct path, and keeping to it. Whatever else one has to be concerned with is an issue of navigation and willful persistence. No undertaking of a lifelong ambition to find oneself in the midst of all other earthly ambitions should be the object of a fad. It should only be a matter of utmost importance to uncover a truth which only you can know, requiring appropriate measures of diligence and sincerity. And the why is in the making.

When embarking upon a quest for knowledge, one does not usually know where it will take them. Yet you start from where you are, and you can never be certain of where you are going. At the outset there is no plan except to move forward and set a course for self-improvement. Each step you take view it as ascension of intellect and spirit. Envision it transporting you from the entangled web of conflicted emotions to the clear light of transcendental wisdom. You are a passenger on a spiritual crossing of transfiguration wondering what you will see in the mirror at journey's end. Comprehend where you have been and what you have collected along the way. Be without a list of expectations, but at the same time entertain the hope a personal renaissance is dawning. Even the most agile of foot stumble on occasion, but as long as you stumble upward instead of tumble downward, it is only a misstep.

To excel everyone requires a mountain to climb and a reason to climb it. The impetus to climb that mountain is to reclaim one's innate right to know the Truth and express it with each breath. But each individual must come to this realization of their own accord for the reasons they determine. Perhaps the only thing most are lacking is the inspiration to do so. Consider your quest to be an awakening to the knowledge that there is an underlying Truth that never changes. One can maintain one's anonymity until one takes a stand. Once one does, concealment of one's prescience is no longer possible. If one sees things others don't see nor has thoughts others don't have that doesn't make one dangerous. The jeopardy only lies in how one uses them. If one realizes that the aim of ideology is not to free humanity from its bonds but to tighten them that should be enough of a warning in how far to take it.

In all hybrids of falsification the essence of error remains unchanged. A human being can land on the moon, or measure the depths of the oceans, but he or she cannot seem to solve the puzzle of his or her self. While one can appreciate the tree, one cannot seem to fathom the seed, and while one realizes the tree grows from a seed, one does not understand why the seed exists. Yet it does not prevent one from devising elaborate fantasies and then believing in them when the simple truth of the Here and Now is plainly evident. The result of this miscalculation is form without substance and data without wisdom, and the mind is consumed with what is not, and what can never be.

A metaphorical observation from the study of Cosmology seems to be apropos at this juncture to describe the purpose for the quest for knowledge. When a star explodes, a scattering of crystal lights is evidenced, rushing away from the center of the explosion. You are one of those lights seeking reunification with the One that explodes. And the subliminal urge to reconnect with God is thus revealed as a conscious desire to retrace one's steps, and reunite with the One that explodes. It is coupled with a subconscious understanding you belong to the One that explodes.

An Armageddon of the Mind

One who lives a life devoid of accusations, prejudices, and litigations shall live a life of peace; for calmness is its own reward. One who causes few ripples on the surface of life suffers fewer disturbances. The fewer the ripples, the clearer the reflection is in the ether of soul. A clear definitive image results in a minimum of disturbance on the surface of the water. As the image is formed, pixel by pixel, the life unfolds inch by inch, second by second. As the image is shaped so is one's life experience as it is played against the backdrop of the Universal Mind. If the river stopped flowing, it would become a stagnant pool, therefore to circulate to new heights, one must move.

Common sense may be an appropriate guide for the material life, but it knows not the realm of the soul. An individual's common sense will automatically deny the existence of what cannot be sensed in a physical way; for one is recognizing only the perceptions of the five physical senses. When one neglects the input derived from the metaphysical senses of insight and intuition, one's perception is significantly limited. Therefore one's decision-making capability is short-changed because it is dependent upon reason alone. In the decision-making process, it is appropriate to consider what facet of self is best equipped to deal with them. The collective consciousness of mind-body, soul, and spiritual essence must become harmonized before one can lead a fully-functioning life.

When dealing with the practical matters and issues of material life, the mind is best equipped to resolve them. When dealing with topics of a metaphysical nature, the soul is best equipped. However, what is of primary importance is composing a concert of mind-body, soul, and spirit. They coexist within each other like concentric spheres of influence intersecting without collision. Spirit instructs; soul commands; and mind-body performs. Those minds which are guided by Spirit lead individuals to virtuous lives. For one to be a fully-functioning human being, the harmony of all aspects of self is necessary because each aspect has its own expertise. The desired end result is perfect balance, a governing triumvirate in which each element contributes its expertise: the rationality of mind, the insight and intuition of soul, and the life-giving Truth of

Spirit. When all three elements of being are fully-functioning partners, anything can be realized and anything can be accomplished. A concert of discord is transformed into a celestial harmony after proper tuning. Hence it is incumbent upon the individual to find his or her *key* and play it upon the heartstrings of one's inner self.

Giving, taking, sharing, and hoarding span the range of human interaction, and for each individual there is an unequal bounty that the full force of Universal Law attempts to balance. One accumulates what one dispenses and one is deserving of what one gets in return. Whenever the will is exercised to achieve an end, there are consequences. There are consequences to every decision made, and every action taken. Do not ever believe that one is insulated from consequences because a result is delayed by the length and breadth of time and space. Every action has an equal and opposite reaction however long it takes to complete. The interrelationship of cause and effect always provides circumstances which are forever relevant to physical beings. All that one creates becomes a part of one's being, and thus is carried forward in the building blocks of transmuted vibration. One lives to create, preserve, or destroy until Creation itself is dormant.

Where individuals error is the assumption that death is the end of life, and their lives are lived accordingly. That belief is a figurative condemnation of soul and denial of the continuation of life principle. It has been embodied in Newton's first law of thermodynamics -- *'energy can neither be created nor destroyed'*. Like the waves which crash upon the shore, the vibratory energy they release upon impact is absorbed by the sands of the beach, not dissipating but changing form. Represented in the phrase, as above so below, the vibratory wave of spiritual energy rolls eternally across the broad expanse of the celestial landscape. And matter, being composed of a vibration in solid form, is an expression of life subject to the very same laws of cosmic interoperability.

Positive and negative, masculine and feminine are manifestations of the duality of action; protons and electrons of force which engage and disengage at calculated intervals. In actuality, masculine and feminine express creative principles which have been in motion since the dawn of Time. The interplay of these forces is embodied in Newton's second law of thermodynamics -- *'for every action there is an equal and opposite reaction'*. The aggressive action of masculine has always attracted the receptive action of feminine, as protons attract electrons within the atomic structure of cells. As positive and negative are not value judgments, but values, masculine and feminine are likewise equal and opposite units of reactive material. From their electromagnetic union is issued a physical manifestation. One is not superior to the other, nor should one dominate the other. They interact and interoperate to achieve the fullest possible expression of each. To each side there is a complement, an inverse proportion that is seeking balance, likened to the principles of the yin and the yang. It is meant that one should seek the completion of this equation, and learn from one's complement the lessons necessary to be whole. Completion of the image of the divine human is the only perfect state that one can achieve. Willful persistence in the pursuit of Truth, and acting within the precepts of Universal Law, is the only way in which to achieve it.

Atonement is the attractive movement of self toward the Source. Without a commitment to the process of atonement, there can be no actual progress made toward achieving it. Therefore to varying degrees all are attuned to the pulse of the cosmic beat of life whether it is realized or not. Subconsciously one strives for fulfillment, but may fall short of its attainment due to a lack of understanding as to what it entails. Thus it is incumbent upon you to know what you seek. Willful persistence brings the mind into alignment with the Spirit's design for self. What this design may be, or how it may manifest is for you to decide within the limits of what is attainable. The responsibility for devising a master plan for oneself cannot be diverted to a second party. It belongs to you alone. How this individual responsibility is manifested is largely dependent upon the degree to which the individual is attuned to the forces that cause.

Realize that which is easier is not best. How can one achieve a highly-evolved state of being without substantial effort? Very simply, if no effort is made, nothing is achieved. If one is not prepared to make the effort required to move oneself, one has no right to expect movement. If one chooses to move at one's own pace, patience is required; for impatience breeds carelessness. There are no shortcuts in the process of atonement. Errors come from mental frustrations arising from a desire to proceed at breakneck speed when caution is warranted like traveling on an icy road. Every human being is subject to error. This especially applies to those who believe it is not possible for them to commit an error. The worst mistake is made when one is unwilling to admit an error was made. It is compounded by the arrogance of self-righteousness. Therefore never assume you wear the cloak of infallibility no matter what your station in life is; for if you wear a physical form you most certainly do not. Discretion is truly the better part of valor, and humility the savior of arrogance; lest one box oneself into a corner from which there is no escape.

Do not browbeat yourself for failures, past transgressions, or present errors in judgment. Do not waste energy in condemnations and punishments of the outer self like an outraged parent. If you do, your prospects will be bleak. Do not be self-righteous with the self; it only diverts the focus of what should be the real intention. That is correcting mistakes and clarifying misgivings to bring oneself into alignment with the true path. One can spend so much time in chastisement, that the object of chastisement can be forgotten. Forgive yourself for your errors, but do not forget them, lest you repeat them. Put your energy into identifying and correcting them; for one's success rate is predicated upon effective remediation. A balanced scorecard is a noteworthy goal. A perfect one is an unrealistic expectation. The overriding purpose of the Creative Life is the remediation of error, and how it is accomplished depends upon an individual bias; that bias being the manner in which it is achieved. Freedom of mind is an invaluable asset in avoiding the establishment of a bias which can serve as a handicap in attaining that goal. If one sees each transgression as only a misstep along the path of light then it is treated like a bump in the road -- a slight turn of the wheel, and one proceeds on one's way. Conversely if one sees a transgression as a mortal sin then it is treated like a roadblock -- where a detour is required so that one can proceed on one's way.

Every soul has incarnated again and again to be tested in the crucible of material existence. Once the impurities of carnal instincts have been burned away, an elemental being remains which is the shell of soul. Life has been engineered to cause realizations of the possibilities for escaping the prison of the emotions, or for lengthening the term. Unfortunately, many squander their freedom by choosing not to be individuals. They wish instead to be run-off an ethereal assembly line, carbon-copy personalities as instructed by their respective faiths. Be wary of those who wish only to stamp out a mold because it is a convenient solution for leveling the playing field. It is not a fair exchange for the price of one's individuality.

Those who believe their ticket to heaven is their religious affiliation are grossly mistaken, and promise to be sorely distressed when confronted with that realization in the hereafter. What matters only is the progress toward atonement with the All-in-All one makes for oneself, and each incarnation is indicative of spiritual evolution or devolution. Many struggle to style an ideal image of themselves as a precursor for enlightenment because they perceive a metamorphosis is necessary for one to become what one truly is. But it is only an undercurrent of self-doubt that causes one to believe in magic. One has to be nothing but a window for the soul that is infused with the pranic energy of the God within each individual. As it shows forth through the cracks and seems of one's fabricated concepts, one is confronted with the disparities these concepts cause when laid against the true pattern of mandated spiritual force.

Alignment with the First Cause is the noblest goal to which an individual can aspire. Attaining this end is not without its difficulties or setbacks, but from its accomplishment follow the rewards you must receive to truly be a fully-functioning individual. The rewards received upon atonement are transparent to the uninitiated; being spiritual in nature and defying an accurate literal interpretation. They are revealed in the individual as an embracing of the principles of understanding, faith, justice, insight, and truth. These are not gifts of Grace from an invisible God, but consciously achieved principles of enlightenment congealed by the willful persistence to apply them to one's daily life. Living them liberates the Spirit within. And by repetition, the mind, by awakening the Spirit within, achieves the state of being required to exhibit the sublime image one seeks. Each individual which achieves his or her goal of at-one-ment will eventually rise in triumph and unite with Spirit in the final glory of Creation. However before this can occur, distinctions must be made between what is real and what is illusion, and what is fact and what is fiction, and most importantly what is intended by the Law of One and what is not. Until these distinctions are made, there can be no actual movement toward Truth, only away from it.

Know that any human being who hates is lost. Conversely any human being who loves has found him or herself. He or she is in touch with their feelings and understands them. Anyone who judges another unjustly shall be judged more severely; for one has compounded the original offense. Anyone who does not give of oneself shall be forgotten. As the Master said, when one gives freely without anticipating a return, a thousand-fold of returns shall be realized. Those who give to receive are prone to disappointments and frustrations. They will never be satisfied with what is offered in return because they have already anticipated what they deserve to receive. When one gives without consideration of receiving, however, one lives a life free of expectations. True happiness then lies in the absence of expectations, and despair is the result of them. When one settles into the flow of life, and asks for nothing, they are positioned to receive everything. If one seeks comfort and pity for one's afflictions, one will never be at rest. The obsession for absolution will expand the karmic horizons without broadening the spiritual goal. Thus one trudges on the treadmill unable to jump off, and the karmic wheel spins eternal.

The more one knows oneself, the more humble one becomes. The more one is cognizant of their circumstances and one's interactions with others, the more one is sensitive to the consequences of one's actions. The closer one gets to an understanding of self, the Eternal, and the life, the more one becomes tolerant and patient. The more one depends upon the calmness of the inner self, the more one discards the delirium of the outer self. The more one realizes the less one has to be told. The more one listens, the less one has to talk. The more time spent in purifying the mind, the less time is left to muddy it. The more time one spends clarifying, the less one languishes in confusion. The more one worries, the less one acts, and the less one acts, the more there is to worry about. The more effort one devotes in comprehending the self, the less time is left for the trivia of life. Conversely the more energy expended in experiencing the trivia of life, the less energy one has left to tackle the issues of life.

Be still, and flow in that stream of cosmic consciousness that like a river rolls through the cerebral landscape. Be unaware of trauma and foreign to inner turmoil. Purify the mind and a clear expression will follow. Watch the dew dropping from the leaves, and know it is in the Plan. Be advised that all things happen according to the Plan. Watch carefully the world around you, and you will come to understand the Plan. As one invests more in self-discovery, the more one grows. However, one must come out of the shade to grow; for one is certain to grow if exposed to the Light. A seed does not sprout from the soil until it feels the warmth of the Light. But it must sprout before it can grow.

As you float from day to day on the Stream of Life, swim with the current, and feel a part of it. Learn to appreciate the simple things in Life because they are of pure origin. Give in to what you feel, but know the reason you are feeling it. That is your measure of control. Many have deluded themselves with illusionary emotions because they are over-anxious to share their visions. Separate what you think from what you feel so that you can clearly see the difference. In that distinction, trace the path of reason to where they meet and understand the difference.

If you are in rush to talk, a fool's words come out. Do not be anxious to talk. Be eager to listen; for learning only occurs after listening. When you wish to speak the right words will come if you wait to formulate them. Fill your vessel with a passion for life and you will never regret, but clinging to any concept, you will always be in debt. To align with the God-Concept, you must express it with every breath. Adapt your concept to your life, and you will rise above the storm. Walking upon the waters of discontent, you will point the way like Moses, leading the homeless to a home.

There are no slot machines in the soul, nor educated guesses to make, or blind-faith potions to drink. You must chart a course within to find your creative purpose. When you find the right path to travel, you will be guided to your destination. When the tumblers fall into place, all will be opened unto you. What you create with your thoughts, words, and deeds is irrevocable. You cannot undo what has been done. You can only make what is to be done, and what is to be done is within your power to shape if you will it. One who has misplaced his or her will to shape, has forfeited his or her ability to rule oneself. The powerless seek a ruler from outside themselves. But no ruler who usurps your throne can rule as wisely as the ruler within. When one hands the scepter of power to another, one succumbs to destiny. He or she is a ship without a helmsman carried by the current to a destination unknown. Each man and woman must will to be that helmsman because the gauntlet cannot be passed to another without the cup being spilled.

Within the well of soul dispel the murky waters of discontent and self-doubt that erodes the self-esteem. Still the turbulent seas of sentimentality and the swift current of thought slow to a crawl through your consciousness. Watch the vivid scenes of casual sensation and examine what ambles like a turtle through the space where rabbit thoughts generally race. As the veil that shrouds the spiritual senses disperses, you will witness the ghosts of thoughts you believed were haunting you become your friends. Watch closely what thoughts arise and understand why. Once you understand what the mind can create, you can begin to learn how to control it.

Striving to be the Perfect Being

Perfection is ordered balance in the harmony of all realities, material and spiritual. Perfect functioning is expressed by the cell as it operates its eternal instructions passed from generation to generation in the space of milliseconds. The eternal soul is a spiritual cell that has refined its instructions over the course of lifetimes until the instructions are perfectly executed. Without the continuity of refinement, or art of applying the principle of at-one-ment, an individual would not be presented with the opportunity to evolve toward perfection. The wishful thinking of some theologians that one human life is all that is needed or even that perfection can be accomplished in one is the epitome of blind optimism. Obviously they misunderstand the true import of the task at hand. If it were that easy the accomplishment could not be considered worthwhile in human terms. The supposition that life is a mansion with many rooms certainly applies. It lends credence to a belief in reincarnation.

To be perfect in all expression is a monumental task, fundamental but also radical in the extreme because it necessitates a rejection of materialism's sacred cows of power, fame, and fortune. The ascetic's rejection of the life experience is unwarranted because it defeats the purpose of living at all. Detachment from the pleasure and pain of human existence can be accomplished through denial, but it is an unnatural act that will not result in the resolution of desire. By denying desire one acknowledges its existence, and the tension it creates for its fulfillment. If unfulfilled, one will be forever haunted by the craving of the ego. To resolve desire, one must focus it upon spiritual accomplishment, and forsake forever materialism-in-excess. If successful, the human temperament will be pacified by the recognition that moderation is the true way, and selfishness will be shunned forever. Moderation in all ways is infinitely better than the rejection of any. However many have yet to learn this, and will continue to suffer with their selfish appetites until they do. They focus upon the desires of the ego instead of those of the soul. This simple realization is beyond the understanding of many whose eyes are fixed only on the far distant object, thus casting out of focus what is near. Blurred vision prevents them from concentrating upon the needs and concerns of the Here and Now.

The purpose of setting the goal is to make one aware one has a long way to travel to reach it. But it also discourages many from trying. By setting the bar so high, it serves notice that for all practical purposes it is out of reach. One may appreciate fine art but it doesn't mean one has the capability to duplicate the effort. Perhaps shorter distances and intermediate goals may need to be set in-between whereby one realizes the progress made. When one falls short of the mark, one picks him or herself up, and tries again. Though it is left unsaid, God does not anticipate the perfection of human thought, word and deed. HE patiently waits for one to achieve it in one's own time. It is the ego which is impatient, and when deadlines and timetables are not met looks for something or someone else to blame. The God within could wait an eternity. The ego cannot wait for a few moments; for underneath it all the ego realizes its time is measured by the biological clock.

Most individuals believe in their heart of hearts it is not possible to be perfect in an imperfect world. Consequently they have given up trying. They may imagine the goal is not worth achieving, too difficult to achieve, or is a figment of theological imagination. Whether or not this is true, should not the objective be to get as close as one can? Is it the individual's judgment call to give up the attempt? There are historical individuals who defied these odds, and persevered to the best of their ability. If one were to follow their example, instead of listening to the nay Sayers, who knows what could be achieved? Were it not for the existence of a benevolent Deity, the possibility would not have ever been introduced into the collective thought processes of humanity. The human individual would have been relegated to being a large-brained animal foraging in the forest, and been satisfied with it if no other alternatives were possible. But since there is no accounting for the differences of opinion concerning the human condition, what is the excuse for desiring to remain at best an intelligent animal? After partaking of the apple of the Tree of Knowledge, one can never return to a blissful state of ignorance. Once one's eyes have been opened, and the mysteries of the garden are revealed, one sees what's really there. And the realization dawns that what one sees is a reflection of what one feels inside. It is projected forth despite any efforts one makes to maintain the illusion that one can hide it. As a perfect image is distorted by the ripples on a pool of water, one's self-image is determined by one's thoughts and feelings bubbling up to the surface.

Thus perfection is made impossible for many by virtue of their defeatist thinking and resignation to imperfection. No advice seems appropriate when one has already prepared the concession speech. It is not so much that one decides to be a failure in this endeavor, but that one recognizes the degree of difficulty of this effort may be too much to be overcome. While the celebrated rituals and ceremonies of mystics and theologians were instituted to grease the path to Nirvana, success is not guaranteed. Unfortunately the success of such an endeavor is only revealed by the relative state of unworthiness felt in the human heart. The reliance upon magical potions, formulas, and transformations is symbolic of the acceptance of a failure to perform in a natural way. The desirable last resort of supernatural intervention is an acceptance of the inability to perform at all. To quit striving for perfection is to quit improving oneself, and is an abdication of individual responsibility; for it is the primary directive.

Soul is the place you must go to realize yourself, and the path you must travel lies over its terrain. Each individual has his or her own vehicle. There is no car-pooling allowed. You must go to that place inside you, and dwell there in silence. Then slowly all of the phobias, neuroses, compulsions, and delusions that arise because one lives a physical life will fall away, and you alone will remain -- the essence of yourself. When you look into the face of the soul with love, the place, time, and being of existence will be realized. With that realization you will be initiated into the Law of One. The man or woman of fortitude builds his or her fortification upon a pureness of character. The soul's quality of translucence is predicated upon one's innate understanding and alignment with the seven laws of spiritual cause and effect. If constructed upon the firm foundation of Truth and Understanding, it cannot fall. Because life is a process of gathering experiences from the environment, the mind, and the Primal Force, the process of at-one-ment is not complete until a perfect specimen is forged. One must brave the fire of repeated rebirths in a continuous effort to achieve perfect functioning. Since perfection of the human formula is the underlying reason for life, it is the one overriding reason to live a physical life, and the goal is to profit from it in a metaphysical way.

To be attached and detached at the same moment in time with the essence of being, the All-in-All, is the directive of the soul. No one can tell you that their way is better for you than your way because one can truly live in one way at a time. Such a judgment would be one of ignorance. The way for you is inscribed into the spiritual DNA by the source of memory, feeling, and will. The individual mind converts that impulse of Spirit into an impulse of matter. It is a subconscious vibration that pumps the blood and stirs thought in the mind with each breath. Each collective breath serves to purify the temple of oneself if one is committed to enacting the living Truth.

All the tools required to forge a virtuous character are located within the human being, one has only to uncover them. And with that discovery, one must trust again in one's native intuition to initiate the appropriate change of venue. The quandary of doubt is not remedied by treating the symptoms, but rather by understanding the cause for the dis-ease. Thus an earnest effort must be made to determine why one should doubt the Truth when it is presented, or on the other hand, promptly reject falsehoods that are laid at one's feet. No effort is ever wasted if the motive is pure, and no cause is ever doomed to failure if it comes from pureness of heart. Where failures occur is when one allows just feelings to fade because one fears to trust in them.

When the temple has been purified of waste and malcontent by the flood of understanding, what is truly you will remain. What is *you* will be manifested by all of the senses that the conscious mind does not know: the sense of insight, the sense of compassion, and the thrill of the third eye. Do not hope and pray for a better tomorrow. Do your best now to make it happen. NOW is all that ever exists within your consciousness replayed over the lifetime of a sun. Do your best now for you create your future. Do not try to reform past mistakes, instead make your effort in the present; for you have within you the right or the wrong, the weak or the strong for the moment and beyond. But it is not enacted upon a whim. One must be alert to small voice within you that declares: Be Here Now.

The goal of perfection can only lie in being in the now; for if it does not, one can be assured not a single human being could ever achieve it. The only roadmap one truly needs to find the Truth that underlies the width and breadth of God's Natural Creation. One has but to delve into it to reveal the essence of its concealed wisdom. However, in his infinite wisdom, humankind has superimposed its own invention like a Mylar over the natural world, annotated it, and called it Theology. It basks in the artificial luminescence and beckons humanity like unto moths attracted to the porch light. And like a moth who flies too close to the flame, one day one finds oneself without wings, and like Icarus tumbles headlong to his or her eventual demise. In its impatience to spread its wings, the ego neglected to learn how to fly, throwing caution to the wind. Before spreading one's wings, it is always the wisest course of action to derive the most one can from the flying lessons offered before flying solo.

From the human perspective, destiny is created by interjecting free will into the Universal Mind. From the universal perspective, there was one beginning, and there will be one end that is unified by a preserving nature. Hence one images a path before it is taken, and after it is traveled an imprint is left behind. All that occurs within the Universal Mind is ever becoming something else with the passage of Time. While the human being perceives demarcations of space and time, form and substance, they really exist only for a perceptible moment. The Universal Mind is an unbroken Stream of Consciousness. The River flows unimpeded. For many it is the failure to view life as a spiritual process that keeps them stagnant and dissatisfied with their spiritual progress; for they measure life only in terms of material progress, and thus misunderstand the actual representation of their birthright. It is founded upon adherence to a Principle, and commitment to a goal; not being measured strictly in terms of space or time but in the quality of feelings filtered through the mind. When you turn out a quality product, you have reached your goal.

Michael L. Kilday

Truth Never Changes: The Genesis of the Path

Reclaiming Your Idealistic Purpose

The orthodox Christians chiseled statues from marble and granite, and idolized them. In their eagerness to demonstrate the living art of spiritual perfection, artifacts were exhibited like art in a gallery to which the rich patrons donated their valued pieces. This expression of reverence became to many a substitute for the reverence of Spirit that created it. The gnosis of that Spirit became locked in the object which represented it. As representations of Faith, Truth, and Understanding these objects were utilized as symbols to trigger consistent responses from the congregation. Hence the effectiveness of the faith became dependent upon the ability of those who effectuated it, rather than the altruistic principles upon which it was founded. Orthodox beliefs were modified periodically not because new truths were discovered, but because the populace could no longer tolerate the current form. Scriptures have been reviewed and re-interpreted by every generation of scholar-saints, ostensibly to shed more light upon the Truth. However, there is no accounting for the diversity of human opinion; for it must be remembered that only humans have the need to write scripture. The Record of the All-in-All is eternal and inalterable; for it is the very fabric of so-called Ether, or Spirit. If our human beliefs were the Truth, no change would ever be required. However, doctrine needs to be revised and modified to conform to the living truth; for if it does not it ceases to apply to the human condition.

Without an idealistic cause to center upon, the spiritual efforts of the individual have no focus. And without a focus, they seem like the incessant ramblings of simple-minded romanticism which is not taken seriously by the rational mind. As humanity strives to excel in its outer manifestations, they come no closer to creating a heaven on Earth. It can only mean the cause of the inner man lags behind. The proof of this statement lies in the simple fact that the Golden Rule, arguably the most idealistic statement of all time, carries so little weight in molding human behavior in our day and age. While no one will deny the veracity of this statement, yet no one can explain why after two thousand years it is ineffective in making a heaven on Earth. Without the prospect of achieving an Ideal, the individual will resort to the satisfaction of physical need and neglect any spiritual inclination; except for the bare minimum of going to a house of worship one day a week. Hence what is neglected remains hidden, and a resource untapped is not a resource at all. It is an esoteric curiosity that goes unfulfilled; for the needs of Spirit-in-Man are unknown to the great mass of humanity which takes for granted the God within.

Witness that in the Information Age, the experimenter has been supplanted by the spectator. The electronic media has replaced the teacher as a digitized Socrates whose oral instructions are replaced by infomercials. Its students are mesmerized by the green-glow of high-tech jargon issued by the electronic media icons. However efficient its delivery may be, no warm touch comes from the plastic keys of the keyboard, nor are comforting words spoken by laser tongues. No wisdom can be gained from a programmed mind, or a church, temple, or mosque full of them. Instead what is revealed are sound bites that must be provided meaning by authority figures. They can do little else but comply with canned responses to earnest pleas for spiritual guidance from their congregations.

By contrast to the modern methods of logic and reasoning, the ancient adepts drew upon the divine man. The progenitor of the Idea in the human mind was recognized as the Infinite Source or Plethora[lii], rather than the individual himself. Masters of philosophy like Socrates, Pythagoras, and Hermes Trismegistus fine-tuned the aesthetic appreciation of early Mediterranean civilizations in deference to the actual brutalities of life around them. The feelings of ancient sages were invested in the progress of their respective civilizations. But the few documents that have survived and monuments of their civilizations now have to be interpreted by the uninitiated. The feelings that created ancient wonders are not necessarily lost, but rather are forgotten by a modern civilization that does not remember its origin in Spirit. Hence the margin of error in this interpretative process has become significant with the passage of time.

The idealism of Western Civilization has been animated with a reverence for Intellect, what the Greeks called *Mind*, dating back to the lectures of Socrates at the Academy in Athens. Philosophical debates conducted then are considered art now, and their influence is still felt today in the halls of academia, but virtually nowhere else. Since the golden age of Greece, the elements of philosophy, the sciences, and Cosmology, have been interpreted from an intellectual viewpoint because that has become the accepted method of understanding them. Since the Renaissance, the scientific method has been applied to nearly every phase of life, and still no one knows quite what 'It' all means. Instead steady diets of mental gymnastics and short-sighted solutions have contributed to a further complication of the issues of concern. It's as if the populace was being intentionally paid lip-service to give the impression that their concerns were being addressed, when in fact the opposite was true. While feigning sympathy for their plight, the powers-that-be have been conspiring to further enslave them economically, politically, and spiritually at every opportunity. Economics, politics, and religion are used to bedazzle and confuse the inquiring mind. Therefore the proper spin must be applied to the proposition that quality of life is the concern. It makes it appear there is an altruistic motive which underlies it all; when in fact it is merely a device to increase a profit margin.

The passion to learn, to know, and have a desire to expand one's awareness has become subverted in a world stricken with a fever for the easy answer and fast buck. The yearn for wisdom and justice has taken a backseat to the desire for sensual gratification in all its conceivable forms. These hedonistic urges have been accentuated as reliance upon technology to do the thinking and the labor has been realized. Thus relieved of one's devotion to one's work because of living in a mechanized world, the individual can devote more time to leisure, but it is generally spent seeking entertainment rather than enlightenment. And this has led to an unfortunate circumstance whereby the ability to create has been diluted with a solution of antiseptic *mind-wash*. As crass commercialism fills the void created by a dearth of ingenuity, one cannot help but wonder to where originality has fled. The abilities remaining are carbon-copies of ancient talents, remnants of great innovations, and echoes of magnificent thoughts. No new Einstein has stepped forward to postulate a new theory of relativity, nor did a new DaVinci appear to style an ideal form. Sadly it is apparent humanity lives in an age of sequels where if one were to have an original idea it would likely languish in obscurity because it would be too difficult to find someone to bankroll it. The moneyed interests only want to finance guaranteed returns-on-investment. Supposedly the people get what they really want rather than what they need. Or that is what the polls are manipulated to say because the right questions aren't being asked. Unfortunately, to assume individuals merely want to hear the same story over and over again as if they never tire of it is an intentional device to avoid telling them what they need to hear.

The contemporary man or woman has exhibited a desire to recreate, and he or she is achieving it splendidly; not realizing he or she is in the process of digging themselves into a rut. Far more energy is expended in the pursuit of audio-visual entertainment than in the reading of books, a sad commentary of our age. Tragically, the ability to witness firsthand is foregone in favor of media presentations. It is these packaged-opinions and their effect upon the masses that really shape the thought-processes of generations of individuals, rather than the events themselves; capitalizing upon the human drama to elicit pity instead of instilling valor. Intellectual minutia seems to be the order of the day – short, sweet, and to the point. If it cannot be explained in a New York minute, the attention-deficit syndrome sets in, and the public loses interest because it has been trained to react that way. The media has become the event, and the interpretation derived: the opinion of the week. And as long as each individual dutifully lines up for one's fifteen minutes of fame, the segment is replayed as if on a tape-loop. Ironically with the overdose of sensory gratification, a human being's sensory talents have not been sharpened. Instead a deterioration of awareness is revealed in daily life primarily because of the denial of the spirit-in-man. To succeed in this denial, the individual anesthetizes the mind with every kind of sense-numbing substance; the purpose being, not to feel the Truth nor realize the Lie. The result is form without substance and data without wisdom. The human mind confuses itself with endless riddles trying to solve a philosophical Rubik's cube, instead of recognizing the eternal wisdom of the statement: Be Here Now.

While artistic endeavor can serve the need to explain unknown quantities, and fine tune the aesthetic sensibilities of the human race, it can also be elevated beyond the understanding it inspires in the mind and heart of the beholder. In other words, artistic endeavor can be a source of idealism in humanity's time of need, but it has been denigrated by its misuse to stir in the public hero worship of media demigods. Though the talented deserve respect and recognition for their accomplishments, they should not be accorded the role of royalty; simply because one can act, sing, or dance. With the magnification of their virtues, comes the subsequent magnification of their vices. Hence the two-dimensional image of celluloid heroes does not compare favorably with the three-dimensional view. The art forms, objects of human creation, are revered and imitated as if they were the Creator. When life endeavors to imitate Art, and celluloid personalities usurp the place of real people, the quality of the life of the common man will decline because the observer would not consider it satisfying enough to lead a normal life. Inevitably he or she yearns for the stature of superstardom as well as riches beyond one's wildest dreams, and is disappointed with anything less.

In general, the conceptual theories of Western Civilization have centered upon the mastery of the Intellect: in taming the environment, solving societal problems, and probing the mind itself. As the dynamic mechanism of Intellect has modified the understandings of self, soul, and Spirit, the human being has evolved attaching new values to those understandings. In this manner, humanity has reshaped its existence with ideas derived from the interplay of intellectual forces. Consequently, the scientist can rearrange DNA strands and produce viruses in hermetically-sealed laboratories that could extinguish life on Earth, or with a slight modification of the same DNA strands produce a cure for cancer or Aids. Seemingly the intellect has been divorced from the spirit and soul. Only an antiseptic intellect cleansed of any knowledge of forethought or the workings of spirit engages in a steady diet of mental gymnastics and short-sighted solutions. Both religion and science have contributed to a further complication of the issues of concern by allowing politics and economics to pervert their expression. Fundamentalism blends myth and superstition with the *good news* of the prosperity gospel to herd the sheep. Science whips up a batch of modern miracles, and then makes people pay through the nose to use them. Just when humankind may have thought it had progressed beyond the point of adhering to a religious philosophy that relies upon smoke and mirrors, it takes a giant step backwards. Just when humankind may have thought it had progressed beyond the point of being at the mercy of Nature, it realizes it cannot live without it.

Whenever a philosopher rearranges his thought-patterns a new philosophy may result, but it is not necessarily a true or effective one. New meanings and expressions have forever been created to replace those that have out-lived their usefulness, but the source data has forever remained the same. The Intellect re-engineers and re-interprets the data in an obsessive attempt to find the Truth that it is destined not to realize because that realization is beyond the scope of intellect. It requires an understanding of how all things are connected at the Source which requires intuitive insight. The reason for Faith defies what is considered to be a logical explanation; logic that is, as it is defined by the scientific understanding that comes from a computer print out or a laboratory experiment. Generally the scientific method is devoid of any higher purpose or understanding of the spiritual meaning of life. The relationship of metaphysics to physical reality is normally not a consideration. While logic is used to correlate and extrapolate the facts uncovered to produce a conclusion, it is at odds with insight and intuition. If no conclusion is reached, it means there are not enough facts to produce one, not that there is necessarily none to be reached. It then becomes obvious that if the facts are continually misinterpreted, the correct conclusion can never be reached. However one goes round and round demanding the spiritual answers from mental processes ultimately not capable of comprehending them. But there is a logic one can use if one will suspend their prejudice, put trust in their intuition, and follow the heart. It is the understanding that one individual cannot know everything all the time, some things cannot be explained by laboratory tests, and that's the way it's supposed to be.

Nonetheless the contemporary efforts of the powers-that-be have been geared toward a mastery of life through scientific means without a full commitment to the mastery of self, or understanding of the workings of the soul. Therefore evidences of human moral and spiritual progress are lacking in the accompanying technological achievements. This is because human beings are not encouraged to balance the activity of the hemispheres of the brain, nor use them appropriately, nor consider what their use should actually be. Despite the fact the left hemisphere is the province of reason and primarily uses the scientific method in its processing, we often misuse it to ponder spiritual and religious issues. These rightfully belong in the province of intuition, a function of the right hemisphere which uses a processing method of divination through *feeling*. Presently the right hemisphere has become a source of psychic entertainment only, and its functioning denigrated to the point where individuals can no longer trust their intuition to provide credible and meaningful information. Its usage has been relegated to a tool for psychic entertainers, rather than a credible resource for mystics and philosophers. As a result, abstract ideals become impossible to grasp without the balancing of hemisphere interaction. By disregarding right hemisphere input, technocrats of the modern age have short-changed themselves in the development of their mental faculties. With only the weights and measurements of empirical science to guide them, knowledge becomes a one-dimensional commodity. The meaning is lost upon an obsessive/compulsive, results-oriented mentality. The total reliance upon left hemisphere activity has created a void in the human mind, a blind spot; that cannot be accessed by the engineer. Rather it needs to be sketched by the artist; for it assumes a capability to wonder what should be there.

The inability of many to keep abreast of change has left them floundering between the old ways and the new. They find themselves earnestly desiring the old values, but having new values repeatedly shoved in their collective faces. This inability to adapt to a runaway technology has bred a recklessness whereby material progress is not handled with care. Hence there will always be chemical dumps to be cleaned up, and radioactive waste to be disposed of. And it breeds a new brand of cultural lag developing where material achievement is out of balance with spiritual growth because there is an absence of warning labels. The Western intellectual establishment entertains a Victorian view of moral, social, and spiritual issues which is in basic conflict with basic technocratic aims. However, all cohabitate in a world which runs a rat race on weekdays where anything goes and runs religious routines on the weekends where there are rules and regulations to follow. It enables one to break every commandment during the week, and then confess at week's end. One who intends to live one's faith is no doubt sorely distressed. A point of equilibrium is desperately needed if only to save humanity and its home from the purveyors of waste and perversion.

While technocracy demands a pragmatic approach emphasizing the analytical abilities of the individual to the detriment of the clairvoyant faculties, the Victorian super-ego feverishly attempts to prop-up the impotent values of Church and State. However, the preoccupation with the intellect has made the Truth un-findable for those who over-analyze, and they are consigned to the realm of doubt. Unfortunately the processes of Intellect cannot examine themselves, or Science and Engineering would have solved all human dilemmas eons ago. Yet they are still haunting humanity like ghosts in the machine. Thus material achievement is out of balance with spiritual growth. Balance is drastically needed if only to save humanity and the environment from the purveyors of waste and perversion.

Regrettably technocracy is no respecter of individuals because it recognizes them only as functional parts of the economic engine. Institutionalized theories of specialization have corrupted the ideals of generations of these *working parts* without the least bit of consideration for the spirit that drives them. The attitudes of social Darwinism leave little room for a compassionate view of human plight, and it is only a faint hint of Conscience that keeps this flame of recognition flickering at all. With technocracy being results-oriented rather than process-conscious, the cheapest and fastest way to perform a task is usually the chosen way because the first priority is always to balance the books. Little consideration is given to whether or not the chosen way is the ethical or the ergonomic way to achieve the goal. The consequences for ecological disasters like Love Canal or Times Beach cannot be avoided in future if the profit-driven mentality continues to operate without moral compunction.

It is apparent in their behavior, the despoilers of the environment seek to obliterate the natural way, and replace it with an antiseptic version of their choosing. Considering what one can observe of the execution of the business plan of corporate America, their modus operandi should not be confused with the altruistic principles of any idealistic cause. A love of money drives the grinding wheels of economic progress and technological advancement, and it has fostered a system of values that are justified by the profit-gained. Thus the means are justified by the desired ends, and value of the effort expended is measured strictly by material gain. The very thing for which capitalistic societies condemned communistic societies, the capitalists are guilty of themselves. How perfectly ironic! When communism declared ideological and economic bankruptcy, the capitalists rejoiced. When knee-deep in the muck who will be left to applaud Capitalism's fall from grace when the last of Mother Earth's natural resources are spent?

Truth Never Changes: The Genesis of the Path

Despite the human tendency to cling to golden ages, mythical or actual, it is never correct to reach back into the past to re-establish one. It is meant for the son or daughter of man to look forward to a new expression that more aptly fits the human need of the moment. No progression of soul occurs when the attempt is made to relive a past experience or recapture a pure emotion. Golden ages did not occur in the past because attempts were made to rekindle a dying flame, but rather because a renaissance of thought and feeling had dawned among men. Forward-thinking visionaries should be leading the way in humanity's climb from darkness into the light. Instead the way is blocked by the ideological baggage of social reactionaries who cling to the notion that ascribing to a belief in king and country will inevitably pave the way to a glorious future. What glory is to be had in missions of world domination and unification by conquest? Rather it promises to doom humanity to further enslavement to a status quo where the Almighty Dollar remains King, while its subjects bow and curtsey before the gilded throne and those who sit upon it. And unbeknownst to the servants even the masters must wonder why they are so revered; for they realize their positions of power and influence are not earned by merit or good works. Most often they are the result of clever manipulation of markets that excel in the art of buying and selling ideology.

Literally humanity is trapped in a whirlpool of neo-conservative media banter that spins its way through the cesspool of human opinion flowing into the airwaves fomenting ideological strife. The underlying message is to keep the rabble focused upon the enemies in their midst instead of who is behind the curtain pulling the levers. The constant barrage drowns out the weeping and gnashing of teeth of under-privileged brothers and sisters who shiver in the darkness, bereft of hope, languishing in the absence of charity. No one profits from it except the usurers looking down on them from their penthouses in the air, clapping their hands in glee; for they have cashed in handsomely on the despair of the less fortunate. Sadly human progress has been linked to the proposition that it has little chance of happening without the rich getting richer, and the poor getting poorer. But in actuality no ascent of fortune in human endeavor has ever occurred in human history without a searchlight going forth from the inquiring mind. And no progress has ever taken hold if not validated by the selfless spring of altruism arising from the human soul. It falls to a new version of the Renaissance man to come up with the answer that resolves our current woes; for he alone can bridge the gap between soul and intellect that theologians and scientists apparently fail to realize.

At this juncture in history it is exceedingly important for the human being to be mindful instead of mindless. The consequences for mindlessness could be the total loss of self-determination; for as individuals suppress their creativity, the chances to use it will dwindle. Any opportunity lost to exercise one's inalienable rights in any venue will encourage those who have no respect for them to redouble their efforts to obliterate them. Any opinion-not-expressed is assumed to be agreement by those who do not wish to hear them or feel threatened by them. Thus the silent majority is granted ideological viability with its unwillingness to become involved in any purpose beyond the private sphere. What they fail to realize is that their silence provides motivation for the unscrupulous segment of humankind who wish the silent majority to remain forever silent. A docile populace plays into the hands of the despoilers of the spirit-in-man who are undeniably self-involved, and unabashedly focused on self-aggrandizement. In league with them, are the swindlers of spirit who preach daily the word of the Father of Lies, Belial, while professing it to be the word of Yahweh. In HIS name, they drive the final nail into the coffin of humanity, professing all the time, HIS will be done, but in reality, it is the will of Belial they enforce with every breath. Thereby diminishing the will of the All-in-All in their lives, and this legacy they wish to imprint upon humanity with evangelical fervor.

Any perceptive individual who is sensitive to the growth-pains of humanity can recognize an urgent need for self-rejuvenation. The evidence lies in times of frustration and despair when cynicism takes root in the mind. It requires effort to maintain a positive outlook on the fate of humankind when all the news seems to be to the contrary. When confronted with the atrophy of Western Civilization before one's very eyes, one cannot avoid feeling a bit overwhelmed, and willing to succumb to what a weakness of spirit wills. And the feeling is perpetuated when individuals desire only to physically survive from one-day-to-the-next because it is too hard to try to uplift themselves to the stature of altruistic purpose. However the answer lies not in vilifying the messenger for retelling a tale of woe, but to hold those accountable who continue to weave the tale. The attention they receive encourages bad behavior because the voyeuristic tendencies of the public has unleashed a monster which feeds upon publicity be it good or bad. If the unscrupulous purveyors of excess and perversion were not handsomely rewarded for their moral turpitude by receiving the attention they crave, their behavior would change immediately. If individuals were not encouraged to be nihilistic of spirit they would cease to be. If no profit could be derived from it, they would give consideration to changing their ways.

With a proposed renaissance of thought, a new logic can be fashioned to reason new solutions for the prevailing dilemmas of humankind, and a fresh method of divination can be introduced to understand the workings of Spirit. However one must be prepared to embrace them. Whether it be spiritual or scientific, when knowledge is held against the Light within, it casts the shadow of a refreshed version of the human being. A fresh analysis of the son and daughter of man must be accompanied by a compassionate treatment of the human spirit; for that is what modern technocracy lacks, and what accounts for the failures of religion and politics in alleviating world-trauma. Because of a persistent streak of vested self-interest, they cannot bridge the gap between ideal and real in a believable fashion. Unfortunately the result is ideal and real conceptions which are not foreseen to line up because ill-gotten knowledge is Belial's handiwork. And subsequently a misunderstanding is wrought of what is truly important in life -- honor, compassion, integrity and self-respect. These are forgotten commodities in a world order which places a premium upon fame and fortune, and is willing to stonewall the idea there might be something wrong with that assessment.

An awakening waits in the wings, awaiting the cue to be called out for the final act. A solution is in the offing that can tie together the loose ends. And the first step to be taken is the synthesis of reason and intuition to form a new partnership of Intellect in which neither overshadows or dominates the other, but rather work in harmony. In this fashion, the left and right hemispheres of the human brain will become synchronized, so that their activity may become balanced finally in the expression of Universal Law. Thus in the spirit of Plato's Academy, the union of these faculties will finally provide the answers the individual seeks, and ground them so that they can be acted upon reasonably in the resolution of real problems.

Michael L. Kilday

If the Innovator is turned loose in an environment where one is empowered to develop one's grand ideas, is free to act upon them and bring them to fruition, the sky's the limit. When financial cost, vested interests and ideology no longer hinder human progress, and the unencumbered ascent of the enlightened intellect is the prime directive, anything can be accomplished. And humanity will find its way out of the darkness with knowledge as Plato envisioned. Until then humanity will continue to be ruled by ideology where the way is predetermined ensuring the shades of darkness over one's eyes will be an inhibitor to knowledge until the eyes become accustomed to it. And if humanity is not able to shed its ideology when it conflicts with the evidence of common sense, it may be consigned to dwell in darkness unable to witness the Truth.

In the material world, the waste of human thought has diluted the pure Ideal, and the pure has been mixed with the impure until the Ideal has been mistaken for its manifestations. It is your responsibility and yours alone to find the Ideal to which to aspire. Then make every effort possible to make it real. In the end, it is only your effort that will be judged. All that matters in the end is that you be a sincere seeker; for it is your substance of character that determines if you have reached your goal. The results achieved are inversely proportional to the effort made to achieve them.

Without personal commitment, idealism has no cause or meaning. One has no cause for idealism without an Ideal in which to invest. Without an investment, the cause would seem to be lost. Thus it would seem to be the Ideal that is misplaced. Until humanity realizes its error and returns to living dynamically rather than vicariously, a positive change will not come over the world. When the realization dawns on humanity, it will be recognized that the greatest work of art is the perfect life accomplished in real-time. And this can only be accomplished when idealism once again reigns in the human mind; not sectarianism under the guise of idealism. True idealism comes from the understanding that all is One. A sincere seeker seeks the Light. He or she does not expect it will be simply cast upon him or her by virtue of one's beliefs. A sincere seeker realizes the Light shine from within not upon one.

Sectarian Salvation Comes with a Price Tag

The purpose of belief systems is to make broad thoroughfares of the path to the Light. The track has been divided into ideological lanes so that the sprint for the trophy will be awarded to a clear winner at the finish line. But the quest for illumination has never been nor will ever be a competition. There are no trophies to be had for the mantelpiece; nor is there produce to sell in the marketplace. What the wise man or woman knows is enough to be humble. Furthermore the wise ones realize they could not have come as far as they have without being connected to the One. The sincere seeker is lead to the truth by unseen forces that have a vested interest in making the Truth known. The reason for their intervention in the affairs of humanity is its disclosure at the opportune time. A timely revelation will strike a chord within each individual who feels it to motivate them to take inventory of their most treasured possessions. Those are the substance of one's character and the integrity to adhere to principle under the severest of influences. Humanity is squeezed in a vise grip of unrelenting economic, societal, and psychological pressures. Its only protection is wrapping itself in the Truth. At the very least, it will provide a reason why.

However looking backward through the haze, the human being has forgotten his or her place of origin (believing it is Earth), and the ancient directives of life-in-spirit are masked by human needs. Thus human actions primarily serve the purpose of the outer man -- the Earth man or woman who lives then dies. The divine man or woman is made a figment of imagination, or shrouded in so much mystery he or she is exceedingly hard to know. As a result, the cause of the outer manifestation is judged to be more tangible, and is preeminent because the cause of the inner manifestation is not understood anymore by most human beings. They envision a grand battle scheme of the eternal struggle of good vs. evil sold to them by the mind-controllers of religious institutions, or in rejecting that view, worship the demigods of science and technology who have whipped up a batch of modern miracles, brought humanity to the brink of self-destruction, and will leave it hanging until it puts one more dollar into the miracle machine. The spiritual answers one craves one imagines they can be found in an inanimate object like a book instead of lodged in the higher mind or eternal soul. In the guise of idealism the pious have applied their own unique take on salvation. Under any name sectarianism operates the same, and produces the same results.

There is a reason why the Jews are still waiting for their messiah to come. Their expectations for deliverance require a super-human capability. One might assume that is the reason they continue to wait, but the issue is more complex than that. In their case, a messiah will vanquish their enemies, delivering the faithful from evil. This hasn't happened yet, and it's doubtful it ever will. Their situation on Earth deteriorates because they make as many enemies as friends. That's why the Jews are still waiting. Conceivably they could wait forever. What they ask for they could conceivably do for themselves. But their methods seem to breed more evil instead of less. Violence simply begets violence with no end in sight. Where there is enmity no one wins in the end.

For the Christians, their messiah already came. His First Coming was a dubious success. He spoke the truth, so his enemies tortured and killed him. Even though his followers pretend his death is by design, it only serves to ease a guilty conscience. A rational conclusion is that it is the inevitable cover-up for mishandling his untimely demise. The faithful await his return in the form of a Second Coming. Perhaps it is also symbolic of the ancient Egyptian's conception of the Great Return. More likely it has already occurred in the Resurrection. Humanity's desire for it is evidenced in a latent disenchantment in one's own performance to envision a triumphant return. To complicate matters, humanity has failed to do what the messiah Jesus expressly told them to do to be saved. That was to love one another. Until that commandment is fulfilled, *spiritual victory* is not achievable because the pre-requisite has not been met. Again what they wait for they could conceivably do for themselves. They choose not to for it is a hard thing to make peace with one's enemy. It is easier to look to skies for the coming of the heavenly host to do battle with one's demons, than it is to forgive the transgressions of the ones who are possessed by demons. The faithful yearn for them to be cast out; for they cannot be converted to righteousness.

For the Muslims, the Scripture they adopted from Judaism should convince them not to take the hard line. Their faith builds another floor upon the foundation of an existing edifice, but they neglect to see it from that vantage point. Instead they imagine it is an entirely new structure that supersedes all others in its magnificence. They neglect to see it is constructed of the same materials using universal design principles. Estranged sons of Abraham contend for the same turf as a legacy of birthright. While the peacemakers posture, the zealots claim what they believe is rightfully theirs without consideration of compromise. Their faith cannot be compromised and still be considered faith. Their combativeness will only ensure an exchange of death for life. Their error manifests in the belief that a *spiritual victory* can be won by combat. With any crusade, no one wins in the end.

What exactly does one expect a messiah will do for them that they cannot do for themselves? Neither Jews nor Christians nor Muslims could probably handle the shock when the epiphany dawns that the messiah is already here and 'he' is in each one of us. 'He' is not a person but a seed of Universal force and intelligence, namely the Christ Consciousness. It has always been with us. It has never left here so it cannot return here. Each individual carries the *seed*. The true believer waits for the messiah to reveal himself so it is very unlikely he or she will actually recognize 'him' when 'he' does. He hides in plain sight as the faithful look past him, and concoct their own glorious vision of him as the conquistador. Sadly that is a desire for justice that cannot ever be fulfilled in the manner they desire unless one is pure of heart. An old adage *'love conquers all'* suggests a glorious victory of spirit, but love only needs to overwhelm one's heart to succeed in its objective. So the semantics implied are self-defeating if one is geared for victory over the powerful enemies of love when one should only be poised for surrendering to it.

No more messiahs must be expected for the purpose of deliverance because that expectation keeps humanity from making an earnest effort to resolve any of its problems. Humanity is ultimately paralyzed by reliance upon a super consciousness that purportedly can fix anything with a wave of a hand. The resolutions of human problems take time, effort, and a commitment on the part of individuals to do the difficult work that is necessary to affect a resolution in real time. It is really a handicap for individual growth to think that responsibility for the task at hand can be passed to a God, through a church, temple, or mosque. It rests always with the individual, and no delusion to the contrary can ultimately succeed. It is one of the individual responsibilities no one can take from you. Ironically, it is the one duty that a great many God-fearing individuals are seemingly anxious to give away to what is perceived to be a higher authority. The belief must be it rests with the one who is most qualified to perform it, but the truth is it is incumbent upon each individual to rise to the occasion. Your ascension to the status of a son or daughter of God begins when you accept responsibility instead of trying to dump it on your chosen Master. Until such time, you remain a son or daughter of man who aspires to be a son or daughter of God, a journeyman who yearns to be the master of the craft.

Hence the destiny of the son or daughter of man really lies with no ideology; rather instead it abides with the prime directive from the God within each individual. Regardless of what the inventors of religious faiths have said throughout the ages, you are not chosen to serve God. You choose to embark upon that path of your own volition. It is your birthright. If you choose to select it from all of the options that are available to you, you can rest assured the effort will not be wasted. However if you cannot find God within yourself, you certainly will not recognize HIM outside yourself. Conversely if you fail to look for HIM, you cannot expect to lead the life of a fully-functioning, spiritually-minded individual. To achieve that objective one must realize the import of the teachings of Socrates embodied in the phrase: *'To thine own self be true'*. No one individual can receive a higher accolade than to be acknowledged as one who will say what they mean, and do what they say. No one can expect any more than that from a life well-lived. Any higher reward is a figment of theological imagination, akin to the search for the fabled city of El Dorado. Truly the radiance of gold the sincere seeker craves is the treasured possession of a pure soul, shining through a crystal clear image of self in perfect alignment with the motivating spirit within.

Pre-conceived notions of theological pomp and circumstance are an opiate for the masses to divert attention away from seeking the simple truth. Like space savers their function is to occupy one's time, subvert one's effort, and lead nowhere constructive. Ultimately they will not satisfy; for you are erecting castles made of sand that cannot withstand the elements of Nature indefinitely. Change is the universal constant to which all living things are subjected. Evolution is an aspect of the universal movement of spirit and matter through the processes of Universal Law. It is enacted by the force and intelligence of Universal Law which is the only Truth which is sustainable, measurable, and relevant to all living things, all

Truth Never Changes: The Genesis of the Path

of the time. Ultimately any attempts made to circumvent Universal Law are doomed to failure because Truth never changes. What does change are human perceptions of Truth embodied in the tribal traditions of religious faith until the individual mind settles upon an appropriate representation for him or herself.

The nature of the human condition is aptly expressed in a statement made by Julius Caesar in Shakespeare's play of the same name. The quote comes from Act I, Scene II, in which Julius Caesar muses, *"The fault lies not in the stars, dear Brutus, but in ourselves"*. No statement made by anyone at any time provides a more perceptive analysis about the nature of the human condition. At the same time we are the problem as well as the solution. Certainly we could make matters worse or we could make them better. But we tend to look everywhere possible but in ourselves for the solutions to the problems we face. And to complicate matters that is the only place where the solution resides.

Apparently our hope is the problem lies not in us. We would prefer to think there are external forces at work which influence us to do all of those things which cause the problems we face. We live under the misconception that it is a demon that can be exorcized from us by the heroic efforts of our ideological guardians, and kept at bay by magical formulas and rituals. Despite the fact the exorcists have tried for countless generations to cast the demon out, the demon lives on. Anyone who believes this demon will just give up and release its hold on you is drinking the proverbial Kool-Aid. It will never simply go away because it feeds upon your selfish appetites, your ego trips, and your grand designs on fame and fortune. Until those fuel sources are eradicated, it will remain. It cannot be otherwise because the demon doesn't sit on your shoulder tempting you; it is in your head driving you.

The demon to dread is the attitude that causes one to worship celebrity and bemoan their own obscurity. It causes one to embrace physical beauty and disparage ugliness, and to judge others on personality instead of character. It causes one to embrace privilege, power, position, and patronage while discarding equality, fraternity, and justice as the governing principles of social interaction. This causes one not to recognize that merit is the true measure of one's worth. Under the demon's spell one cherishes their outer manifestations while disregarding the essence of their inner selves. And worst of all, the demon mandates that this behavior never be corrected. That demon feeds upon one's wants and desires, and its voracious appetite makes one deaf to the instructions from the higher mind. In substance those instructions would tell one to put all of that aside. Yet that seems to be not persuasive enough to cause a change in behavior. When the seminal moment arrives, will it be realized?

In fact this malady even encroaches upon the doctrine of the faithful; in that the prosperity gospel currently being spread to the masses encourages them to pray for material things. This is the *good news* they preach that serves to keep one in bondage to materialism. If one harbored a doubt about how Jesus would have responded to the prosperity gospel, remember what he did to the moneychangers in the temple. He did not equivocate on the subject. His message was clear and unequivocal and it hastened his end. Apparently the faithful have convenient memory loss when it comes to comprehending his true message; that of sharing one's abundance. His way demands giving and taking be balanced for the good of all. When the bounty of the Earth is not shared equally amongst all of its inhabitants, he considers it an abomination. Humanity languishes in a poverty of the soul because we do not share as he instructs us to do. The prosperity gospel Jesus taught does not lend itself to the acquisition of material things which are rightfully God's property. His message pertains to each individual's share of a storehouse of Love. That is to say: it belongs to all in equal measure. The bounty one reaps by sharing it is returned a thousand fold because it accumulates as it radiates outward.

If one is willing to share his or her love with one's neighbor, material prosperity is shared as a matter of course. When abundance is not shared, it causes disharmony, inequity, and strife. When one is fomenting turmoil, it is difficult to spread calm. Until that is rectified it presents an obstacle for the advent of peace and harmony foreseen in the coming age. Because it is apparent humanity is not hearing the message, it sinks further into its ideological quicksand. Because of a belief that *'those not with us are against us'*, the battle lines are being drawn. As Lee Brown suggested more than two decades ago prophecy truly is an either/or proposition. The critical component is choice.[liii] In this context, it is a choice between self-sacrifice and self-aggrandizement.

It's not that wanting things is inherently wrong. The issue lies in how much is enough to satisfy you, and how those things are used. When they are used to ingratiate the rich at the expense of the poor, sharing becomes an afterthought; like offering sustenance to the poor when the rich have had their fill. When one hears the chant of the latest prosperity gospel coming from the hallowed halls of worship, one realizes the moneychangers have invaded and held the temple. Their *good news* is now made to serve Caesar. The law of attraction that is currently being preached to the masses that may not get their daily bread from the church of their choice is the prosperity gospel under a different name. It is not that getting what one desires is inherently wrong, or what is being preached is technically incorrect, but it is being offered without qualification. No one is being cautioned first to examine the legitimacy of his or her desires. People are being told to vent their desires indiscriminately as if desiring whatever one wants is the appropriate thing to do in all cases. One whose heart is not pure should not be given carte blanche to order from the menu. Sometimes the answer should be NO. The selfish do not intend to leave anything for anyone else. While one may be hard-pressed to think of a way to prevent it, good or bad are strictly perceived alternatives.

There is a good reason why The Buddha taught self-denial. It wasn't an arbitrary decision he made. He understood the danger in giving in to one's heart's desire irrespective of what was being desired. The free enterprise system now runs rampant because the greedy and the selfish shift the gears and operate the knobs on the financial engine of Society. That was not what John Locke or Adam Smith intended either[liv]. They merely wanted the common man to get his fair share of the earthly goods because the powers-that-be had always hoarded all of it for themselves. Throughout history, the selfish have perverted every noble intention, wittingly or unwittingly. A corporate aristocracy lording it over humanity is not a substantial improvement over nobility doing the same. In practical terms, it amounts to the same thing -- the lord and master reaping the benefit of your labor instead of you. When one sees clearly through the haze of desire, there is no denying it.

Addiction to excess is nothing more than object lessons for the faint of heart. One could muse: was it not that this was so, but such is the human condition. The accumulation of things is not meant to be the driving force of anyone's life, but yet it is for the great mass of humanity. The fault lies in how they are used to define oneself. That puts artificial parameters upon one's feelings of entitlement by denying their expression because they do not possess the things they crave. This is what needs to change, and the sooner, the better; for what will you do when you no longer have them? Is your identity at risk? It is if you define yourself by your things, and you no longer have them. If you are defined by your things, you also run the risk of never being satisfied. Worse still you are saying the love in your heart is not enough to sustain you.

The following is a premier example of cognitive dissonance, perhaps one of the most perplexing one could encounter.[lv] The proposition of this incongruity unfolds as follows: our economic systems are faltering because the gap between the haves and have-nots widens into an unbridgeable gulf. With each fiscal year, the rich get richer and the poor get poorer. And no serious attempt is being made to rectify it; especially since every attempt suggested that even infers redistributing the wealth, is met with cries against *socialism*. And it is not captains of industry and the usurers who raise the objection. It comes from the people they exploit. How the exploited have become so thoroughly trained to rally to the aid of their oppressors truly boggles the mind. Whereas the general public should be literally up-in-arms over that disparity of income, strangely they are not. It makes one wonder if there is a bizarre variation of the Stockholm syndrome in effect here; whereby those held hostage protect the interests of the hostage takers, even if it means one would never be free of their chains. Over time Capitalism has evolved into the financial equivalent of Darwin's law of natural selection. Does anyone truly believe Capitalism when it is a synonym for imperialism is a fair and equitable system of commerce? Or are they so thoroughly brainwashed they can't tell anymore what is fair and balanced in accordance with spiritual law? Furthermore what maladjusted belief system would ever cause one to forsake spiritual law in deference to the *law of the concrete jungle*? To ignore the signs of the unbridled Ego, unleashed in the marketplace, and do nothing to curtail it, is a silent endorsement of the behavior.

Sectarianism demands a division of purpose for a cause that could only be achieved through unity. Worship is idolatry. It is of no profit to a seeker of Truth. No one else is responsible for your illumination but you. Thus one who offers to serve as intermediary between you and your God warrants scrutiny; for intermediaries are not required. If you've spent your life on your knees you've primed yourself to be a sacrifice to the god of someone else's choosing. One may toil in their fields tending to the fruit of their labor. But it will bear the sourest of fruits if one plies their skill in another's orchard. Then your workman's wages signify that you are a servant to a master other than yourself. When you owe tribute to no one, only then are you free to be yourself. And only then are you empowered to be yourself.

Michael L. Kilday

The Declaration of the Son of Man

HE WHO HAS NO NAME creates, destroys, and preserves ITS Creation complying with the precepts of the Law of One. From a universal perspective, creation and destruction are but singular events joined by the stabilizing influence of a preserving Nature. The harmonious continuity of the Creative Cycle of Life denotes a purpose both singular and plural that engineers a manifestation through the application of Universal Law. Toward this end, the evolutionary processes of body and soul were mandated to fulfill the need for Growth, and laboratories like Earth were created where that growth could occur. The world was created to be a proving ground for virtue where each individual tests his or her mettle in the crucible of material existence.

Virtue is described by the relative purity of one's mind. It determines the performance of the instruction achieved through the mental and emotional discipline over the inebriate of selfishness. Inevitably human actions and reactions will exalt or pervert the instructions transcribed within. But it is made to be an arduous process when one fails to abide by the precepts of Universal Law. Respect for the individual should replace a reliance on Piety because a respect for Virtue will naturally evolve from it. The attainment of a virtuous state of being is the one Ideal that needs to be maintained in the Society of Man. Its enactment is the completion of the self-divine. The objective is to grow beyond any self-imposed limitations, with the goal being ultimately, a perfection of self. However before that can be accomplished, each individual must know his or her microcosmic universe completely, and express that knowledge with each breath. As one begins to understand how to separate Truth from fantasy, derive from it a Faith that comprehends the difference, one can deliver a compassionate Justice to all who seek it. Only when one learns the art of selflessness, can the promise of peace, justice, and the brotherhood of Man be realized. In this way only can knowledge be truly enacted; for the knowledge issued forth by the raving of the ego is truly a seed sown among thorns.

When the divine self is brought forth as the Master Jesus suggested, actions will be tempered with Compassion, thoughts will be founded upon Truth, and words will be bolstered by Faith. Once expressed, what was lacking in self will be replaced by the desire to achieve a fuller expression, and the willful persistence to accomplish it. When the divine self is neglected, it is forgotten. Therefore one must remember his or her divinity because this realization is the only avenue to freedom. Without it, the karmic wheel spins eternal, generating countless lifetimes of toil and travail. Spiritual evolution requires an effort from within to continuously improve, and carries with it an obligation of providing aid and comfort to one's fellow man. To abolish selfishness one must change the motive for material pursuits, by striving to be just, individual-to-individual. If one is ever to gain, one must not fear to lose. However if one fails to put aside his or her egomania, one can never be satisfied with oneself, with what is offered, or with what is gained. The perverse passion of interpersonal relationships can be turned to joy when the effort is made to give instead of take away.

Many try to force a natural evolutionary process, that of becoming, because their impatience forces unnatural conclusions. Because they have not grasped the truth about Universal Law, many are talking when they should be listening, and acting compulsively to fulfill their obsessions. Silence, not debate, is the threshold to wisdom. Within one's own being are all of the answers worth knowing, but few realize it. They cannot wait for it to unfold naturally. They must unfold it by force. Most are constantly casting into the depths of uncharted waters attempting to find what lies close to the surface. They are unable to see beyond the scum that clouds the surface, and thus the pure waters beneath remain untapped.

To assemble the mosaic of humanity into a coherent whole is the goal of the All-in-All. It has charged each individual soul with a need to accomplish this feat. As each feels the urge to unite, he or she remembers the directive that has been encoded. Until that need can be brought forth into consciousness, no individual realizes why he or she has been placed here. Until realized the need resides in the recesses of the individual subconscious awaiting the moment of recognition like a seed waits for the warmth of the sun before it can grow. When it is touched by the Light and nourished by the water of life, the process of growth begins. No growth can occur in the vacuum of time and space. It requires the diversity of human circumstance and the fertile soil of material existence to take root. Truly human beings must find it within themselves to do the right thing at the right time for the right reason. And depend upon nothing other than one's native intuition and Conscience to advise one to do so. The transition from son or daughter of man to son or daughter of God is an open invitation to all individuals to experience without the coercion of institutionalization, but each chooses whether to be enslaved or free.

Faith should not be subjected to the weights and measures of four-dimensional space, but rather tested in the pure waters of the soul. Strength of faith is determined by the seriousness of conviction to the Truth. Balance is a prime component of the Law because what is given is received in equal measure. However, when thoughts are enriched with virtue, exponential gains can be realized. The reiteration of virtuous thoughts produces virtuous deeds which as they enumerate constitute a virtuous life. The continuance of virtuous living is the express lane to a paradise on Earth. And when humanity joins in the spirit of Harmony and free will, all societal crises, divisive economic issues, racial injustices, and religious conflicts will be realized to be inconsequential because spiritual equality overrides all human conditions.

This is the one lesson which the Declaration of Independence attempts to relay which humanity in its blind allegiance to political one-upmanship fails to recognize. In the face of those who seek to divide humanity, unity can be forged in spite of the efforts, they who foster all expression of political and societal enmity for their own gain, expend to divide and conquer. As long as humanity continues down the path of conflict and disharmony, they revel in a job well done to preserve their cherished fiefdoms. Whether or not the purveyors of dissension and discord fully realize it, they have an equal share in the failure to unite humanity in a common cause under the auspices of Universal Law. Odds are that those who do not submit to Universal Law do not understand it. They may labor under the misconception that striving for balance and harmony is not a divine mandate. While equality, fraternity, and justice are man-made jurisdictions, they do spring from Universal Law to promote Harmony in human relations.

Love alone is not enough to reach the heights of spiritual expression. Unless that Love is directed by the union of Force and Intelligence, it becomes the aimless romanticism of the simple-minded. The eloquent expression of the Triune God (Force, Intelligence, and Love), cannot be expressed by the simpleton who must be told what to believe. It can only be expressed by one who has mastered his or her Gnosis (knowledge) of self and God, realizing it is ONE. Truly it is the wise man or woman who does not worship at the temple of another, but instead purifies the temple of his or her self to be a fitting receptacle for the God within. Since God is the acknowledged source of the spiritual DNA all living beings carry, one can rightly say that God is the Father. But the equation of spiritual life cannot yield a product without a unification of the masculine and feminine principles within the matrix materialized by spiritual force. It is provoked by the catalyst of Love. The true Trinity of masculine principle, feminine principle and transcendent Spirit is expressed in the embodiment of body, mind, and soul united as ONE. Hence the relationship engenders spirit-in-flesh, and the transition from son or daughter of man to son or daughter of God is the realization. There is but One Thing from which all manifestation springs.

Humanity's greatest failing is the assumption that Truth can be mandated by faith, justice can be legislated by government decree, and compassion can be enforced by human institutions. The ultimate success of human endeavors operates from the inside out, rather than from the outside in, and from the bottom up rather than the top down. When one comes to the realization that the onus is upon each individual to be the manager of one's own life, then one's thinking is aligned with the natural course of human events. Of one's own volition, an individual must feel the urgency to perform to the pinnacle of one's ability for there to be everlasting success in any endeavor. The sooner one adapts one's thinking to preserving Universal Law, relinquishes the futile attempts to make it, and realizes the individual's role is only to interpret it, the more fortuitous his or her journey promises to be. To make the world a better place in which to live, each individual must be engaged in the spirit of free will, and reconcile one human heart at a time, starting with oneself. There is no pot of gold at the end of the rainbow, lest one put it there. It essentially means one reaps what one sows. Be satisfied with the fruit of one's labor. It is all one is owed.

In the final analysis, it will be discovered that the divine consciousness you have been invoking for aid and comfort all of your life is actually the divine part of you. You have simply failed to recognize this because your attention is focused upon the grandest of ideas, not the simplest. The simple truth can be the most elusive truth of all. It is easy to overlook the minute details when one is contemplating the intricacies of a grand design. When one has been instructed to dream the impossible dream, anything less than that seems mundane, unthinkable. Your task is to become the best you it is possible for you to be, nothing more. It is far better to live each day for itself than to abide by an expectation of things to come that may never come to pass. Revelation is too much to expect when one cannot follow the simplest of instructions; that is for individuals to love one another unconditionally, without reservation. In actuality, no further revelation is necessary; for the door to eternity will be opened wide when one accedes to the Master's request. Otherwise it will be shut tight; for love lubricates the hinges, while hate causes them to rust. The value of any revelation achieved in the absence of the Master's prime directive is thereby diminished. If one cannot accept his message of selfless service and compassion for one's fellow man on its own merits, then one hasn't heard the message. If one does not do everything in one's power to incorporate it into every waking minute of one's life, then all further acts are futile. How much more simple can it be? If one chooses to be selfish instead of selfless, it merely proves one doesn't understand the message.

 Herein lay the ambivalent meaning of the simple truth: it is what it is, but it is what you make of it. The way it is, is the way it is supposed to be. One cannot prove otherwise, and should not devote any energy to do so. In the end you are measured by how much you love, as well as by how much you are loved. There is little else one can do to secure a place in paradise, but earn one's way by placing virtue before all other achievements. One can be assured no one is keeping any scorecard that is binding, except your internal auditor that records every move you as a matter of record. Your code of conduct is self-regulatory. Not abiding by the dictates of Conscience is your own cross to bear. Certainly no one can carry it for you, nor would that meet your need. It is the epitome of blind ignorance to believe that you will ever stop learning and growing. No one can open up a book, and point the truth out to you. The living truth you discover yourself by living the simple truth. Only you know when you have found it, and only you can actuate it for yourself. Truly it is the most personal of revelations.

Even a realized being must continue to evolve on a designated pathway. Because a complete understanding of the Creative Cycle of Life is probably beyond the scope of human comprehension, the individual may imagine that Life has an end, but these speculations are a result of limited insight. While may be correct to say that human existence has a beginning and an end, the life of the soul is neither on a time clock, nor is it limited to a space of four dimensions. Having no discernable beginning or end, it exists extemporaneously. It needs no reason nor relies upon faith, and understanding its agenda is beyond the scope of human capability. It exists even without an acknowledgement of its existence. Thus the fog of human miscomprehension clears when one makes the effort to resolve the rumor and innuendo that inevitably accompanies the quest for knowledge. One should not merely assume one's association with the conceited truth-tellers of ideology guarantees enlightenment. More likely the opposite is true; for their ulterior motives are too often masked by feigned sincerity. No foregone conclusions substitute for the Truth because it is an acquired taste. It pre-exists the human need to know it, and would exist even if no human being existed to believe in it. Understanding the objectivity of Universal Law can be circumvented by one's portal view. Therefore to realize it one must see it from God's perspective rather than one's own. After one has purged all vestiges of self-interest from one's agenda, one's view is refocused. It is the view from the God Within.

Embrace your experience whatever it is; you worked hard to earn it. But realize you owe allegiance to yourself only. Your experience helps make you who you are and your only choice in the matter is to embrace it or deny it. It won't change who you are, but it will set the stage for how it will be manifested. Your life is guaranteed to be a mixed bag of pleasure and pain, but it is no more one than the other. It only seems so as desired by those who strive for an advantage. If you fear your pain it will destroy you. Thus you must embrace it to rob it of the chance to hold dominion over you. When you can, you are poised to carve out a destiny. Only then can you say you truly lived. Until then you merely occupied space.

The principles of secular humanism stand alone as the absolute testament to the merit of the Golden Rule. Without the trappings of human ideology, the fatherhood of God and the brotherhood of Man are given expression. Their driving force is to live in accordance with

Truth Never Changes: The Genesis of the Path

Universal Law. Love does not insist upon its own way. It is only personal bias that demands compliance. Only the obsessive compulsive personality demands that everyone follows his or her rules. The All-in-All does not demand it. IT doesn't have to because Universal Law makes it unfold naturally. It is inherent in the system; a natural outcome if one has the foresight and willingness to make the correct choices. It is one's duty to recognize this, and act accordingly.

In accordance with the Law, your sole responsibility is to *connect* to the One within you. Within you, the messiah awaits. You venture inward to latch onto it instead of reaching outward to gather it in. In essence the proposition is to strive to be more spiritual and less materialistic. A connection to the higher mind is enabled by a re-establishment of the chain of command. Know that an untapped resource is no resource at all. If you follow the dictates of your higher mind, you cannot take a wrong turn. That is the answer you seek. There is no other to impart that is of value. Thus we revisit the topic of purpose to declare you must find it within yourself. No one else can give it to you; nor would you want anyone to. It is your obligation to know what it is and go with it. It is incumbent upon you to choose wisely. Remember no principle is worth upholding if in order to uphold it you have to hurt the one you love.

Knowing is not an end in itself. Doing is its end. To seek is not enough, but it is a valid beginning. Finding initiates a second beginning, and when it is no longer enough to know, it becomes time to effectuate. Let compassion reign, lest one's endeavors be perverted by self-interest. Let love radiate through one's motivations, lest one's character be stained with self-interest. Where the love-light leads, others are certain to follow.

Michael L. Kilday

Truth Never Changes: The Genesis of the Path

The Road Ahead

In the era in which we live, the heralded Doomsday Clock is on the verge of striking 12. As the needle of the tolerance gauge inches perilously close to the red line, the unspoken question in everyone's mind seems to be: does it have to be this way? We can do little else but try to keep it from crossing the line; much less understand what is causing the needle to spike in the danger zone. Since quite literally staying the course would invite disaster of a preternatural kind into our midst, a course correction is urgently needed. What are the alternatives available to us? As the fabric of life unravels like a ball of twine bouncing down a winding staircase, one must wonder if it was meant to be, or it was made to happen this way. In reality both statements are true. How one decides to view it, however, is an individual perspective which isn't guaranteed to influence the outcome. The scope of human influence extends just so far; then it dissipates into the mist of Time.

To say that *the end is near* is too cryptic a phrase to make it a compelling statement. The phrase has been overused to the point it's become cliché. Since the 1st century of the Common Era when the Book of Revelation was written, a day of reckoning has been anticipated. Whether the reason is a subliminal death wish or feelings of guilt over complicity in the death of the *lamb of God*, the prophet's visions speak to an earnest desire for justice. Ironically it is the thing that is hardest to get because each individual's perception of what justice is differs. What may be justice to some is a miscarriage of justice to others because inevitably we each see the same transgression from different angles. Although one man's pleasure is another's pain, empathy alone cannot account for the difference. Whereas one can be certain of their uniqueness, it is difficult to imagine to what extent lives intersect and why. Since the only certainty in life is change, it becomes the focal point of a common experience; one that all are compelled to share.

At the present moment, the probability is that we stand upon the threshold of monumental change if we can trust what our prophets and seers tell us. And we would know what to do if we could correctly interpret the signs. We find ourselves at the bend in the road when it is necessary to come to terms with the Earth changes that will manifest soon after the Aquarian Age begins on 12/21/2012. The fact that there will be changes in the Earth is a foregone conclusion. It has been ordained by unseen forces beyond the scope of any single human being's influence. That cannot be changed because it is part of the Earth's cyclical life cycle. When the Earth moves, we can do little else but move with it. Common sense would dictate a scramble for shelter. Whatever changes are in store for human beings are a different matter because choice is involved. Therefore the impact of change upon human beings is a variable in the equation. The severity of the impact is predicated upon the human response to its effects. Human beings can buffer themselves against the effects of change, but they don't have the power or influence to stop change from occurring.

The coming changes are spiritual effects which have a physical component primarily because the coin is one.[lvi] The physical changes will be the result of how humanity responds to the spiritual effects, and vice versa. As the effects accumulate, it spells the destiny of the human race. It is one of those things one just accepts or goes crazy denying it is real. Denial is a curtain one draws in the mind when it is too painful to realize the truth. Be advised Earth changes are for real from the viewpoint of climate change, economic deprivation, and global ecological imbalance. A spiritual crisis of confidence is just as real however. It is the effect of the Canopy of Light that has descended upon the entire planet. It has been stimulating the human reaction to change for decades now. Primarily the impact has been upon the human psyche, and has resulted in shifting belief systems. The effects of global change it has spawned are pervasive and comprehensive. Forces are set in motion that defies explanation. Yet we see and feel the effects. Nature has its own systemic influence which has a purpose of its own. While it is folly to deny reality, it is worse to cling to a superstitious belief that change is entirely predetermined. Free will is the rule, not the exception to the rule. That is why forecasts are sometimes wrong. It is a moving target.

Change is a paradox. While it is true that change is pre-destined to a degree by the macrocosmic instruction path of Universal Law, on the microcosmic instruction path of free will, it is determined by cause and effect. Even though this seems to be a contradiction in terms, it is nonetheless true. Those who fail to recognize this have an ulterior motive for doing so. That stems from the belief they have more control over the situation than they actually do. Perhaps that is because they do not comprehend the nature of Change. Change on a cosmic scale cannot be wished away. Moreover no amount of prayer will make any difference. No supplication will forestall the inevitable. Placing burnt offerings on the altars of demigods are merely confirmation that superstition can displace reason in the human mind.

Undeniably the deprivations of which Spirit admonished three decades ago[lvii] are happening now before our very eyes. They are of every conceivable variety and there is no mistaking their meaning. We have less and even less to do it with, but still no one seems inclined to alter their ways and means. Permeating the fabric of daily life, the greed, selfishness, and gluttony practiced by the greater portion of humanity knows no bounds. While so many go to bed with hunger pains, the gluttons feast upon what they have hoarded for themselves. The gluttons feel no remorse, only a hunger to quench their appetites. The desperation in the eyes of the disadvantaged and disenfranchised are the signal flares of imminent upheaval. As the need becomes overpowering, the closer humanity approaches the brink of dissolution. The recognition of deprivation settles into the heart, soul and mind of humanity. If want and misery of one's fellow man does not tug at the heart, something is certainly lacking in one's perspective.

As a consequence Nature is withholding its abundance so it will no longer be delivered to the gluttons. As it is slowly withdrawn, a scarcity sets in; the scope of which widens as it radiates outward like a ripple on still water. An economic downturn is the least of humanity's worries. Economists call it a recession, but it really is a tightening of the screws on human needs and desires. Truly it is the beginning of an anticipated global tribulation; one that has been rightfully earned. The bounty extracted from the Earth will be less than it was before, and it will offer less of a return in each season. Naturally those who do not wish to acknowledge it will deny it is happening. They will say it is the natural course of events, and *"it too shall pass"*. But these think in terms that profit their wallets and pocketbooks rather than their souls. Their eyes are clouded by the haze of desire for material possessions. Anyone who turns a blind eye to misery and despair has a reason why they do so. Whether it is because of ignorance or an attempt to profit upon another's misfortune it amounts to the same thing. It is a symptom of imbalance and disorder due to a lack of compassion. Nature will seek its state of equilibrium. It can do nothing else but follow its laws of operation. The servants as well as the masters reap the same harvest because they all work the same fields. Destinies are interwoven, causing consequences to be shared. The causes and effects of global change are equally distributed. One can choose to be aware or be taken by surprise. But one cannot refuse to participate in the coming harvest of souls.

Humanity's optimal course of action is to stop obsessing over change, and start preparing for the consequences. The time for recrimination and regret is long past. The seeds have been sown by our destructive ecological and economic practices as well as a spiritual deprivation. The worship of false idols like fame, fortune, and material possessions permeate Western Civilization. We reek of the stench of ill-gotten gains, and the Society at large praises those who benefit from them; deeming it to be entrepreneurship. We even fill our churches with idols, and pray on our knees before them, as if they can save us the pain and misfortune of the bad choices we have made. And not once does the epiphany dawn it is because of our ill-gotten gains we could pay the ultimate price. This verdict is not a judgment from the All-in-All. It is a penance we earned by not obeying its Law in the true spirit of the Law.

Regarding Earth changes, the best one can do for oneself is to be open-minded and adaptable. It is not wrong to hope for the best that could happen, but at the same time one should be prepared for the worst. That is not a defeatist attitude. That's good common sense. Open-ended optimism is often a belief in fantasy. One needs to temper their optimism with a pragmatic approach if they expect to succeed in their endeavors. A pragmatist will never be taken unaware. A pragmatist who has a solid optimistic base will try to make the best out of any situation. No matter what it is, he or she will bring the full force of their intelligence to bear in solving the problem at hand. When it comes to surviving Earth changes, that's what is required from each of us. Have no expectation, and deal with the reality of the situation as it presents itself. No sane person would ever suggest you ignore the warning signs or close your eyes to the Truth. But the sage person would suggest the wise course of action is to deal with actualities, rather than prognostications. Look at the evidence and analyze the root causes of problems. Don't get bogged down in the effects. Resolve the causes of the problems rather than wasting precious time obsessing over their symptoms. An optimistic approach will guarantee you can deal with it, while a pessimistic approach will ensure you cannot. Unless they have the ability to see around the bend in the road, they cannot see the ruts in the road, or any obstacles in their path. They could imagine they are there, but won't know it for a certainty until they bump into them. Now the seeds we have sown are bearing the sourest of fruits and one cannot turn back the clock.

Closing one's mind so one doesn't hear what they don't want to hear is never an advisable course of action. It is far better to face one's fears than to allow them to fester inside. If they dominate the discourse, nothing of substance ever gets accomplished. Quite the opposite occurs. One is forever handicapped by one's fears. It is preferable to illuminate the darkest corners of one's mind rather than keeping the curtain drawn. Just maybe one may discover their fears are unfounded, and the act of casting those fears into the light of day has the net effect of nullifying them. It may turn out to be one's saving grace because one may find hope where there was none; just because one looked for it. Eventually the sincere seeker manages to turn over enough stones to reveal what had been hidden from view. One's prospects for illumination are inversely proportional to the time and effort it takes to make one's way down the path. In other words, it is relative to one's qualities of insight and perseverance. It is also a function of whether or not one says what they mean, and does what they say. That is indicative of being an individual of character. The expectation is that goal is within anyone's reach if they ascribe to the Truth, rather than surrender to an untruth for convenience's sake. If nothing else that is the prerequisite to get one's foot in the starting block.

Rather than talk around the issue like human beings are prone to do, it is time to speak from the heart. If not now then the opportunity may never arise. Will the partnership of egoism and ideology continue to hold sway over the public health and welfare? Will the Beast and the Harlot waltz casually over your grave in their dance of death and destruction? It is up to you to decide when a change of perspective is due. It would be wise to make that decision before there is a sudden and irrevocable change of venue. The Earth changes prophesied for the beginning of the 21st century should be cause enough for one to sit up and take notice.

After it comes it is too late to turn back the clock. Meanwhile life on Earth hangs in the balance. If one harbors a doubt this is a true statement, one need only observe the world around them. The cadence of change plays in the background but soon it will move to the foreground as it has been ordained. Like a refrain that is an undercurrent in the stream of consciousness, the volume will be turned up until it cannot be ignored. All will hear plainly a call to change their ways. The saving action required is a change of perspective, from materially-oriented to spiritually-minded. Those who are unable or unwilling to make the transition in their thinking will rue the day that choice was made. The lesson has been noted: be careful of what you wish for. You may just get it, and it probably isn't what you really want. But you will definitely get what you do because you earned it.

If you define yourself by your inherent qualities of character, however, you will find contentment. If you align yourself with the One Thing that the teachings of Thoth suggest you should, you just may adapt to the Earth changes successfully. For you it could be just a bump in the road that you could negotiate quite easily. This is not to suggest you will not be impacted. Everyone will in some way, but some will be impacted more than others. That is because some have more to lose than others. It will depend upon what each individual cares about the most. The alternative may be you will drive yourself into a ditch, or worse you may be lost in the wilderness of despair because you are unable to let go of your things. Many already sense this intuitively because they are turning to religion to provide the fulfillment that is lacking in their lives. But there is no opportunity for salvation if you don't change yourself in the process. This not only includes resolving character flaws, what you value, but also changing your behavior. Only you have the power to help you. No one can do it for you. If you cannot find in it within yourself to make the changes necessary, they simply won't happen.

Are your principles founded upon a Truth that never changes? If they are, you have nothing to fear. If they are not, your fears are not unfounded. Can you keep your head about you while all around you everyone is losing theirs? To be honest you won't know that until the critical moment arrives, but you stand a better chance of emotional stability if your head is on straight to begin with. This speaks directly to one's values. Your salvation lies in freedom from material things. That is your route to salvation. And as Thoth says we are *'one and the same'*, all part of the One Thing. Therefore gravitating to the center of the wheel of life is the only route to salvation for all humanity. All human beings just need to realize that and act accordingly. It is easier said than done when one is continually pulled to its edges by their desires.

What one can know for certain is that if a person has to profess an ideology, or a political preference, or take a philosophical stance in order to save themselves, then we are all doomed to failure in whatever endeavor we undertake. It is a cause for more division of purpose instead of unity of purpose. Frankly the ideological baggage one carries is always going to be different, and it shouldn't matter one bit. It doesn't change who you are biologically or spiritually. All of our belief systems are human inventions. Salvation could never be based upon personal preference. A Supreme Being would never make that mistake because a Supreme Being knows better. Only one living in their separate reality would because he or she is counting upon the fact they are someone special. How you really achieve it is by acknowledging your humanity, and that all human beings regardless of their lifestyle or belief system have the same rights to life, liberty and the pursuit of happiness as you do. That is the democratic ideal and the purpose for it is a fair deal. Democracy was invented as a framework for free will, and provides an opportunity for achieving that fair deal.

We all should share in the belief system of equality, fraternity, and compassion for every living thing. In the estimation of the All-in-All, we are all equal because it has expressed no preference. It is only human beings who have, and they jealousy guard its lineage as if it is not freely-given and has to be earned. We all share the same biology, but not the same mindset. We share Nature with other livings things but we don't afford them the rights we imagine we have. The difference may only be in how we perceive our place in the grand scheme of things. It may be that some have grander schemes than others, but we are merely different grains of sand on the same beach. At the core, no one is any different than anyone else. We simply *think* we are. All of our problems stem from how we perceive ourselves and each other in our own minds. Everyone is guilty of it in some degree. Certainly that is something we can change provided we possess the will to do it.

Perhaps if we stop *thinking* so much, and start *feeling* more, most of our problems wouldn't seem insurmountable. All of those differences we fabricate with our minds would evaporate as well. The more one feeds the ego with their thinking, the stronger it becomes. And the more willful it becomes the harder it is to control it. What makes anyone believe they are always right and anyone who disagrees with them is always wrong? It is evidence of all the sludge clogging the streams of human commerce that keeps us apart and at each other's throats, nothing more. From time immemorial all of that crap we've been fed by religion, government, economic institutions, the media, and ideological superiors, serves to impress upon us what they want to mold us into for their own benefit. Under the guise of serving and protecting, it keeps us chained to their wheel. Look at what it is has wrought upon the Earth. Need there be any more proof on display? The time has come to put that aside, and begin listening to the One within us. It has a different story to tell and a different purpose laid out for us. Its intent is to guide not exploit. The One has your best interest in mind rather than its own because it's "one and the same". For that reason alone you can trust what it has to say. What one needs to do is stop believing in what the ego has to say. You will become a prisoner of its own success in meeting its many needs.

Do you honestly think the All-in-All cares about what you think? It really cares more about how you treat its Creation, and each other. This points back directly to your feelings and if they are in line with its laws of operation. If you start with the one commandment of Jesus[lviii] and abide by it in the best way you know how, free will takes care of the rest. If you want to do the will of the All-in-All, you first have to correct your thinking, and then act in a way that unites rather than divides. This would be the only thing the All-in-All actually wants, if it had needs and desires. But the All-in-All only operates on Principles, and the Laws from which they have been formed.

Chuck all of the ideological rules and regulations that have come down through the ages, attributed to needs and desires of unseen forces. They represent a mind control exercise orchestrated by the powers-that-be to keep you obedient, dutiful, and compliant. If you can control your own cravings, you've erased the need for external measures of control. If you have not, perhaps you need some guidelines to make you toe the line. But they do not supersede the one commandment you are obligated to obey. The purpose of ideology was to provide some guidelines for human behavior. It does little more than differentiates the human circumstances of compliance with the One. The ego cannot profit by the Golden Rule so it will fight tooth and nail to subvert every effort to comply.

How could one profess to love the All-in-All, and then proceed to despoil, obliterate, and destroy every vestige of its Creation – Nature? If we simply respected all life for what it was, acknowledged it had the right to exist, and did our best to preserve it, there could be peace and harmony in the world. No one needs to be converted to any belief other than the Live and Let Live philosophy toward all living things to make this happen. Unfortunately as long as people put a monetary value on the physical world, this isn't going to happen; especially since all contend for a fraction of that value. And ironically they show a willingness to extinguish life to preserve life. It is only a contradiction if one thinks in terms of one and equal instead of separate but equal.

If humanity loved the Earth a lot more, and loved material possessions a lot less, it wouldn't be in the position it is currently in, but it isn't as simple as that. Moreover it is not an individual judgment call to decide what the penalty is for non-compliance with Universal Law. That will take care of itself without any interference from the do-gooders. It's one of humanity's many *sins* to presuppose it has the right to judge. These *sins* one can only atone for one at a time. If the emphasis was placed upon putting one's own house in order before passing judgment upon the condition of another's, that would be an appropriate first step toward setting one's feet on the right path. A second would be to rein in one's own wants and desires to determine if they fit their need and the operation of the Law. The third would be to ensure one is fulfilling their moral and spiritual responsibilities in the spirit of the Law. These steps will determine if one goes out in a blaze of glory or sinks into the bottomless pit of despair. One may think of it as the difference between going to heaven or hell. But ultimately it is the same place and same space they exist in. The difference of appearance is determined by the pureness of the heart that projects it. The next whistle stop is only a different set of circumstances to give the physical life another try.

To say that the glass is half-full or half-empty is the tactical ploy of a con-artist trying to sell you something. The perception that it is half-full or half-empty is an illusion. Moreover it is bone-dry unless one fills it oneself. In that way one controls the content of the glass. Furthermore to think that perception is reality, and consciousness is entirely a matter of selective perception is ludicrous. That does not take into account the source of causation. If *you* didn't exist, the source would anyway. And the proof is the objectivity of Universal Law. Imagining one's reality the precise way one wants it to be to showcase an idealized image of oneself is a fool's errand. You simply are what you are. If you want to argue the fine points of ideology that's your prerogative, but it gets you no closer to your goal. It's the game plan of the Children of Belial to keep humanity distracted from uniting in a common cause. As far as their game plan is concerned, it will work to perfection until the realization dawns you've actually gained nothing but strife. Therefore you play the hand you are dealt. Whether you win or lose the hand depends upon the cards you hold, and how you play them.

But everyone is entitled to their own opinion however misguided it may be. One should never be denied one's inalienable right to an opinion even if exercising that right results in a perversion of the Truth. But perhaps what the purveyors of error may fear is that the realization of their error will be revealed, and the pious will awaken from their trance, and stop pretending everything will work itself out in the end if they pray long and hard enough. This is not to say that prayer does not have its place. However if one assumes it substitutes for good works in the name of the Lord, then one has consigned oneself to being nothing more than a leaf in the wind. The truly righteous man or woman should not have an agenda except to terminate the reign of ego in the ways and means of human endeavor. It is ego alone that causes one to demand his or her reward, grab another by the throat and beat it out of another to get it. It steers the course of human history in whatever direction the weight shifts to satisfy a duplicitous need. No angel or demon has any power over human thought, feeling, or deed which of itself can cause a single thing to happen. No influence can be wielded which affects a consequence against one's will. In as many ways as one can say it, for you, the future is not written until a choice is made. There is no other way to say it, except to remind the reader the future is in your own hands.

No playbook can really be offered to survive Earth changes because it is a living document. For each seeker the plays are run differently; so in this sense, innovation operates upon the rigors of a personal psycho-spiritual scientific method. In the oral tradition of seeking enlightenment, the novice learns his or her lessons from the master. The seeker receives the principles and observes the teachings in action. As far as the lessons are concerned, they provide instruction for the seeker like a morality play. Modern liturgy substitutes doctrine in place of the master so contemporary man is forced to improvise. As far as the plays are concerned, all that can be offered are diagrams for the most commonly used scripted plays. What you do with them is entirely up to you. No one is compelled to follow a script written for them; no matter what they are told the ideological requirements may be. There are none which are binding, and none which are not freely chosen. The only requirements which are binding are those which are necessary for growth. Each individual chooses in which direction they desire to grow. It is determined by one's willingness to accept Universal Law as the rule and the laws of cause and effect as their guide. Regardless of the pace one wishes to set, growth is manifested one step at a time. Since it is a marathon rather than a sprint, endurance and perseverance are key components of the seeker's quest.

What have been characterized as leaps of faith are giant steps one is prepared to take when the situation calls for it or the opportunity arises. The Earth changes prophesied for the 21st century are billed as one of those opportunities. How this is to be accomplished each individual must determine of his or her own accord. Clues are provided in the communications from the masters that point one in the right direction. Whether or not one chooses to take heed of their advice is the seeker's prerogative. There are no commandments that apply. No one can make you do anything you really don't want to do. You have to feel it is the appropriate thing for you to do. Whenever free will is abridged it is an abomination. Such is the way of belief in the All-in-All and the methodology of the Law of One. It must flow freely from the Source within without the impediment of doctrine. Belief is most often predicated upon understanding the scripted plays involved because one may have similar experiences from which to draw upon. But what matters most is: who scripted them and why, and if they are effective in *moving* the spirit within.

In each human being there is a chain of command. As the masters have noted, Spirit instructs, Soul feels, and Mind thinks. The evidence shows human beings are subverting the chain of command. Their egos are permitted to run amuck. It should be obvious to the dimmest of bulbs. The walls they erect to protect their fiefdoms will come tumbling down. All of the possessions to which they lay claim will be returned to the Source that actually owns them. It has been foreseen. We will be laid bare. That is the purpose of the Great Purification. It signals a return to the simple life. Your misery will be eternal if you can't adapt to it. When the change comes, will you be ready for it? Only you can answer that question because only you know the answer to it. The best any individual can do is to prepare to meet their Maker with a clear Conscience, and accept what may transpire. The worst is to bemoan the loss of a complicated life because one is afraid to let go of it.

The avatars of pure intent have always said the easy path of desire is the false path. Therefore the implication is that nothing worthwhile ever comes effortlessly. Effort is required to achieve any goal worth achieving. The true path is most often the difficult path to traverse. It doesn't take a genius to figure this out. But it takes the endurance of a marathon runner to finish the race. Willful persistence and intestinal fortitude are noteworthy virtues. When the world expects you to give up or give in, if you can forge ahead, you will always be miles ahead of where you expect to be.

Take a lesson from the tortoise. He may be slow afoot, but he gets where he's going. He'll finish the race. He just won't do it in record time. He's not looking for a trophy for his mantle. He is just satisfied not to be clutching his chest at the finish line. The simple things in life are those which are worth keeping. The extravagance, the excess, and the selfishness humanity exhibits in daily life are what need to be expunged from the human condition. If collectively we are to make it to the finish line, we owe it all to a willingness, in the words of Jiminy Cricket, to *let your Conscience be your guide*.

In history, the seminal moment will be if and when the balance between those who observe the Golden Rule and those who don't is tipped in favor of those who do. When the great mass of humanity comes to the realization greed is not good, gluttony is an abomination, and it is better to share than hoard, then humanity will be primed for ascension to a higher state of consciousness. After the realization dawns and steps are actually taken to correct the behavior that permitted greed, gluttony and the remainder of the Seven Deadly Sins[lix] to flourish, only then will humanity save itself from a harsh fate. One cannot wait for the All-in-All to do it. And if one really understands the teachings of Jesus that's exactly what he was telling humanity to do all along. His way was absolute alignment with the ONE in Principle. He called IT the Father. This had to be done by choice. Until it is accomplished one's growth is stymied because we are all part of the One Thing.

Human beings may be destined to revert to their baser instincts – called the survival of the fittest. The only thing that could prevent it is a universal commitment to secular humanism. That is what the avatars of every cultural persuasion actually preached – a way of life that was in harmony with God and Man that owed nothing to any particular ideology. None of them intended to see their wisdom institutionalized because it would suck the life out of their teachings. Moreover all of these belief systems are founded upon the principles of the Children of the Law of One. The fact that the institutionalized belief systems have gone so far afield in their growth process cannot be blamed upon their founding principles. The blame could only be placed upon the role of ego in that growth process; specifically in those who wished to profile in their accomplishments. The content of one's character will always determine the direction growth takes. And one's system of values will provide it force and intelligence. Due to the nature of the human condition there are no guarantees of success or failure. Inevitably your intent shines through and one is found out for who and what they are.

At the seam between Ages, the Cosmos will reach out to each of its inhabitants. The manner of this communication will be left to the imagination, but a *last call* will be sent. It will be clear and undeniable that epic change is on the threshold. What is graphically displayed will show the consequences of our actions like branding a scarlet letter upon the sinews of the human heart. Once branded the mark cannot be erased. Each individual will be shown what they are and what they have become. The key *communication* will come just before the pole shift occurs when the magnetic fields of the Earth are disturbed. It will be a preview of coming attractions of what lay in store for humanity. Unlike the showcase Hollywood presented which featured a disaster film of epic proportions (the 2012 film) for the sake of entertainment, virtually no one will be entertained. Potentially the changes will reach into the soul of Man, and rip the heart out of those who have not guarded it. Throughout history men of exemplary character have given all the warnings that are necessary. Humanity has not heeded any of them. In fact in many cases, they have done the opposite by feeding their egos to the bursting point. Soon the trumpets will play taps. There will be no more warnings that will go unheeded because it will be too late to give them.

Honestly what will be, will be anyway no matter what is written or said about it. Your fate is determined by how well prepared one is for the inevitability of change. Even though many would like to imagine they could predict the outcome, they only succeed in deluding themselves when they attempt to. How it will unfold, and how humanity will be affected by it is yet to be determined. Events on the ground will determine that, rather than the words on a piece of paper, or the symbols carved into stone monuments. It is the human interest story par excel lance of our generation. More importantly it is what one makes of oneself that matters most. Those that believe wishing and hoping for the best is all that is required shortchange themselves because it requires effort to make the world and the people in it sane again.

Regarding Earth changes, truthfully no one can say what will actually happen until it does. But considering the prodigious amount of evidence compiled to support the contention an apocalypse is imminent, to dismiss it out-of-hand would be foolhardy. Conversely to walk down Main Street every day with a placard that announces '*repent, the end is near*' would be equally foolish. No one seems to know precisely when the appointed time will be. Thus it appears a common sense approach needs to be adopted that treads the middle way. Furthermore it is logical to believe one's saving grace will not be the product of any ideology, political platform, or philosophical stance. A personal response is called for, and that can only come from each human individual, in turn. Realistically any semblance of order and civility is likely to disappear in any worst case scenario of cataclysm. Therefore a firm foundation in moral values and social conscience is what will enable the human race to endure, and nothing less than that. It all boils down to a single decision each individual faces. Will one go the way of selflessness, the inclusion of every noble virtue into one's behavior, or selfishness, the exclusion of every noble virtue from one's behavior? Your destiny lies along the path you choose. Humanity will ride the wave of the collective choice.

Truth Never Changes: The Genesis of the Path

Until the day of reckoning arrives, we perch precariously on the fence; not knowing to which side we will fall. The wise man and woman knows he or she will fall to their death if they fail to understand what course of action is in their best interest, and neglect to act upon it. The proof lay in the making. There is nothing else to add to it or take away from it. The results of seeing with a clear eye and thinking with a sound mind will reveal it is time to turn the page. The challenge then is to harness the rational mind to do the bidding of the God within. Believing doesn't make it true. You must translate your beliefs into action to make them live in yourself. According to Mahatma Ghandi, "*You must be the change you wish to see in the world*". If not now, then when? End of story.

Michael L. Kilday

Index

2012............................. *10, 11, 17, 19, 20, 22, 194, 205*
Abdominal brain *112*
Adam Smith........................... *181*
Aether *163*
Akashic Record *51, 77*
Albert Einstein *20, 165*
All-in-All.................................
78, 133, 153, 160, 163, 172, 186, 191, 196, 199, 200, 201, 203, 205
Anti-Christ *105*
Anti-Christ consciousness *105*
Aquarian Age.............. *10, 28, 194*
Ardipithicus *62*
Aristotle *59*
Arthur C Clarke........................ *50*
Aryan........................ *90, 91, 92, 93*
As above, so below.....................
23, 96, 99, 101, 102, 108, 126, 150
Atlantea *90, 91*
Atlantean Masters *1, 7, 45, 71, 72*
Atlantis.............. *14, 22, 30, 95, 96*
Atonement *135, 151, 159*
Automatic writing *74, 78*
Baha'i Faith *29, 30*
Be here now *160, 166*
Becoming *186*
Belial........... *92, 104, 142, 172, 173*
Bible ....
... *1, 14, 56, 59, 60, 68, 129, 131*
Book of Enoch...... *56, 77, 87, 95*
Book of Revelation *104, 105, 193*

Buddha *34, 181*
Canopy of Light................ *10, 194*
Capitalism *170, 182*
Carl Jung *51, 77*
Catastrophism *23, 64*
Charles Darwin *55, 56, 57*
Charles Hapgood *20*
Chaucer *31*
Children of Belial............................
.... *103, 105, 106, 109, 202*
Children of the Law of One... *10, 30, 67, 69, 77, 78, 88, 93, 95, 96, 97, 100, 103, 104, 105, 106, 108, 109, 126, 127, 205*
Christ *105*
Christ Consciousness ....
.... *105, 108, 177*
Clarence Darrow........................ *53*
Climate change.......................... *26*
Cognitive dissonance............. *182*
Collective unconscious *51, 77*
Columbus.......................... *59, 65*
Conscience....................................
.... *122, 170, 187, 189, 204, 206*
Copernicus....................... *59, 65*
Creationism...................... *55, 68*
Creationists *55, 58, 65, 68*
Creative Cycle of Life................
.... *145, 185, 190*
Creative Life *6, 139, 140, 152*
Crown of creation............. *60, 65*
Da Vinci................................. *165*
Dark energy *67*
Dark matter *67, 77*

Dead sea scrolls *103*
Declaration of Independence......
.... *187*
Demon.............................. *179, 202*
Deprivations *195*
DNA *61, 62, 65, 66, 69, 167*
Dome of the Rock *8*
Doomsday Clock *193*
Dr. Frederick Fischer ....
.... *13, 30, 33, 37, 71*
Earth changes ....
  6, 7, 10, 17, 18, 31, 108, 109, 194, 196, 197, 198, 202, 203, 206
Earth's wobble *25, 26*
Eden *90, 91, 92, 93, 95*
Edgar Cayce *17, 18, 20, 77*
Egyptian *97*
Egyptians *14*
Elohim *88*
Elwood Babbitt *3, 5, 37*
Emerald tablet *98*
Enoch *77, 95*
Erik Von Dainigan *64, 78*
Essene *67, 103*
Euclid *58*
Evolution ....
  53, 54, 56, 61, 63, 64, 65, 127, 143, 153, 178
Evolutionists *55, 58*
Fifth Age of Man *8, 110*
First Cause *99, 153*
First Coming *176*
first law of Thermodynamics . *52,* **150**
Galileo *55*
Garden of Eden *55*

Genesis ....
  53, 55, 57, 59, 65, 68, 69, 77, 78, 127
Gilgamesh *95*
Global warming *26*
Gnosis *163, 188*
Gnostics *67*
God Within ....
  122, 124, 140, 153, 158, 164, 178, 190, 207
Golden Rule ....
  ..... *108, 146, 163, 190, 201, 204*
Grand Architect *61, 66, 139*
Great Purification *7, 204*
Great Return *11, 12, 13, 176*
HAL *49, 50*
Hammurabi *131*
Harold Camping *21*
Here and now *148, 158*
Hermes Trismegistus ....
.... *96, 97, 98, 99, 108, 164*
Hopi *7, 10, 11, 14, 17, 28, 110*
Horus the Child *11*
Human condition ....
.... *179, 181, 204, 205*
Idealism *166, 174*
Isis *11*
Jesse Ventura *27*
Jesus the Christ *100, 122, 185*
John Locke *181*
Julius Caesar *179*
Krophron ....
  77, 79, 80, 81, 82, 83, 85, 89, 90, 91
Krophronite ....
  78, 79, 80, 81, 82, 83, 84, 85, 86, 87, 88, 89, 90, 91

Kundalini............................ *33, 34*
Lao-tzu *44*
Law of attraction *181*
Law of One...........................
   30, 73, 78, 88, 89, 92, *97, 103, 105, 106, 110, 115, 133, 134, 141, 142, 153, 159, 185, 203*
Lee Brown.............. *28, 30, 180*
Lemurian *88, 92*
Library of Alexandria *97*
Mahatma Ghandi *207*
Manifest destiny *60*
Maya................... *10, 11, 14, 92*
Messiah *176, 177, 191*
Michelangelo........................... *60*
Missing link *54, 64*
Mordach *92*
Moses............................ *131, 155*
Napoleon................................ *60*
NASA *17, 19, 20, 25, 28*
Natural Law *63, 65, 66, 100*
Natural Selection...........................
   .... *55, 57, 62, 65, 182*
Neophilm *87, 88*
Nibiru.................................... *11*
Nostradamus *11, 14*
Nous *66*
One Thing. *99, 102, 188, 198, 199*
Original sin............................. *67*
Osiris *11*
Osiris/Isis Mystery *11*
Panspermia............................ *64*
Phoenician........................ *93, 98*
Planet X *11*
Plato *14, 93, 101, 146, 174*
Plato's Academy *164, 173*
Pole shift *20, 23, 24, 205*

Posideia *90, 91, 92, 93*
Prosperity gospel *167, 180, 181*
Pythagorus *58, 164*
Quran *131*
Rapture *21*
Renaissance................. *58, 60, 165*
Renaissance Man................... *172*
Ring of Fire............................. *18*
Scopes.................................... *53*
Second Coming................... *176*
Second law of thermodynamics
   .... *150*
Sectarianism............. *174, 176, 182*
Secular humanism................... *190*
Set *11*
Seven Deadly Sins................... *205*
Seven Laws of Creation... *87, 115*
Simple truth *125, 189*
Sincere seeker.................................
   3, 4, 7, 73, 107, 174, 175, 178, 197
Sir Issac Newton................ *52, 70*
Six days war *8*
Socrates *164, 178*
Solar flare *20, 22*
Son of God...................... *178, 187*
Son of man *137, 178, 187*
Sons of darkness *103*
Sons of light.......................... *103*
Spiritual DNA *132, 133, 160, 188*
Spontaneous Generation *64*
Summer of love.......................... *8*
Technocracy *169, 170*
Temple of Solomon *8*
Temple of the Living Spirit.... *93, 95, 96*
Ten Commandments *146*

The Beast ***104, 197***
The Harlot......................***104, 197***
The Other Side.... ***2, 5, 45, 72, 73***
Theosophical Society.......... ***10, 11***
Thomas Jefferson............... ***42, 43***
Thoth ....
... ***11, 95, 96, 106, 108, 198, 199***
Torah ***56, 131***
Tree of Knowledge.... ***47, 54, 158***
Triune God ***188***
Uniformitarianism.....................***23***
Universal Law...............................
97, 100, 101, 105, 126, 133, 134, 137, 151, 173, 177, 178, 179, 185, 186, 187, 188, 190, 191, 194, 201, 202, 203
Universal Mind..............................
102, 103, 110, 144, 149, 150, 161
Uriel ***95***
Vishnu ***87***
Watchers ***95, 132***
What the bleep ***23***
William Jennings Bryan............***53***
William Miller............................***21***
Yahweh ***172***

Bibliography

Brown, L. (1986). *Shamanic Teachings*. Retrieved from Shaman Website.

Clarke, A. C. (1968). *2001: A Space Odyssey*.

Darwin, C. (1859). *The Origin of Species*. London, England.

Gordon, J. (2004). *Egypt, Child of Atlantis: A Radical Interpretation of the Origins of Civilization*. London, England: Inner Traditions.

Heinlein, R. A. (1961). *Stranger in a Strange Land*.

Kilday, M. L. (2009). *Truth Never Changes: Earth Changes*. Wolcott, CT: Green Dove Press.

Kubrick, S. (Director). (1968). *2001: A Space Odyssey* [Motion Picture].

Levine, S. (1986). *Who Dies?*

Luther, M. (1517). *95 Theses*. Wittenberg, Germany.

Peniel, J. (1997). *The Children of the Law of One and the Lost Teachings of Atlantis*.

Plato. (5th Century BCE). *The Critas*. Athens.

Proyas, A. (Director). (2009). *Knowing* [Motion Picture].

Shakespeare, W. (16th Century). *King Henry IV, Part One*. Stratford-on-Avon, England.

Times, N. (1989, March 13). NY Times. *Large Solar Flares Erupt Anew*.

Trismegistus, H. (unknown). *collection*.

Vastag, B. (2005, 15 12). North Magnetic Pole is Sifting rapidly into Siberia Toward Russia. *National Geographic News* .

Veilikovsky, I. (1950). *Worlds in Collisions*.

Ventura, J. (2010, April). Conspiracy Theory. Denver, Colorado, USA.

Vivekanada, S. (1980). *Raja Yoga*.

Von Dainigan, E. (1968). *Chariots of the Gods*.

Waters, F. (1963). *Book of the Hopi*.

webmaster. (2010). Retrieved from canada.com.

webmaster. (2010). *Harold Camping*. Retrieved from Harold Camping.

webmaster. (2009). *NASA document on Earth's magnetosphere*. Retrieved from NASA.

webmaster. (2005, 12). *NASA document on magnetic pole shift*. Retrieved from NASA.

webmaster. (2010). *NASA document on the Chandler wobble*. Retrieved from NASA.

Truth Never Changes: The Genesis of the Path

Endnotes

On the back cover at the top of the 3 dimensional pyramid is a photograph taken by the Hubble Space Telescope. It is a photograph of Sirius A and B. The Egyptians believed their home planet was in the Sirius constellation. *NASA, ESA, H. Bond (STScI), and M. Barstow (University of Leicester)*

[i] The Atlantean wise men were disembodied entities inhabiting the ethereal realm. As their identification suggested, they were associated with the fabled land of Atlantis as the guiding force of that civilization. During a deep-trance session in 1979, certain claims were made by Spirit that they were a source of information for the author, and were in constant contact with him. Virtually all of the communications with these wise men were received intuitively and recorded in this manuscript in the form of 'automatic writing'. Their influence was felt strongly throughout the entire manuscript, but they speak directly in Chapters 7 through 18. More details concerning these wise men and the deep-trance session were provided in the first book of Truth Never Changes series, TRUTH NEVER CHANGES: EARTH CHANGES.

[ii] Falstaff's quote came from the Shakespearean play, KING HENRY IV PART ONE.

[iii] A three day music festival called, The Woodstock Music and Arts Festival, was held in White Lake, NY in August of 1969. The phrase *Woodstock Nation* was coined to represent the massive numbers of young people who attended the festival; estimated to be in the range of five hundred thousand to one million by the media and festival promoters. The term was used to signify a constituency of the 1960's counterculture movement which advocated progressive change. It was believed this change encompassed a social and spiritual awakening that would blossom into a renaissance of the human spirit. Though it was yet to appear, the belief was it had only been delayed until humanity committed to the cause.

Michael L. Kilday

[iv] TRUTH NEVER CHANGES: EARTH CHANGES was the first offering in the Truth Never Changes series. The book was published by Green Dove Press in February of 2009.

[v] In general, a Great Purification was the prognosis for Earth changes as presented by the North and South American Indians. Typically it was focused upon in the 'end-times' prophecies of the Hopi, Sioux, and Mayan Indians. Specific references to THE GREAT PURIFICATION can be found in THE BOOK OF HOPI as well as BLACK ELK SPEAKS. The idea spoke to Nature's need to purify itself of that viral infection known as 'man'. It delved into an understanding of planetary life cycles which of necessity all nature-oriented religions always possessed. Ultimately it meant change which humanity had little or no control over occurred at regular cosmic intervals. These had been divided into 'ages' in accordance with the cosmic clock (the precession of the equinoxes). Hopi tradition cited four ages, presumably of 25,920 years each. The beginning of the 21st century denoted one of those intervals (e.g. the beginning of the Aquarian Age). Native American philosophy had always represented the Earth as a *living thing* with a consciousness and purpose, a la the Gaia theory. Throughout history most indigenous tribes maintained an existence that was in harmony with Nature. The phrase '*Nature is God; God is Nature*' was an apt way of capturing the essence of that belief system. The natural theory of Western Civilization tended to ignore that view; preferring instead to adopt ethnocentric views. Therefore the white man tended to view himself and his civilization as being separate and distinct from Nature. He mistakenly believed he was the master of the natural domain. And that fact was recorded in THE BIBLE. It was the source of his error that he compounded with every breath he took.

[vi] This phrase harkened back to Plato's climb to the light. Essentially it represented the ascension of the human intellect to a status of knowing the truth through one's reasoning faculties. The *cave* symbolized the darkness of ignorance, while coming out of it into the sunlight symbolized the light of understanding. Plato's metaphor describes the goal of sincere seekers from time immemorial.

Truth Never Changes: The Genesis of the Path

ⱽⁱⁱ The Children of the Law of One were alleged to be a group of survivors who fled the continent of Atlantis during the final phases of its destruction about 11,000 years ago. They settled initially in Egypt among other places on the African, North American, South American, and European continents. Under the leadership of Thoth, to Egypt they brought with them the spiritual teachings of the elders of Atlantis. These teachings were revealed in the ancient mysteries of Universal Law and the Seven Laws of Creation (Order, Balance, Harmony, Growth, God-Perception, Love, and Compassion). In short they taught that God, they termed the ALL-IN-ALL, was One, and that every physical manifestation of the Universe emanated from One Source. It was manifested in accordance with the principle of *'as above, so below'* and was dispersed throughout the Universe. Their expressed purpose was to teach the Truth and thereby fulfill their mandate to show the way back to union with the One. Throughout this manuscript there were numerous references to the Children of the Law of One and their teachings in many different contexts. Further information concerning the Children of the Law of One regarding their history and teachings could be found in the book, THE CHILDREN OF THE LAW OF ONE AND THE LOST TEACHINGS OF ATLANTIS. It was published by Network Publishing in 1997, a subsidiary of the organization, The Children of the Law of One.

ᵛⁱⁱⁱ Theosophy is a doctrine of religious philosophy and mysticism. Theosophy postulates that all religions are attempts by the Occult Brotherhood, sometimes referred to as the Great White Brotherhood, to assist humanity in evolving to a higher level of consciousness, and that each religion therefore has a portion of the truth. The founding members, Helena Petrovna Blavatsky (1831 – 1891), Henry Steel Olcott (1832 – 1907), and William Quan Judge (1851 – 1896), established the Theosophical Society in New York City in 1875. Rudolf Steiner created a successful branch in Germany and subsequently in 1913 founded his own successor organization the Anthroposophical Society.

ⁱˣ This quote was from the book, EGYPT, CHILD OF ATLANTIS: A RADICAL INTERPRETATION OF THE ORIGINS OF CIVILIZATION. It was published in 1997 and reprinted in 2004 by Bear & Company which is a division of Inner Traditions International.

[x] IBID ... TRUTH NEVER CHANGES: EARTH CHANGES

[xi] This item was copied from the NASA web site.

[xii] IBID ... NASA web site

[xiii] According to an article in NATIONAL GEOGRAPHIC, "Magnetic north, which is the place where compass needles actually point, is near but not exactly in the same place as the geographic North Pole. Right now, magnetic north is close to Canada's Ellesmere Island. Navigators have used magnetic north for centuries to orient themselves when they're far from recognizable landmarks. Although global positioning systems have largely replaced such traditional techniques, many people still find compasses useful for getting around underwater and underground where GPS satellites can't communicate. The magnetic north pole had moved little from the time scientists first located it in 1831. Then in 1904, the pole began shifting northeastward at a steady pace of about 9 miles (15 kilometers) a year. In 1989 it sped up again, and in 2007 scientists confirmed that the pole is now galloping toward Siberia at 34 to 37 miles (55 to 60 kilometers). A rapidly shifting magnetic pole means that magnetic-field maps need to be updated more often to allow compass users to make the crucial adjustment from magnetic north to true north."

[xiv] Charles H. Hapgood was a college professor in New Hampshire who was a close associate of deep-trance channeler Elwood Babbitt. He wrote and published, THE EARTH'S SHIFTING CRUST, in 1958. After it was published it was criticized by many in the scientific community. The general feeling was the theories Hapgood proposed were speculative, and the research was not persuasive. A foreword written by Albert Einstein didn't appear to make much difference. However the book was written before the theories of plate tectonics were fully vetted by the scientific community. Hapgood was no longer roundly criticized, but neither was his theories heartily embraced. One sensed a grudging acceptance that he

may have gotten something right from the scientific community. But no one was doing cartwheels over the implications his theories proposed in light of recent discoveries concerning pole wandering.

[xv] This quote was from TRUTH NEVER CHANGES: EARTH CHANGES. It briefly described how making assumptions made an ass out of you and me. The hope of the Millerites was that the message of their savior, William Miller, was true and accurate. " I am cognizant of the plight of the Millerites who after selling all of their earthly possessions saw 1847 come and go without incident. Imagine pinning all of one's hopes and dreams upon a prognostication only to have it evaporate in the ebbing light of a May evening. Had William Miller never had his vision of the end of the world, the day would have come and gone without notice. To a select few, that day had special significance. To most of humanity that day was a day like any other. Perhaps that is the lesson to be learned -- expectations are a common source of disillusionment. The more expectations one has, the greater the opportunity for disillusionment. Belief is dogged by a similar proposition, but one does not need to take it that far either. And one will not if one allows reality to be factored into the equation from time to time. After their disappointment, the Millerites started a new religion called the Seventh Day Adventists who to this day shy away from making doomsday predictions citing specific dates. Ironically the seventh day is a day of rest. The name implies that the Millerites have 'retired' from the prediction business." One would hope Harold Camping took the hint and did the same.

[xvi] Jesus said the following concerning those who sought to predict Judgment Day, the End of Days, and the Second Coming. In Matthew (24:36-37), he said: "But of that day and hour no one knows, not even the angels of heaven, but My Father only. But as the days of Noah were, so also will be the coming of the Son of Man be". "Watch therefore, for you know neither the day nor the hour in which the Son of Man is coming." Matthew (25:13). Clearly it would seem this event is unpredictable.

Michael L. Kilday

[xvii] According to reports on March 13, 1989 a solar flare knocked out the power grid in the Canadian province of Quebec for ten hours. The NY Times reported the event in a story, "LARGE SOLAR FLARES ERUPT ANEW", on 3/13/1989, (section B, page 5). The following report described events of the day the Quebec power grid went down. It attested to the possibility of this happening again because it had already.

[xviii] Catastrophism was the idea that Earth had been affected in the past by sudden, short-lived, violent events, possibly worldwide in scope. The leading scientific proponent of this theory in the early 19th century was French anatomist and paleontologist Georges Cuvier. His motivation was to explain the patterns of extinction and faunal succession that he and others were observing in the fossil record. The Great Flood by polar ice cap melting or the mass extinction of the dinosaurs by meteor impact might be considered to be explanations of such events. The dominant paradigm of modern geology, in contrast was uniformitarianism in which slow incremental changes, such as erosion created the Earth's appearance. Of course, it was obvious the giant meteor crater of Arizona was not caused by erosion. The uniformitarianism view held that the present was the key to the past, and that all things continued as they were from the beginning of the world. The view of catastrophism held that *extinction events* were interspersed throughout that record causing global change. Recently a more inclusive and integrated view of geological events had developed, changing the scientific consensus to accept some catastrophic events in the geological past.

[xix] Rather than confuse the reader with a diverse array of sources from which the information came, suffice it to say the information came from a variety of sources. It would be exceedingly difficult to decipher the list. The information was gathered from several internet sources that forecast global change was on the horizon. An array of information was gathered from diverse sites like NASA, miscellaneous scientific organizations, biblical researchers, New Age researchers, and bureaus of statistics. It all led to the conclusion that change however one wished to view it was inevitable, and was happening as we speak.

Truth Never Changes: The Genesis of the Path

xx This organization attempted to link theories of quantum mechanics with consciousness. Their presentation attempted to cross the boundaries of physics and metaphysics and show the links between them. It rekindled the age-old debate concerning objective and subjective reality – which was it? An old Buddhist proverb hinted at the same dichotomy of experience and being. *'If a tree falls in a forest, and there's no one there to hear it, does it make a sound'*? But what it really boiled down to was the question: Were the seen and the unseen co-joined at the Source?

xxi This information was presented by Princeton professor, Immanuel Velikovsky in his book WORLDS IN COLLISION. He wrote "It is no accident that their frozen state indicates the crust of the Earth moved into the polar circle. This is what happens during pole shifts. The Mastodon [or mammoth] is a species that went extinct during the past few pole shifts, primarily when the grasslands they browsed in Siberia were drawn rapidly into the new polar circle. But where drawn into water and drawn into water and drown, and then far enough north, the Mastodons were flash frozen. If the Mastodons were not flash frozen, they would be in some sort of decay – perhaps the skin preserved, but the internal organs a mush."

xxii Scientists claimed the most beneficial gauss strength of the geomagnetic field strength was between 7.0 and 12. To coincide with an increase in solar output, solar flares, sun spots, and geomagnetic storms had increased. The geomagnetic shield surrounding the Earth was getting weaker. It was approaching zero. Recently a satellite reading of the field showed it was a mere 0.4 to 0.7 gauss. Between 1835, when measuring the field became a regular practice, and 1965 the geomagnetic field strength diminished 14%. The seminal moment when it hit zero could occur in due time. When the protective shield of the Earth was down, the Earth would be vulnerable to celestial bombardment.

xxiii From an article posted on the internet site, Canada.com, the following statement spoke to the effects of climate change. One of

Michael L. Kilday

Canada's five remaining Arctic ice shelves – the 4,500 year old, 50 square kilometer, Markham ice shelf, had broken completely away from Ellesmere Island and drifted into the Arctic Ocean. It was the most dramatic sign yet of how rising temperatures and retreating sea ice were creating 'irreversible' changes to the country's polar frontier. A century ago, Ellesmere Island was covered with one continuous, massive ice shelf up to 70 meters thick and extending 500 kilometers along its coastlines. Since then about 90 per cent of the former Ellesmere Island Ice Sheet had disappeared – much of it during a warming period in the 1930s and 1940s. By the 1990s, the single Ellesmere Island ice sheet had been reduced to six smaller, distinctive ice shelves: Serson, Petersen, Milne, Ayles, Ward Hunt, and Markham. Markham was the latest casualty. As one could readily witness the melting of these ice shelves had been happening for a long period of time; probably precipitating the rapid shift of magnetic north to the east since 1950.

[xxiv] Overall the global temperature of the Earth had warmed up 2.5 to 3 degrees Celsius in the last 50 years. In addition to that fact, what was happening in Antarctica was of particular concern. By visual confirmation it had been cited that in twenty years (1966-1989) 502 square miles of the Wordie Ice Shelf had melted away. By the spring of 2002, the Larsen B and Wilkins Ice Shelves, the two largest on the peninsula had lost 1100 square miles of ice. That represented an area about the size of Rhode Island. The rate of ice shelf loss was 5 to ten times normal. It was clear something unusual was happening to accelerate the rate; particularly because the central section was stable, and the eastern section was cooling off. No scientist had yet offered an explanation. But it was significant that the meltdown was occurring on the western side of the continent. Geographically it provided a geographical correlation to a similar meltdown in the Arctic.

[xxv] Al Gore's book, AN INCONVENIENT TRUTH, had made projections of sea rise based on a variety of factors. The factors largely depended upon how much ice would melt in the Arctic and Antarctic respectively in a given period of time. The culprit for the meltdown was largely due to excessive levels of CO_2 in the atmosphere. Thus estimates

ranged between a 20 to a 40 foot rise in sea level all over the globe. Whether it was 20 or 40 feet, this rise in sea level was enough to engulf coastlines on every continent.

[xxvi] Information gathered from a Cable TV program, CONSPIRACY THEORY, on the TruTV network in April of 2010.

[xxvii] Lee Brown, a Cherokee shaman, revealed to the world more than two decades ago an interpretation of Hopi prophecy. No doubt his hope was that this epiphany would instigate a revelation of the coming fifth age of humanity that the Hopi foresaw. Western civilization had signified this fifth age as the AGE OF AQUARIUS. On a shamanic web site, the author found the full text of the five videos, and encouraged the reader to view them. They were not included here in their entirely. The only thing included in this text was a section of the discourse that referenced the advent of the one true religion to unite humanity in a common cause.

[xxviii] Dr Fischer's inference of the one true world religion was terse and to the point. He did not actually call it a religion. But a belief system by any other name would still be a belief system. If the way prescribed led out of the darkness into the light, it qualified as a path one wanted to take. Whether it rose to the level of being a religion was probably a point that needn't be argued. The way of the Children of the Law of One did not vary substantively from what Jesus said during the course of his teaching in describing himself as *the way*. The way to which Jesus referred, however, differed greatly from what his orthodox followers prescribed. His *way* was the way of achieving *Christ-Consciousness*, while theirs was to populate a *body of Christ*. This reference could be found in the Gnostic Gospels; specifically in THE GOSPEL OF THOMAS, among others. But it had been continually misinterpreted by the powers-that-be in every generation to support their agenda of mind-control through doctrine. It was a doctrine they dispensed and controlled since the Council of Nicaea in the fourth Century CE when the Christian canon was established. The way they established was to deny humanity the opportunity to achieve Christ-Consciousness. As long as human beings were trained to follow, no threat

Michael L. Kilday

existed any one of them would get off their respective knees and realize they were qualified to lead.

^{xxix} IBID ... Children of the Law of One

^{xxx} The Baha'i faith was founded more than 150 years ago, by the prophet Baha'u'llah in Persia. He was considered to be the latest in a series of divine messengers; the others being Abraham, Krishna, Zoroaster, Moses, Buddha, Jesus and Muhammad. According to his followers, he brought new spiritual teachings for our time. He taught the oneness of God, the oneness of the human family, and the oneness of religion. He said, *"The earth is but one country and mankind its citizens"*, and that, as foretold in all sacred scriptures of the past, now was the time for humanity to live in unity. The followers of the Baha'i faith believed the crucial need facing humanity was to find a unifying vision of the nature and purpose of life and of the future of society.

^{xxxi} The book purchased was entitled RAJA YOGA. It was written by a Hindu yogi, Swami Vivekananda, master of the craft whose skill and method far exceeded anyone I was likely to meet in the flesh. It was doubtful he would be paying any visits to the Woodbury Yoga Center where I was taking lessons in the craft.

^{xxxii} A book, called WHO DIES? was written to assist individuals with coping with the passing of loved ones. It was highly recommended for that purpose because the author blended personal experience with the psychology of loss to make it an informative as well as enlightening read. In essence, it served as effective therapy for the grief-stricken.

^{xxxiii} This was a fragment of a quote from THE GOSPEL OF MATTHEW (7, 7:8:9:10:11). The full text of the quote was as follows. *"Ask, and it shall be given you; Seek and ye shall find; Knock and it shall be opened unto you: For every one that asketh receiveth; and he that seeketh findeth; and to him that knocketh it shall be opened. Or what man is there of you, whom if his son ask bread, will he give him a stone? Or if he ask a fish, will he give him a serpent? If ye then, being evil, know*

Truth Never Changes: The Genesis of the Path

how to give good gifts unto your children, how much more shall your Father which is in heaven give good things to them that ask him?"

xxxiv This film, released in 1969, topped the list for one of the most tantalizingly inscrutable films of all time. Many a young person spent hours upon hours contemplating what it meant. If one saw it 'under the influence' there was really no hope of understanding the profound message it presented. Thus its meaning eluded many. It wasn't until many viewings later when 'straight' did the viewers finally grasp the subtle meanings of the film, and was able to draw the appropriate correlations to Science, religion, Genesis, and evolution it offered.

xxxv From Wikipedia, to grok was to share the same reality or line of thinking with another physical or conceptual entity. Author Robert A. Heinlein coined the term in his best-selling 1961 book, STRANGER IN A STRANGE LAND. In Heinlein's view, grokking was the intermingling of intelligence that necessarily affected both the observer and the observed. In the novel this explanation was provided: *"Grok means to understand so thoroughly that the observer becomes a part of the observed – to merge, blend, intermarry, and lose one's identity in group experience. It means almost everything that we mean by religion, philosophy and science – and it means as little to us (because of our Earthly assumptions), as color means to a blind man"*. The Oxford English dictionary defined '*grok*' as "*to understand intuitively or by empathy; to establish rapport with*" and "*to empathize or communicate sympathetically (with); also to experience enjoyment.*" Other forms of the word include 'groks' (present third person singular), 'grokked' (past participle), and 'grokking' (present participle). In an ideological context, a 'grokked' concept became part of the person who contributed to its evolution by improving the doctrine, perpetuating the myth, espousing the belief, adding detail to the social plan, and refining the idea or proofing the theory.

xxxvi The Butler act prohibited schools in Tennessee "*to teach any theory that denies the story of the Divine Creation of man as taught in the Bible, and to teach instead that man has descended from a lower order of animals.*" Presumably this statute had since been repealed. However it remained ensconced in the hearts and minds as literal truth by the main body of Fundamentalist

Christians. Their literal interpretation of the Bible will not permit any manner of scientific evidence to supplant views implanted by piety. Where reason feared to tread, ideology rushed in to fill the vacuum.

xxxvii For scientists finding the missing link of evolution would lay to rest the ages-old controversy of whether or not man had descended from ape. Proving the existence of a transitional state between apes and men that possessed attributes of each would settle the score between Creationists and Evolutionists once and for all. This author was of the opinion that both Creationists and Evolutionists missed the mark. As process, the principles of Creation and Evolution were dissimilar events in the planetary life cycle. One could not be substituted for the other. Hence the concept of a missing link was a red herring. It was proposed to create an argument rather than settle one. The human being's point of origin was an open question. Dissimilar viewpoints were expressed by Religion, Science, and Philosophy. The purpose of resolving the issue was to move on to the real question. That was: what is the purpose of life?

xxxviii Charles Darwin's book, ORIGIN OF SPECIES, had perhaps been one of the most misunderstood, most misrepresented, and most controversial of all time. At the same time it was revered by many and maligned by just as many. In the scientific age in which we lived perhaps it was the first time the balance of power had shifted in its favor. On one hand, it was accorded the stature of a scientific bible, while on the other, it was considered to be heresy of the highest order. And it was all in the mind of the beholder. Ironically Charles Darwin was a very religious man who took his faith seriously. In this author's opinion, if he had realized the uproar his book would have caused throughout the ensuing ages concerning the origin of species, it would never have been published. He would have kept his opinions to himself. It was too late, however, to retract what so many take to heart as gospel on the scientific side of the equation. One supposed an appropriate question to ask concerning the theory of Evolution was if the human being fit into the genealogical profile it presented.

Truth Never Changes: The Genesis of the Path

xxxix This line was a lyric from a song entitled "THE BOXER" by Paul Simon. It was apropos to the argument presented; for it provided a rationalization for holding on to preconceived notions. Ironically the boxer took his lumps because he may be unable to dodge the punches thrown; not because he was sacrificing himself for the greater good. It spoke to the human penchant for rising to a desired level of incompetence.

xl A recent archeological find in East Africa, termed Ardipithicus, threatened to overturn previous theories concerning the course of evolution. Uncovered remnants of a fossilized skeleton, dated at 4.4 million years ago, predated the appearance of the homo sapiens on the African savannahs some 3.2 million years ago. The Ardipithicus displayed traits of both the simian and hominid branches. It had led researchers to postulate that simian and hominid may had developed along parallel lines. The physical evidence suggested both lines may have come from a common ancestor. It was previously thought simian and hominid development was on a single evolutionary line, primate, which split millions of years ago. Anthropologists and archeologists continued to search for that common ancestor. Regardless of what further evolutionary details were uncovered, it still will not solve the mystery of Creation. Solving these mysteries required the interaction of both sides of the human brain.

xli This was an allusion to some content from THE BOOK OF ENOCH, and THE EPIC OF GILGAMESH. These were the product of the Hebrew and Sumerian civilizations respectively. However, Greek, Roman, and other mythologies around the globe did have quite a few instances of *gods* mating with human females. Often giants, titans, monsters, or simply individuals with superman qualities like heroes were thought to be the offspring of that union. Unless all of these civilizations copied from each other, which was likely only in a few cases, it appeared the experience was widespread.

xlii The autonomy of the separate self was in fact an illusion. Thinking of humanity as a colony of cells within a single being, the One, was more appropriate. An individual cell's autonomy' existed just as far as one's cell membrane. It operated the processes within the cell. But since all cells were really connected to the One Thing, they shared that spiritual lifeline to the Source of Spirit, and drew upon it for sustenance.

[xliii] IBID ... Atlantean wise men

[xliv] THE BOOK OF ENOCH was a Jewish apocryphal text in which the main character Enoch, the great-great-grandfather of Noah, ascended into heaven and conversed with the *angels*. One of these angels, named Uriel, guided Enoch on a journey through the seven levels of heaven, and instructed him on the *ways of the angels*. Enoch was given knowledge concerning the Cosmos, the Natural world, and the nature of God to which, he believed, only the angels of the Lord were privy to at the time. In our day and age, this information would equate to a rudimentary education in the sciences of geology, astronomy, psychics, mathematics, and biology. At one time the book was widely read by Christians, and was an integral part of Hebrew tradition. After the Council of Nicaea circa 325 CE it was declared to be heretical and excised from the canon. Now the reasons for its exclusion were a matter of conjecture. The reference to the historical personage of Enoch in GENESIS was relegated to a two-liner. '*Enoch walked with God. Then God took him*'. If one was to believe what was written in the tome of Enoch, of which there were five books, ostensibly written by his hand, there was much more to the story. This knowledge was deliberately withheld from humanity. In this author's opinion, a footnote should have been placed in Genesis to indicate that the Book of Enoch existed. Then humanity could be advised if one wished to investigate forgotten pages of history one had the opportunity to do so. Labeling it speculative (another word for apocryphal) and hiding it away only served the interest of ideologies which strove to keep the knowledge it contained from prying eyes. Much of the information contained in the BOOK OF ENOCH was also contained in the BOOK OF JUBILEES. The latter was also excised from the Christian canon at the same time. Whether keeping this knowledge secret served the purpose of keeping it out of the hands of those who would abuse it, or spoke to the motives of the powers-that-be; these motives served the belief that knowledge should

be kept under lock and key. The reason for secrecy at this point was purely speculative. But if history taught us anything, it was that knowledge was power. The reader may take from that what he or she will, concerning the motivations of the powers-that-be.

xlv Discorporation as a procedure would be challenging to explain. In the deep trance session in 1979 it was suggested by Spirit that the Krophronites had *"discorporated into a further star known as Earth"*. Suffice it to say it was taken at face value that they had simply materialized on the Earth plane; as opposed to traveling there in a spaceship. From this statement came the information contained in the chapter, Atlantean Genesis.

xlvi Traditionally Belial was a name for the force representing materialism in opposition to the spiritual force of the Children of the Law of One. The approaches were antithetical and contentious. The word, Belial, appeared in the literature of the Dead Sea scrolls; notably in the writings of the Essene, the Children of the Law of One and in the psychic predictions of Edgar Cayce. Metaphorically Belial was equated with leadership of the *sons of darkness*, while Thoth was equated with the leadership of the *sons of light*. During Atlantean times, Belial as well as Thoth inhabited physical bodies. Afterwards their respective energies came to represent the force of Spirit they emitted. The meaning this representation conveyed was strictly a matter of interpretation in the race memory to which it was applied after the fact. In biblical literature like THE BOOK OF ENOCH and THE BOOK OF JUBILEES, all of which were catalogued by the Essenes, there was a hint that the terms *Belial* and *Anti-Christ* could be considered interchangeable. It depended upon the perspective one wished to take in detailing the enduring conflict between the *sons of light* and the *sons of darkness*. Traditionally it was known as the eternal battle of good versus evil.

xlvii IBID ... Belial

xlviii With the destruction of the Library of Alexandria in Egypt in the 2nd century CE (Common Era), Hermes Trismegistus (Hermes thrice-greatest) became one of those historical personages lost in the fog of

Michael L. Kilday

Time. His contribution to humanity was now considered to be a product of mythology. Reportedly for one who was considered by many to be a fictional character, Hermes was a prolific writer. His accomplishments were legendary almost to the point few would believe one man could accomplish them. Hermes was credited with writing 20,000 books by Iamblichus (ca. 250-300 BCE), a neo-platonic Syrian philosopher, and over 36,000 books by Manetho (ca 300 BCE), an Egyptian priest who wrote the history of Egypt in Greek, perhaps for Ptolemy I. In the combined mythology of two individuals, Thoth and Hermes, who purportedly were the same person, it was reported that both Thoth and Hermes revealed to humanity the healing arts, magic, writing, astrology, science, and philosophy. According to legend, Hermes Trismegistus was said to have provided the wisdom of light in the ancient mysteries of Egypt. Reportedly he carried an emerald upon which was recorded all of his philosophical beliefs, and the caduceus, the symbol of mystical illumination. He vanquished Typhon, the dragon of ignorance, and mental, moral, and physical perversion. Physical perversion was a latent reference to Egyptian mythology which featured creatures that were half-man and half-beast. The Nubus and the Sphinx were prime examples of what had come down to us in the form of mythology. Whether it was mythology or actual physical perversion was unverifiable at this time. But mythological references to creatures of this kind were prevalent throughout the annals of early Mediterranean civilizations – primarily the Babylonians, Egyptians, Greeks, Romans, and Sumerians. Was it a case of actual experience in pre-historical times or evidence of civilizations copying each other's experience and recording it as their own? Hermes' only known surviving work was the HERMETICA, a collection of 42 books that have profoundly influenced the development of Western occultism and magic. Reputedly the Egyptian Tarot was one of his many inventions that survive today.

[xlix] It was said to have been discovered in a caved tomb, clutched in the hands of the corpse of Hermes. Legends differed on the discoverer. One said it was Sarah, the wife of Abraham. Another attributed it to Apollonius of Tyana. The nature of legends being as they may, no one knew for a certainty which was true, or if there was another possible

explanation. According to annals of the Children of the Law of One neither explanation could be true because Hermes left Egypt prior to his death and settled in Tibet. Furthermore whether an entire system of magic could be inscribed on the emerald was another topic for debate.

[l] Agape was a Greek word essentially meaning an unconditional love. It represented divine, unconditional, self-sacrificing, active, voluntary, and thoughtful love. There were three generally recognized forms of love. Greek philosophers at the time of Plato and other ancient authors had used *agape*, to denote love of a spouse or family, or affection for a particular activity, in contrast to *philia*, an affection that could denote friendship, brotherhood, or generally non-sexual affection, and *eros*, an affection of a sexual nature.

[li] IBID ... Belial

[lii] In the ancient Greek, the word Plethora translated to *fullness* in the English language. In a sense they used it to represent a cosmic abundance of thought as opposed to the limitations of human thought. In Greek Cosmology, GOD was the first Thought. It was the source of all lesser thoughts.

[liii] IBID ... Cherokee shaman who revealed the esoteric meanings of Hopi prophecy

[liv] It was the author's opinion that the *natural rights* philosophy of John Locke and the Laisezz Faire economic policies of Adam Smith were founded upon a belief that the human being was inherently good. Therefore when an individual was faced with a decision to do so-called good or bad, the assumption they made was that the individual would invariably choose good. All things being equal that meant an individual would follow the Golden Rule, and let his Conscience be his guide in all matters of social interaction. And it was their contention that religion or ethical constructs in Society alone would suffice. No individual need be forced to be virtuous. He or she would do it of their own accord.

[lv] Cognitive dissonance was an uncomfortable feeling caused by holding conflicting ideas simultaneously. The theory of cognitive dissonance proposed that people had a motivational drive to reduce dissonance. They did this by changing attitudes, beliefs, and actions. Dissonance was also reduced by justifying, blaming, and denying. Experience could clash with expectations. For example, with buyer's remorse following the purchase of an expensive item, in a state of dissonance, people may feel surprise, dread, guilt, fear, anger or embarrassment. People were biased to think their choices were correct despite any contrary evidence. This bias gave dissonance theory its predictive power, shedding light upon otherwise puzzling irrational and destructive behavior.

[lvi] IBID ... as above, so below

[lvii] IBID ... TRUTH NEVER CHANGES: EARTH CHANGES

[lviii] In case there was a doubt, one did not know what the Golden Rule was. It was time for a refresher course. It stemmed from a statement Jesus made to his disciples. "*Love the lord your God with your whole heart, mind and soul, and love your neighbor as yourself*". In terms of secular humanism it was called THE ETHIC OF RECIPROCITY. Simply stated, we were to treat other people the way we wished to be treated ourselves. It was the tenet upon which the principles of secular humanism were founded. Human beings needed no other doctrine to follow to accomplish this objective. It was yet to come to pass. Certainly that was the failure of a secret teaching of the ages worth investigating.

[lix] The Seven Deadly Sins appeared in classical literature in the epic poem, FARIE QUEENE, by Edmund Spenser. They were: *pride, lust, envy, anger, covetousness, gluttony, and sloth*. In the medieval age, these traits were particularly important in testing the character of the medieval class of knights. Their existence constituted a moral dilemma every knight should avoid falling into; the result of which he be found unworthy of knighthood.

Truth Never Changes: The Genesis of the Path

Made in the USA
Charleston, SC
19 August 2012